International Political Economy Series

Series Editor
Timothy M. Shaw, University of Massachusetts Boston, Boston, MA, USA;
Emeritus Professor, University of London, London, UK

The global political economy is in flux as a series of cumulative crises impacts its organization and governance. The IPE series has tracked its development in both analysis and structure over the last three decades. It has always had a concentration on the global South. Now the South increasingly challenges the North as the centre of development, also reflected in a growing number of submissions and publications on indebted Eurozone economies in Southern Europe. An indispensable resource for scholars and researchers, the series examines a variety of capitalisms and connections by focusing on emerging economies, companies and sectors, debates and policies. It informs diverse policy communities as the established trans-Atlantic North declines and 'the rest', especially the BRICS, rise.

NOW INDEXED ON SCOPUS!

More information about this series at
https://link.springer.com/bookseries/13996

Sandya Hewamanne · Smytta Yadav
Editors

The Political Economy of Post-COVID Life and Work in the Global South: Pandemic and Precarity

palgrave
macmillan

Editors
Sandya Hewamanne
Department of Sociology
University of Essex
Essex, UK

Smytta Yadav
School of Environment, Education, and Development
University of Manchester
Manchester, UK

ISSN 2662-2483 ISSN 2662-2491 (electronic)
International Political Economy Series
ISBN 978-3-030-93227-5 ISBN 978-3-030-93228-2 (eBook)
https://doi.org/10.1007/978-3-030-93228-2

This Palgrave Macmillan imprint is published by the registered company Springer Nature Switzerland AG
The registered company address is: Gewerbestrasse 11, 6330 Cham, Switzerland

The book is dedicated to the world's low-income workers and informal laborers who are coping with the pandemic and lockdowns while enduring challenging working conditions exacerbated by COVID-19.

Acknowledgments

We would like to express our gratitude to Timothy Shaw, the editor of the IPE series. Tim has been an endless source of inspiration, advice, and support throughout the process. We are also grateful to Anca, Geetha, and the rest of the Springer team. The initial idea of this book comes from a workshop organized by Yadav at the University of Sussex in 2018 titled "Neoliberal Welfare State, Precarity, and Development: Transnational Activism and Solidarity for Global Workers". Hewamanne brought her expertise on precarious work, global production networks, labor rights and feminist political economy to the project.

Yadav is thankful to Abel Polese for mentoring her first book and also introducing her to Tim Shaw. Hewamanne is grateful for her family and friends. She is especially thankful for Sadie, Desi and Barnaby, whose feline antics provided much joy and laughter.

Contents

List of Contributors

Sudeshna Chatterjee University of Massachusetts Boston, Boston, MA, USA

Afshana Choudhury Centre for Entrepreneurship Development (CED), Brac University, Dhaka, Bangladesh

Fahim S. Chowdhury Centre for Entrepreneurship Development (CED), Brac University, Dhaka, Bangladesh

Jashodhara Dasgupta Uttarakhand, India

Sandya Hewamanne Department of Sociology, University of Essex, Essex, UK

MD. Faizul Islam Centre for Entrepreneurship Development (CED), Brac University, Dhaka, Bangladesh

Areet Kaur Government of Punjab, Punjab Rural Health Mission, Chandigarh, India

Kanika Jha Kingra Gurugram, India

Chantal Krcmar University of Massachusetts Boston, Boston, MA, USA

Patrícia Rocha Lemos Centro de Estudos Sindicais e de Economia do Trabalho (CESIT), University of Campinas, Campinas, Brazil

Kundan Mishra University of Massachusetts Boston, Ottawa, ON, Canada

Shahidur Rahman Department of Economics and Social Sciences, BRAC University, Dhaka, Bangladesh

Adam Sargent Western Sydney University, Sydney, NSW, Australia

Sadril Shajahan Centre for Entrepreneurship Development (CED), Brac University, Dhaka, Bangladesh

Nadia Singh Northumbria University, Newcastle upon Tyne, UK

Smytta Yadav School of Environment, Education, and Development, University of Manchester, Manchester, UK

List of Tables

CHAPTER 1

Neoliberalism, Informality and Precarity

Sandya Hewamanne and Smytta Yadav

Uneven development after colonization, imperialism and outwardly influenced internal conflict, have caused many countries in the formally colonized or semi-occupied (literally and metaphorically) countries in the world to lag behind in wealth accumulation, investments in manufacturing and technology and equitable distribution. These countries are not only considered as poorer but also politically powerless at the global stage. The term 'Global South' itself is designed to recognize the historically produced inequalities even as it replaces the hierarchical term the 'Third World.' In late July 2021, the Wikipedia page on the Global South included "a lack of general hygiene and cleanliness among their population scholars hold of formerly colonized, less affluent countries of the

S. Hewamanne (✉)
Department of Sociology, University of Essex, Essex, UK
e-mail: skhewa@essex.ac.uk

S. Yadav
School of Environment, Education, and Development, University of Manchester, Manchester, UK
e-mail: smytta.yadav@manchester.ac.uk

S. Hewamanne and S. Yadav (eds.), *The Political Economy of Post-COVID Life and Work in the Global South: Pandemic and Precarity*, International Political Economy Series,
https://doi.org/10.1007/978-3-030-93228-2_1

world. That this statement (and an apparent widespread attitude of apathy to that fact)" as a defining feature of Global was still included uncontested in a page that countless undergraduate students refer to in late South populations, showing the still prevailing neo-imperialist, essentialist notions some July 2021 highlights how the economic injustices are influencing intellectual, western epistemeological, and ideological spheres as well.[1]

Uneven Post colonial development was not helped by the intensified globalization which saw most of these poorer countries being forced to adopt draconian structural adjustment policies proposed by the world monitory organizations as a way to alleviate the debt dependency. Open economic policies meant an end to protections for fledgling industries in these countries, which in fact led to the success of already affluent countries in the first place. Having dragged into world market dynamics on an equal footing with already developed countries led to the exacerbation of existing economic inequalities at a global scale. One consequence was the rapid burgeoning of the informal economies within poorer countries. Although most of these countries already experienced high rates of unemployment and under employment resulting in large informal economies, the unprecedented growth since 1990s is directly connected to neoliberal models of development touted as the only way out of poverty by international monetary institutions and development agencies. Washington Consensus which encouraged foreign investment in countries of the Global South saw people in these countries being included in global production networks at the bottom most rung. Although this provided employment for newer groups of workers, namely women from marginalized communities, it also resulted in armies of daily-hired workers and home-based workers leading to increased precarity and livelihood insecurities.

To this environment of already unjust, precarious livelihoods arrived the dreaded global pandemic in early 2020. Informal economies and precarious work are highly vulnerable to external disruptions. When COVID-19 struck, western countries locked down leading to unraveling of global production chains. Bankruptcy-filing companies and shuttering of stores in Europe and North America translated into closed factories in the Global South leading to hoards of workers losing their livelihoods

[1] After a scathing critique added by Hewamanne, this sentence was deleted by the end of July 2021.

(Nilson 2020; Nilson and Terazono 2020; Hewamanne 2021). Even people engaged in more traditionally locally-bound informal economic activities such as domestic work and sex work found their livelihoods disappear together with disruptions within global and local production and service hierarchies. This edited volume highlights cascading effects of the pandemic and resultant lockdown on informal economies of varied countries in the Global South. Specifically, it covers three of the most populated countries in the Global South, India, Brazil and Bangladesh with one chapter providing a contrasting case of a smaller state, Sri Lanka. The chapters weave through global economic disruptions as they affected workers in the informal sector who have already been largely invisible within the state development policies and programs. Chapters further question whether existing models of neoliberal development are still conducive within the post-pandemic Global South as it grapples with rebuilding economies, livelihoods, effective institutions, systems of governance and rethinks industrial and welfare policies.

The industrialization in the Global South has already been anti-poor prior to the outbreak of the pandemic (Stevano et al. 2021). The impact of contemporary industrialization and economic globalization on the Global South economies is uneven as compared to the experience of industrialization in the Global North. This is in major part a result of historical processes such as colonialism, imperialism, slavery and the dispossession of indigenous groups that accounted for much of the wealth accumulation in the Global North. The current industrialization and development initiatives follow the highly unequal capitalist model that only benefits those with capital and control over the means of production. The current financial restructuring is also not in favor of equitable distribution or just social changes.

Neoliberalism represents a set of political economic practices that hold 'human well- being can best be advanced by liberating individual entrepreneurial freedoms' (Harvey 2007: 2) within an environment of strong free market policies and free trade. Neoliberalism also works as a form of governmentality by instilling norms of individual selves as autonomous, self-directing agents (Rose 1999; Gunnel 2009; Fevre 2016). Thus a neoliberal subject is an individual who relies on cost–benefit analysis and market-based principles and embodies the spirit of entrepreneurship. As Gershon (2018) notes, such individuals are disciplined, risk- taking and bent on optimizing skills and in short represent a 'company of one.' The flexibilization of capital and labor promotes the so-called gig economy, and neoliberal subjects invest in themselves to engage in this economy by becoming self-reliant, risk-taking entrepreneurs. Thus some define neoliberalism as a mode of governing through freedom that gives individuals choice and the responsibility of navigating and enhancing their own social worlds. Within this neoliberal understanding what it is to be a 'worker' is also redefined leading to conflictual individual desires and expectations of citizenship rights. In neoliberal times the worker has become human capital, and any activity that generates salary or income, gives satisfaction, increases one's status within family and community and promotes travel and civic engagements is an investment in human capital (Foucault 2008: 226–235). With such an understanding of a 'worker,' it is not surprising that the governments wash their hands off workers who are engaged in precarious work as it is narratively produced and reproduced as an individual choice routed in individual aspirations and self satisfaction. The dominant narratives hide how the late capitalist, market-based global economic systems create precarious livelihood opportunities which are presented as opportunities for self improvement, or as enhancing one's own human capital status.

The gig economy refers to how self-employed contractors enable 'just in time, on demand' services, which consists of outsourcing work performed by traditional employees via open call (Todolí-Signes 2017: 194). Such open calls facilitate unpredictable yet plentiful opportunities for appropriately skilled independent providers. This definition applies to varied job and skill levels starting from highly paid and valued skilled computer services to low-paid assembly line manufacturing jobs considered unskilled work. Global assembly line work (which three chapters of this volume cover) is part of the gig economy in that the temporariness of the work is inbuilt although sold to workers as allowing them further opportunities for self improvement via entrepreneurship. The work is further fragmented through the increased use of casual workers for global factory work, to the extent that the regular factory workforce is asked to quit and re-join as casual workers. Again, the workers themselves are made to believe that casual work is a free choice and that they are agents of their own time and bodies as they can choose when and where to work (Hewamanne 2020). Although at one level it allows for agency, the workers by and large have lost sight of how they lose benefits such as paid leave, medical care and factory pension fund contributions through casual work. The awareness that the particular working arrangements within global subcontracting—long hours of target-oriented, backbreaking work that is detrimental to the physical, social and emotional well-being of workers—drive their desire for casual labor is low. Furthermore, large global subcontracting factories train skilled workers to set up home workshops after they are pushed out of factory shop floors in five to six years. This adds to the already existing armies of home workers whose positioning and livelihoods are highly precarious and vulnerable to the disruptions at various points within the production chains (Hewamanne 2017, 2019, 2020).

Gibson-Graham (2006) advocates for reading economic activities for 'difference rather than dominance,' so as not to take neoliberalism as a dominant, totalizing regime but to look for the failures and weaknesses that give credence to alternatives. Even in pre- pandemic times the workers, their families and communities absorbed the worst shocks at different nodal points within global production networks. But when the shock is too great, such as a global pandemic affecting the centers at the top, what happens to informal sector workers in the Global South? This book shines a critical light at neoliberal development models via the economic and social devastation caused by the pandemic and the lockdown. The pandemic and the suffering of hoards of workers at different job levels brought inherent weaknesses in neoliberalism as a regulative technology and the precariousness of gig economy-related livelihoods to sharp focus (Hewamanne 2021). This is as good an opportunity as it ever would rethink neoliberal development models and to propose and experiment with alternative economic paths that are contextually conducive and meaningful. All chapters briefly discuss the need for such rethinking and possible action (See specifically, chapters by Singh et al. ; Mishra , Dasgupta, Sargent and Hewamanne).

Workers; Right to Protest and Unionization

One of the most unfavorable outcomes of late capitalist economic restructuring is the inability of the workers to organize and fight for labor rights or protest uneven impacts of globalization without risking their livelihoods. Precarious work and gig economies result in this vulnerability and it begets further precarity and unequal distribution. Not having legal recourse via unionization is detrimental to labor and human rights especially with the specific kind of 'upgrading' that is encouraged within some parts of economy while 'downgrading' happens within other parts

(Barrientos et al. 2010). It has been noted that the uneven impacts are often differently felt by groups of workers in the same sector or industry as capitalist development produces and relies on segmentation of the labor market (Peck 1996). Not surprisingly, the sectors that are poorly impacted are mostly occupied by women, and other marginalized groups.

Participation in economic globalization generates new employment opportunities for marginalized people in the Global South. However, this participation does not necessarily lead to same results experienced by workers in the Global North such as high wages, good working conditions or systems of social protection. Workers in the Global North have won these rights after unionization and worker protests. Without the ability to unionize the workers in the emerging economies of the Global South have no traditional forms of recourse to move toward obtaining better work conditions and higher wages. The discouraging or downright prohibition of unionization, as in the global factories, and the built in precarities more or less seal the powerless position of informal sector workers within the Global South. The success narratives surrounding neoliberal development valorizes the precarity while simultaneously underlining the futility of unionization when jobs become more like gigs—temporary and insecure. Such narratives also encourage the individual advancement over collective organizing. In fact unions throughout the Global South are disheartened by the worker turnover which does not allow for consciousness raising toward collective organizing. Few unions and internationally funded NGOs have tried to use creative means to educate constantly changing groups of precarious workers within varied informal settings.

Hewamanne's chapter in this volume highlights some of the difficulties these initiatives encounter as a result of the prohibition of unionization within global assembly line production. In addition the built in precarity, and highly unfavorable work conditions and low pay lead to high turnover further discouraging the emergence of organic leadership.

Economic globalization impacts Global South economies by increasing cross-border interdependence and integrating various sectors of economies to facilitate the smooth flow of goods, services, and people through complex flexibilization of production, capital and markets. Moreover, the contemporary form of economic globalization is characterized by a lack of environmental regulations, occupational health standards, and discouraging of unionization and collective organizing to agitate for labor rights. All this means that global pandemics such as COVID-19 are much more devastating to the emerging markets in the Global South than to advanced industrial economies at the center of the world economic system.

It is important to highlight that the economic globalization has also been detrimental to groups of workers in the Global North especially to those with limited skills and qualifications. Such workers were forced to silently witness the manufacturing jobs that they have traditionally relied on the move to countries in the Global South (Horner and Nadvi 2018). The threat of manufacturing jobs moving across borders has been used to curtail the powers of unionization, while workers at many skill levels, including technology workers, have experienced casualization of their work through moving of job categories to 'just in time' gig economic sphere. These parallel yet differently experienced processes underline the need for global level worker organizing for more meaningful economic restructuring that aims for global worker rights and economic justice.

Informal Economies, Urban Poverty and Health Disparities

The urban poor populations in most countries in the Global South are expanding due to the micro fragmentation of industrial production connected to global value chains. This fragmentation results in numerous small workshops in densely populated urban areas where hoards of unemployed poor men and women are only too eager to take up work under any condition. This also encourages rural to urban migration to these areas, which are already poorly serviced with intermittent access to running water, electricity and security. The sub- human living conditions, and deprivation of goods and services including health and medical facilities within urban low-income communities of India, and Brazil are well documented (Hone et al. 2020; Sharma 2019; Richmond 2020). Having no immovable assets in urban areas (largely squatting on state-owned land) or farmland in villages most members of these urban poor communities depend on direct and indirect employment in the informal and unregulated economy. Decades of working in such informal sector jobs characterized by precarity, low wages and the lack of safety nets, make most such workers indifferent to the exploitative working conditions inherent to these jobs.

Even pre-pandemic the urban poor were more vulnerable to infectious diseases. For instance, pre-pandemic rates of diseases in urban low-income communities are much higher than for rural communities (Mohanan et al. 2021). Urban spaces where informal economies thrive have become COVID-19 hotspots due to population density and their inability to refrain from working in crowded spaces that result from not having safety nets. As the chapters by Sargent and Krcmar in this volume amply demonstrate this has both long and short term health and economic implications. Furthermore, it is amply evident that more globally integrated the economy through supply chains, the more severe the economic implications of the pandemic (Hewamanne 2021; Nilson 2020; Sforza and Steininger 2020). All chapters in this volume, but specifically Chowdhuri et al., Rahman and Hewamanne chapters, further evidence this.

The pandemic response has also been unequal and highly unfair to urban poor communities in the Global South. The governments are struggling to develop coherent frameworks for response and recovery while groups and the non-documentation of micro-subcontracting units of global supply chains exacerbate the invisibility of urban poor who are employed within these outfits. The workers are in fact considered transient as hard work and low pay encourage high turnover. Additionally, most urban squatter populations and rural to urban migrants are not registered via local government databases leading to their inability to claim government welfare assistance and other citizenship rights. In the extreme lack of safety mechanisms, impact of the global pandemic is doubly devastating for the urban low-income communities who depend on informal economic activities for survival (Richmond 2020; Sethi and Creutzig 2021). Both India and Brazil are members of the BRICS, a grouping which emerged as a result of their disenchantment with the current world economic dominance of western countries. BRICS is expected to be a vehicle for these emerging economic powers to amplify their voice and influence within the global stage. Several chapters focus on the failure of pandemic response and the immeasurable suffering of informal sector workers in these two countries, prompting us to question the legitimacy of the current glorified narratives of BRICS prominence. Both India and Brazil have much to do in managing the disenchantment of their own citizenry in the post-pandemic future before making claims on global influence. For that end, it is imperative that these governments (as well as others in the Global South) develop sustainable livelihood-security and recovery frameworks. It is equally important to include informal economies as essential sectors to enable COVID-19 recovery and to face any future health crisis of this magnitude.

Road Map

Brazil , India and Bangladesh are three of the most populated countries within the Global South. While India and Bangladesh (and Sri Lanka) experienced quite similar colonial and post colonial experiences, uneven development in Brazil was largely enabled by a different kind of, namely American-led regional imperialism, militarism and internal conflicts. The chapters in this volume traverse through lived experiences of different informal sector workers in these countries to explicate how the pandemic affected already vulnerable workers within the respective informal economies characterized by extreme precarity.

Most of the chapters in this volume cover India's informal economy. India's informal sector is largely unorganized and most workplaces do not even maintain a formal registry of workers. Most such enterprises are small scale and thus do not pay substantial taxes. Even those do pay taxes, are often not monitored by the government (Yadav 2020). As observed by Hensman (2020), workplaces which are exempted from labor legislation have large portions of temporary, casual and 'contract workers,' (or no-contract workers in reality) hired via labor contractors. To exacerbate already unfavorable conditions, under the Modi administration, Indian informal sector workers have become direct victims of the continuing lack of focus on workers' welfare and rights (Miyamura 2021).

Singh et al. analyzes the experiences of women in informal employment in Indian Punjab using gendered and intersectional lenses. Framing their investigation and analysis within those lenses had enabled them to highlight the subjective experiences of women from different social locations and show general and particular forms of vulnerabilities faced by them during the lockdown. Bringing the voices of women who have been relegated to the background in most policy discussions on the pandemic, this chapter fills a crucial gap in Covid-19 related research which hitherto have not particularly focused on how the losses in livelihoods and health vulnerabilities are shaped by gender, race, class, disability and other markers of marginality and disadvantage.

Through a case study of seasonal migrants in Nuapada, in Odisha, Mishra sheds light on another aspect of pandemic-related health aspirations that the states need to take into account before embarking upon substantial post-pandemic changes. Mishra shows how seasonal migrants deprioritize health aspirations and elaborates on the links between health aspirations and migration decisions of rural households. He shows how the public health systems in India continue to fail the poor, most notably migrant laborers and their families. He further focuses on the calls for investment in health infrastructure to highlight the underlying reasons for migrant workers' low health aspirations for their children. For these migrant workers debt related to health expenses is a key factor in influencing high-risk, low- return seasonal migration. This cycle influences lower health aspirations, lack of investment in health, and low access levels to existing health systems. Mishra thus cautions against a singular focus on building infrastructure, and instead argues for thoughtful integration of migrants' aspirations and agency when developing effective future health systems.

While Singh et al. and Mishra take a general approach to the women in the informal sector in Punjab and migrant workers in Odisha, respectively, Krcmar, Sargent, Dasgupta et al. and Chatterjee shine their investigative light on specific groups of informal sector workers—construction workers, 'volunteer' health workers and sex workers. Each, however, uses specific analytical lenses on their research populations, collectively producing a comprehensive set of tools necessary for rethinking social research and policy initiatives in the post-pandemic world. While Krcmar looks at construction workers in Navi, Mumbai through the lenses of human security, Sargent utilizes his research among construction workers to theorize a politics of exposure.

Specifically focusing on women construction workers in sites at Nakas and Bastis, Krcmar argues for a broader understanding of human security. Using women workers' own narratives she demonstrates how they understand human security primarily as achieving economic security. The pandemic and the lockdown have made Indian women construction worker livelihoods even more insecure. But their narratives also show how tenacious they are in securing whatever jobs available even as such jobs further their already existing health vulnerabilities. Following from Krcmar's findings on human security, Sargent's call for a politics of exposure makes immediate sense. His pre-pandemic ethnographic research among several construction sites in and around Delhi provides the background for his analysis where he demonstrates how the dangerous exposures that characterize construction work come to define workers even as they diminish them. His rethinking of exposure as emerging out of a complex interplay of forces in which workers are treated as expendable, enables him to interrogate the ways the pandemic is reshaping the politics of migrant labor in India and elsewhere. Noting that the very same populations that are subjected to environmental pollutants have been hit the hardest by the pandemic, from poor Black and Latinx communities in the post-industrial US (Lerner 2020) to urban slum-dwellers in Mumbai and Delhi (Biswas 2000; Krcmar, this volume) Sargent shows how broader structural processes bring certain bodies and not others into contact with toxic materials and contagions. Sargent thus argues that Indian construction workers who toil without protective equipment or access to clean living conditions are essential to the Indian economy, yet they are essential only as cheap, unprotected workers and thus largely expendable.

Dasgupta et al. focus on how the COVID-19 pandemic is impacting the lives and work of community-based frontline health and child development workers. The authors use Community-Based Front-Line Worker to refer to those women employed within government schemes and given the direct responsibility of implementing programmes and providing services within community settings. They argue that although the state is the employer of these women workers; by labeling them 'volunteers' the state help maintain informal working arrangements and has effectively erased its own obligations for fair wages and social security. The authors propose pathways for a post-COVID economic recovery plan that addresses the multiple axes of disadvantage faced by these women volunteers. They call for an approach that take these women workers as a robust part of a decentralized mechanism for primary health care and social protection to effectively face future pandemics.

Chatterjee's chapter focuses on a group of workers in a sector that has been an enduring part of informal economies throughout the world—commercial sex work. Utilizing a health securitization framework to study reproductive precarity in the Global South, Chatterjee elucidates how sexually precarious bodies are exceptionalized by the virtue of their health-centric vulnerabilities and the potential to threaten 'public' health. She shows how this leads to spatial/moral segregation. Coining the term 'contamination-invisibility' nexus Chatterjee explores how health securitization underlying the HIV/AIDS and COVID-19 governance in India deepens precarity of sexual labor. She argues that this deepened precarity is crucial for the constitution of the gendered neoliberal-postcolonial state and sustenance of global-sexual power relations.

Two chapters by Chowdhuri et al. and Rahman focus on the second mostly populated country in South Asia, Bangladesh. Moreover, the two chapters focus on the Bangladesh ready made garment (RMG) industry. Chowdhuri et al. base their analysis on two rapid surveys using its factory database generated through countrywide factory census. This is the only chapter to squarely focus on surveys. Rapid surveys are important in a climate where qualitative research is more or less impossible. Authors' rapid surveys have yielded a Covid-19 RMG map exploring the operational status of RMG factories during pandemic. As the two surveys addressed two time periods of the pandemic, a pragmatic comparison between these two surveys help analyze the differing patterns of recovery within the industry. Such comparison can also serve as a potential tool to propagate new research endeavors. Authors hold that using data from the rapid surveys local and global stakeholders can play an active role in proposing and operationalizing short and long-term policies targeting the post pandemic challenges. In contrast, Rahman's chapter uses secondary sources to reflect on the impact of coronavirus on the Bangladeshi garments industry. Highlighting how the gains after Rana Plaza disaster and the global response to it were adversely affected by the global pandemic, the chapter sets out to understand the consequences of this pandemic on the suppliers and workers, while shedding light on the role of the buyers in negotiating the pandemic-related challenges and the extent of the support extended by the government of Bangladesh. Not surprisingly, the chapter concludes that the workers are the most vulnerable to pandemic-related disruptions within the global supply chains and predicts a bleak future for the Bangladeshi RMG sector.

Hewamanne's chapter focuses on women workers within global production in Sri Lanka to comment on how the pandemic resulted in workers losing hard won labor rights. Highlighting how the pandemic put a stop to some positive initiatives in the realm of legal and rights education of workers, Hewamanne argues that the pandemic would lead to reversing positive policy outcomes that resulted from decades of labor protests. Based on highly divergent experience and outcomes of occupational health workshops that she herself conducted for global factory workers in 2018–2019 and 2020 respectively, Hewamanne shows how the pandemic had effected several new forms of exploitation. Akin to Sargent and Mishra chapters this chapter also shows the global factory workers of Sri Lanka too find their work as essential yet their lives expendable. The chapter further demonstrates that the pandemic had been detrimental to the legal empowerment and the advancement of labor rights within the global production and argues for rethinking of informal economies beyond the neoliberal development models which have not being conducive to rights empowerment even during pre-COVID-19 days.

Lemos's chapter not only focuses on another highly populated country in the Global South, Brazil, but also shines an analytical light on a group of precarious workers whose work and lives have by and large been invincible in academic literature. Her chapter demonstrates how the pandemic aggravates precarious living and working conditions of supermarket employees in Brazil. On one hand, she shows the precariousness of work in supermarkets such as Walmart. On the other hand, she points out how social inequality and particular Brazilian labor market conditions limit the prospects of these workers. The research draws on qualitative research conducted at Brazilian Walmart Stores, including semi-structured interviews with workers and union leaders, and analysis of national administrative data and secondary data from media. Despite the increased focus on the importance of these workers and the precarious working conditions to which they are subjected, Lemos argues that recognition as essential workers in the context of the pandemic has, unfortunately, been accompanied by further degradation of working conditions and greater health risks for the workers and their families.

Conclusion

Globalization, the resultant global value chains, and abrupt incorporation into world markets had exacerbated already unequal economic fortunes that resulted from historical processes such as colonialism and slavery within many countries in the Global South. The chapters clearly show how precarious workers in different job categories have experienced the worst fallout of the global pandemic and the lockdown. The themes of informality, precarity, expendability and inequalities are intricately interwoven through all the chapters of this edited volume. The lenses of human security, unequal health aspirations, politics of exposure, contagion-invisibility, essential-expendable nexus and human and labor rights education, explicate the inherent injustices within late capitalist global economic formations. The current developments and economic devastation caused by the pandemic within emerging markets makes us reflect on Gibson-Graham's (2006, 2008) call for progressive alternatives to capital and neoliberalism. The current suffering of marginalized masses in the Global South, hopefully, will lead to a clarion call for economic restructuring that foreground equitable justice and global human well-being. The chapters in this volume are a first step toward an alternative economic imagination more appropriate for the post-pandemic world which is more mindful of how our health futures are globally connected and thus cannot be secured without global social, economic justice.

Bibliography

Barrientos, S., Gereffi, G., and Rossi, A. "Economic and Social Upgrading in Global Production Networks: Developing a Framework for Analysis." *International Labor Review*, 150, no. 3–4 (2010), 319–340.

Biswas, A. K. *Water for Urban Areas of the Developing World in the Twenty First Century. Water for Urban Areas*. Tokyo: United Nations University Press, (2000), 1–23.

Fevre, Ralph. *Individualism and Inequality: The Future of Work and Politics*. London: Edward Elgar, 2016.

Foucault, Michel. *The Birth of Biopolitics: Lectures at the College de France, 1978–1979*. New York: Palgrave, 2008.

Gershon, Ilana. "Employing the CEO of Me, Inc.: US Corporate Hiring in a Neoliberal Age." *American Ethnologist* (2018). https://doi.org/10.1111/amet.12630.

Gibson-Graham, J. K. *A Postcapitalist Politics*. Minneapolis: University of Minnesota Press, 2006.

Gibson-Graham, J. K. "Diverse Economies: Performative Practices for 'other worlds'". *Progress in Human Geography*, 32, no. 5 (2008), 613–632.

Gunnel, Gokce. "Producing Neoliberal Subjects. The Case of Koc University". *Berkeley Journal of Sociology*, 53, (2009), 4–25.

Harvey, David. *A Brief History of Neoliberalism*. Oxford: Oxford University Press, 2007.

Hensman, R. "The COVID-19 Lockdown in India: A Predictable Catastrophe for Informal labour". *Global Labour Journal*, 11, no. 3 (2020).

Hewamanne, Sandya. "Crafting Social Change: Former Global Factory Workers Negotiating New Identities in Sri Lanka's Villages." *Identities*, 26, no. 2 (2017).

Hewamanne, Sandya. "From Global Workers to Local Entrepreneurs: Former Global Factory Workers in Rural Sri Lanka." *Third World Quarterly*, 41, no. 3 (2019).

Hewamanne, Sandya. "Pandemic, Lockdown and Modern Slavery Among Sri Lanka's Global Assembly Line Workers." *Journal of International Women's Studies*, 22, no. 1 (2021), 54–69.

Hewamanne, Sandya. *Re-stitching Identities in Rural Sri Lanka: Neoliberalism, Gender and Politics of Contentment*. Philadelphia: University of Pennsylvania Press, 2020.

Hone, Thomas, Saraceni, Valeria, Coeli, Claudia, Trajman, Anete, Rasella, Davide, Millett, Christopher, and Durovni, Betina. "Primary Healthcare Expansion and Mortality in Brazil's Urban Poor: A Cohort Analysis of 1.2 Million Adults." *PLOS Medicine* (2020). https://doi.org/10.1371/journal.pmed.1003357.

Horner, R., and Nadvi, K. "Global Value Chains and the Rise of the Global South: Unpacking Twenty-First Century Polycentric Trade." *Global Networks*, 18, no. 2 (2018), 207–237.

Krmcar, Chantal. "Female Labour Workforce and Precarity in India's Construction Sector." In *The Political Economy of Post-COVID Life and Work in the Global South: Pandemic and Precarity*, edited by Sandya Hewamanne and Smytta Yadav. Cham: Palgrave Macmillan, this volume.

Lerner, Sharon. "What Racism Smells Like: Ravaged by COVID-19, Polluted Communities Demand Justice." The Intercept, Accessed August 8, 2020. https://theintercept.com/2020/08/08/coronavirus-pollution-environmental-justiceracism.

Miyamura, S. "Turbulence Ahead: Labour and Struggles in Times of the Covid-19 Pandemic in India." *Canadian Journal of Development Studies/Revue canadienne d'études du développement*, 42, no. 1–2 (2021), 165–177.

Mohanan, M., Malani, A., Krishnan, K., and Acharya, A. Prevalence of COVID-19 in Rural Versus Urban Areas in a Low-Income Country: Findings from a State-Wide Study in Karnataka, India. *University of Chicago, Becker Friedman Institute for Economics Working Paper*, 2021.

Nilson, P. Garment Workers in Asia Lose $6bn Wages. *Financial Times* (US edition), 2020 (page 10). Accessed August 10, 2020.

Nilsson, P., and Terazono, E. "Can Fast Fashion's $2.5tn Supply Chain Be Stitched Back Together?" *Financial Times* (2020). https://www.ft.com/content/62dc687e-d15f-46e7-96df. Accessed May 17, 2020.

Peck, J. *Work-place: The Social Regulation of Labor Markets*. New York: Guilford Press, 1996.

Richmond, Matthew. "Brazil's Urban Inequities Will Exacerbate the Impacts of Covid-19," 2020. https://blogs.lse.ac.uk/latamcaribbean/2020/04/14/brazils-urban-inequalities-will-exacerbate-the-impacts-of-covid-19/.

Rose, Nicholas. *The Powers of Freedom: Reframing Political*. Cambridge: Cambridge University Press, 1999.

Sethi, M., and Creutzig, F. "COVID-19 Recovery and the Global Urban Poor," 2021. https://www.nature.com/articles/s42949-021-00025-x.
Sforza, Alessandro, and Marina Steininger. "Globalization in the Time of COVID-19." CESifo Working Paper 8184, (2020).
Sharma, Akanksha. "Cities of the Poor: A View on Urban Poverty in India." *Times of India* (2019). https://timesofindia.indiatimes.com/blogs/in-the-name-of-development/cities-of-the-poor-a-view-on-urban-poverty-in-india/.
Stevano, S., Franz, T., Dafermos, Y., and Van Waeyenberge, E. "COVID-19 and Crises of Capitalism: Intensifying Inequalities and Global Responses." *Canadian Journal of Development Studies/Revue canadienne d'études du développement*, 42, no. 1–2 (2021), 1–17.
Todolí-Signes, Adrian. "The 'Gig Economy': Employee, Self-Employed or the Need for a Special Employment Regulation?" *Transfer: European Review of Labour and Research*, 23, no. 2 (2017), 193–205.
Yadav, S. "Precarity as a Coping Strategy of the Gonds: A Study of Insecure and Long-Distance Seasonal Migration in Central India." *Indian Journal of Human Development*, 14, no. 1 (2020), 7–22.

CHAPTER 2

The Covid-19 Pandemic: Narratives of Informal Women Workers in Indian Punjab

Nadia Singh and Areet Kaur

List of Abbreviations

NHM	National Health Mission
OBC	Other Backward Castes
PMJDY	Pradhan Mantri Jan Dhan Yojna
SC	Scheduled Caste
SEWA	Self Employed Women's Association
UNFPA	United Nations Population Fund

N. Singh (✉)
Northumbria University, Newcastle upon Tyne, UK
e-mail: nadia.singh@northumbria.ac.uk

A. Kaur
Government of Punjab, Punjab Rural Health Mission, Chandigarh, India

S. Hewamanne and S. Yadav (eds.), *The Political Economy of Post-COVID Life and Work in the Global South: Pandemic and Precarity*, International Political Economy Series,
https://doi.org/10.1007/978-3-030-93228-2_2

Introduction

COVID-19 is a health pandemic which has afflicted 216 regions of the world and caused more than 3.3 million deaths till date. Simultaneously, the countrywide lockdowns and quarantine measures implemented to control the spread of the virus have resulted in a host of negative socio-economic repercussions including heightened economic vulnerability, business closures and increased health risks for the most marginalised groups in society. In low-income countries like India, the health pandemic has translated into a humanitarian crisis with unprecedented job losses as well as rising hunger and food security. India's migrant crisis received global attention when thousands of daily wage workers started walking hundreds of kilometres to their native villages as the countrywide lockdown robbed them of their earnings in big cities. As many as 198 workers lost their lives in a desperate attempt to get home.[1]

Along with the health risks posed by the pandemic, the strict lockdown measures implemented in India between 22 March and 16 May, 2020 exacerbated the existing socio-economic inequities in society. India's countrywide lockdown was ranked as one of the severest lockdowns across 165 countries of the world, according to the "stringency" index developed by Oxford University.[2] Despite this stringent lockdown, the infection rate of COVID-19 did not flatten across the country and cases continue to rise. On the other hand, the economic slow-down imposed by this crisis resulted in harsh implications for the most vulnerable groups in Indian society. 91.3 million casual workers and small traders lost their jobs during this time[3] and 260 million additional people were pushed into poverty due to the economic fall out of the crisis.[4]

[1] "Coronavirus lockdown: The Indian migrants dying to get home," BBC. 2020, accessed June 10, 2020, https://www.bbc.co.uk/news/world-asia-india-52672764.

[2] Thomas Hale, Noam Angrist, Rafael Goldszmidt, Beatriz Kira, Anna Petherick, Toby Phillips, Samuel Webster, Emily Cameron-Blake, Laura Hallas, Saptarshi Majumdar, and Helen Tatlow. "A global panel database of pandemic policies." Blavatnik School of Government, Oxford University, 2020, accessed May 25, 2020, https://www.bsg.ox.ac.uk/research/research-projects/covid-19-government-response-tracker.

[3] "Unemployment in India." Centre for Monitoring of Indian Economy, 2020, accessed May 20, 2020, https://unemploymentinindia.cmie.com.

[4] Surbhi Kesar, Rosa Abraham, Rahul Lahoti, Paaritosh Nath, and Amit Basole, "Pandemic, informality, and vulnerability: Impact of COVID-19 on livelihoods in India," *Canadian Journal of Development Studies* 42, no. 1–2 (2021): 146.

The trend world over also shows that the impact of COVID-19 is highly gendered with a disproportionate impact on women. India too follows the trend. In India, most job losses have been experienced in the informal sector, which employs 54.7% women in India.[5] In the absence of formal safety nets, and social protection in this sector, it is feared that the pandemic may translate into increased "feminization" of poverty for women already living on the economic margins. The experience of recent epidemics in other low-and middle-income countries also reveals that women face additional burdens during such a health crisis due to their concentration in jobs exposed to the disease, heightened care needs at the household level, and increased exposure to domestic violence.[6]

Despite these factors there has been little attempt to institute a gendered policy response to the COVID-19 crisis. India's initial response to the COVID-19 crisis was focussed on vacuous performative gestures such as candle light vigils to "challenge the darkness induced by the virus." This performative symbolism was combined with a tepid policy response. The structural factors behind the health crisis were relegated to the background. These structural factors however remain crucial to implementing a robust policy response to the Covid-19 crisis. In her seminal work, Mileti[7] has demonstrated that the increased vulnerabilities following a crisis are a manifestation of existing societal relations, determined by a variety of socio-economic factors. Gender relations may be especially important in this dynamic. This is because gender relations in society intersect with other form of disadvantage rooted in class, caste and socio-economic status, and create distinct forms of marginalisation.

This paper contributes to this critical area by exploring enhanced gender vulnerability during the pandemic through exploratory field-based research. We analysed the experiences of women in informal employment in Indian Punjab using a gendered lens. Our empirical investigation was

[5] "Periodic Labour Force Survey (2018–19)." Ministry of Statistics and Programme Implementation, 2018–19, accessed June 6, 2020, http://mospi.nic.in/Periodic-Labour-Surveys.

[6] Clare Wenham, Julia Smith, and Rosemary Morgan. "Covid-19: The gendered impacts of the outbreak," *Lancet* 395, no. 10227 (2020): 846.

[7] Denis, S. Mileti, *Disasters by design: A reassessment of natural hazard in the United States* (Washington, DC: Joseph Henry, 1999): 27.

framed by intersectionality analysis. This framework enabled us to incorporate the "matrix of domination,"[8] represented by pre-existing power structures in society such as caste, class, and socio-economic divisions in our theoretical framework. This framework also enabled us to bring forth the subjective experiences of women from different social locations and the particular forms of vulnerabilities faced by them during the lockdown. Our fieldwork enabled us to illuminate the intersectional nature of the crisis and present the voices of women who have been relegated to the background in most policy discussions on the pandemic. Kabeer et al.[9] have identified this as a crucial gap in Covid-19-related research: "A big research gap pertains to the intersectional dimensions of the crisis, particularly the losses to livelihoods and health by gender, race, class, disability, life course, and other markers of disadvantage. More work needs to be done in this area across countries."

Review of Related Literature

Gender and Multidimensional Poverty

Poverty has been traditionally conceptualised in terms of income deprivation and lack of material sources of well-being. However, some scholars contend that the experience of poverty is much more complex than merely a shortfall in income, and comprises of a range of social, economic, and material deprivations.[10] Sen's[11] capability approach provided a framework to extend the measurement of poverty to the "functioning and capabilities" approach from the "income"-based approach. He advocated a multidimensional assessment of poverty based on individual welfare, basic human functioning, and the freedom to exercise one's individual agency. Within this framework gender inequality is seen as an issue of

[8] Patricia Hill Collins, *Black feminist thought: Knowledge, consciousness and the politics of empowerment* (Boston, MA: Unwin Hyman, 1990): 137.

[9] Naila Kabeer, Shahra Razavi, and Yana van der Meulen Rodgers, "Feminist Economic Perspectives on the COVID-19 Pandemic," *Feminist Economics* 27, no. 1–2 (2021): 28.

[10] Sylvia Chant, "Exploring the feminization of poverty in relation to women's work and home-based enterprise in slums of the global south," *International Journal of Gender and Entrepreneurship* 6, no. 3 (2014): 294.

[11] Amartya Sen, *Inequality reexamined* (Cambridge, MA: Harvard University Press, 1992): 24.

"unfreedom," rooted in multiple gender discriminatory structures and processes in society.

In spite of these theoretical advances in the assessment of poverty, the current multidimensional poverty indices are not able to fully integrate the gendered dimensions of poverty.[12] These measures treat households as a unit of analysis, rather than individuals. However, a large body of empirical research reveals that there are gendered disparities within a household which manifest in the form of inequitable burden of unpaid care work on women as well as unequal access to medical attention, healthcare, and nutritional food.[13,14,15] These multidimensional indices also do not address the disproportionate the impact of poverty on female headed households, referred to as "feminization of poverty" in literature.[16] Mangubhai and Capraro[17] conducted an empirical case study and showed that women belonging to female headed households, not only experience income-based deprivation but also a range of negative societal stereotypes that compound their economic stresses as well as their vulnerability to harassment, evictions, sexual exploitation, and abuse.

The current policy paradigm in India has not recognised these multiple axes of poverty in India and how gender, caste, and class relations permeate at all levels of social life. Existing poverty alleviation programmes primarily target income-based poverty through in kind and cash transfers, and income support schemes. This tendency for policy makers to focus solely on the income aspect of poverty rather than understanding the intersecting form of inequalities in Indian society leads to

[12] Sylvia Chant, "Women, girls and world poverty: Empowerment, equality or essentialism?" *International Development Planning Review* 38, no. 1 (2016): 23.

[13] Nadia Singh, "Gender, intra-household discrimination and cash transfer schemes: The case of Indian Punjab," *Economies* 75, no. 7 (2019): 1.3, accessed August 2, 2020, https://www.mdpi.com/2227-7099/7/3/75.

[14] Esther Duflo, "Grandmothers and granddaughters: Old-age pensions and intra-household allocations in South Africa," *World Bank Economic Review* 17 (2003): 1–25.

[15] Bina Agarwal, "Bargaining and gender relations: Within and beyond the household," *Feminist Economics* 3, no. 1 (1997): 23.

[16] Sharon Bessell, "The individual deprivation measure: Measuring poverty as if gender and inequality matter," *Gender and Development* 23, no. 2 (2015): 225.

[17] Jayshree P. Mangubhai and Chiara Capraro, "'Leave no one behind' and the challenge of intersectionality: Christian aid's experience of working with single and Dalit women in India," *Gender & Development* 23, no. 2 (2015): 266.

individuals lying in two or more vulnerable groups to fall into the gaps of social provisioning. These individuals, especially women continue to experience discrimination and destitution from the deeply engrained and complex social norm in society.

Chagar[18] has theorised that the Indian state is functioning as a "soft state" with hierarchically arranged multiplicity of power relations. It has thus reinforced the patriarchal norms in Indian society and proven to be a major hurdle in the cause of women's empowerment.

In the absence of robust public policy prerogatives, there has been growing involvement of civil society organisations to address the specific material and social forms of deprivation faced by women belonging to vulnerable groups through provision of credit, creating opportunities for self-employment and facilitating legal literacy.[19,20] However, scholars such as Harriss[21] have argued that there are limitations to the efficacy of community-based organisation as a measure for poverty alleviation. While they provide specific forms of relief to resource poor households, they do not address how existing social and class relations of productions that reproduce poverty. These organisations can act as a "conciliatory" space wherein individual societal and economic concerns can achieve representation; they cannot act as a substitute for state provisioning.

We can thus see that the multidimensional aspects of women's poverty in India stem from the inter-linkages between the income aspects of poverty, patriarchal relationship within the household, and absence of robust policy measures to address the distinct forms of vulnerabilities faced by women. In the field-based research in the subsequent sections we will analyse how these existing vulnerabilities, rooted in the structural nature of the Indian economy mapped out against the specific

[18] Rajeni Chagar, "Protection or obstruction? Women and precarious work in India," *Canadian Journal of Development Studies* 30, no. 3–4 (2010): 595.

[19] Jonathan Pattenden, "A neoliberalisation of civil society? Self-help groups and the labouring class poor in rural South India," *The Journal of Peasant Studies* 37, no. 3 (2010): 500.

[20] Thomas de Hoop, Luuk van Kempen, Rik Linssen, and Anouka van Eerdewijk, "Women's autonomy and subjective well-being: How gender norms shape the impact of self-help groups in Odisha, India," *Feminist Economic* 20, no. 3 (2014): 107.

[21] John Harriss, "Antinomies of empowerment: Observations on civil society, politics and urban governance in India," *Economic and Political Weekly* 42, no. 26 (2007): 2716.

socio-economic stresses induced by the pandemic using an intersectionality framework. This framework enabled us to go beyond the "additive" approach adopted by quantitative indices of multidimensional poverty, and untangle the combined effects of different forms of socio-economic disparities on women's lived experiences of the pandemic. We were also able to bring in the specific forms of disadvantages for certain groups of women rooted in intra-household disparities or their position as female headed households. These nuances are not a part of the current assessments of multidimensional poverty.

Informal Employment in India: A Gendered Analysis

The second core aspect of women's poverty in India stems from their occupational entities and employment within the informal sector. India is estimated to have the largest informal, unregistered economy the world over with the share of informal employment in total employment estimated at 80.9%.[22] Employees in the informal employment are not subject to national labour legislation, income tax norms, and social protection entitlements such as sick leave, minimum wages, health and safety regulations in the workplace and maternity benefits.[23] Therefore, any suspension of economic activity in this sector instantly translates into the loss of employment and earnings for this section of the population.

The dominant role of the informal sector in the Indian economy needs to be seen in the context of the liberalisation and pro-market reforms that were carried out in the early 1990s. The growth process in this model was based on the transfer of resources from subsistence-driven traditional sectors of the economy to growth driven formal sectors of the economy. However, the majority of the population in the traditional sectors could not be absorbed in the modern formal sectors. The informal sector thus acted as a "buffer" to absorb these poor people in

[22] ILO, *Women and men in the informal economy: A statistical picture* (Geneva: ILO, 2018): 18.

[23] Elizabeth Hill, "Women in the Indian informal economy: Collective strategies for work life improvement and development," *Work, Employment and Society* 15, no. 3 (2001): 447.

the urban employment.[24] Butler[25] has described informal employment as a "politically induced condition in which certain populations suffer from failing social and economic networks of support and become differentially exposed to injury, violence and death." Thus, the neo-liberal phase of the Indian economy has been a phase of rising inequities, leading to insecure livelihoods, low incomes, and limited access to basic amenities. The recession induced by the pandemic has been used to further these neoliberal reforms through deregulation of agricultural markets, privatisation of utilities, and dilution of existing labour legislations.

A gendered analysis is vital to understand the informal employment in India, as women are currently over-represented in this sector. Existing gender inequities in society intersect with the conditions of informality to create distinct forms of marginalisation for women employed in this sector. Patriarchal norms in Indian society translates into lower levels of skills and training for women, little access to start-up capital and inaccessibility to formal sector employment. Salleh[26] refers to women in informal employment as a class of "meta industrial" labour who remain at the margins of the economic system. While their labour and value produced by it is an essential economic resource, their prerogatives remain unaddressed as economic actors. These women tend to be disproportionately concentrated in more economically vulnerable and insecure forms of employment.[27] These disparities are reflected in terms of wage gaps in informal employment. Female earnings are estimated to be 54% of the male earnings in rural areas and 70% in urban areas of India.[28] Within particular sectors such as the garment sector these wage disparities persist owing to the gendered division of tasks. Male employees are paid a regular monthly salary for producing men's garments, whereas female employees

[24] Kalyan Sanyal, *Rethinking capitalist development: Primitive accumulation, governmentality and post colonial capitalism* (New Delhi: Routledge, 2007): 3–5.

[25] Judith Butler, *Frames of war: When life is grievable* (London: Verso Publications, 2009): 1.

[26] Ariel Salleh, "Green economics or green Utopia: The salience of reproductive labour post Rio + 20," *Journal of World Systems Research* 18, no. 2 (2012): 139.

[27] Martina Ulrichs, "Informality, women and social protection identifying barriers to provide effective coverage," *ODI Working Paper* (ODI: London, 2016): 141.

[28] Periodic Labour Force Survey, *Periodic labour force survey, 2017–18* (New Delhi: Ministry of Statistics and Programme Implementation, 2018): 33.

are paid by the piece for women's and children's garments, which have a lower price.[29]

Informal employment is characterised by an elaborate system of sub-contracting where in traditional employer-employee relations and standard work contracts are absent. This system translates into greater insecurity and exploitation by middle men and sub-contractors. Local middlemen offer loans to women to start their business at exploitative rates of interest without any written contract between these two parties. If these women challenge the lower income accrued to them they fear losing the work.[30] The disempowerment of women in informal employment is further compounded by the absence of traditional trade unions, which tend to be male dominated. However, in recent years some civil society organisations have made positive efforts in organising women from diverse trades within the informal sector and protecting their occupational identities and livelihood rights. These include Self Employed Women's Association (SEWA) which helps to collectively organise women in the informal sector around common needs for credit, education, and legal literacy.[31] A women waste picker's trade union in Pune called *Kagad Kach Patra Kashtakri Panchayat* has launched numerous "soft power" initiatives such as broom worship to win recognition for waste pickers as a critical participants in municipal governance structures.[32] In Kerala, a women's collective called *Kudambashree* assists informal women workers by educating them about their legal rights and getting access to microcredit. They also started a "break the chain" campaign during the covid-19 outbreak to sensitise women from marginalised communities about the importance of mask wearing and maintaining personal hygiene.[33] Even though these civil society organisations have helped to mitigate some of the disparities faced by women engaged in informal

[29] Ibid., 27.

[30] Barbara Harris-White, "Rethinking institutions: Innovation and institutional change in India's informal economy," *Modern Asian Studies* 51, no. 6 (2018): 1727.

[31] Baruah Bipasha, "Earning their keep and keeping what they earn: A critique of organizing strategies for South Asian women in the informal sector," *Gender, Work and Organization* 11, no. 6 (2004).

[32] Naila Kabeer, Kirsty Milward, and Ratna Sudarshan, "Organising women workers in the informal economy," *Gender and Development* 21, no. 2 (2013): 253.

[33] Usha, V.T., *Kerala's gendered response to the pandemic* (New Delhi: Global South and Rosa Luxemburg Institute, 2021): 37.

employment, they continue to face marginalisation owing to institutional structures of informal markets, and lack of any system of social protection for workers within this sector. In our field-based research, we will analyse how these pre-existing vulnerabilities rooted in informal employment mapped on to the economic hardships induced by the Covid-19 crisis.

Methodology

Due to the exploratory nature of the study, we conducted qualitative research, following Sayer[34] who postulates that the choice of research methods should be based on the object of the study and what one wishes to know about the subject. Qualitative methodology provided a sound framework to analyse the subjective experiences of the COVID-19 pandemic among participants in the study. This methodology has been extensively employed in intersectionality research.[35,36] We conducted 34 semi-structured in-depth interviews to capture the lived experiences of women during the pandemic. These interviews took place between May 17 and May 25, 2020 in and around Mohali district adjoining Chandigarh, the capital city of Punjab. This period corresponded to the fourth phase of the lockdown imposed in India. From May 17, 2020 restrictions on movement of people were partially lifted with opening up of shops, public transport, and offices. During this time, we could approach our interview participants to document their experiences during the preceding three phases of the lockdown between March 25 and May 16, 2020. We conducted the interviews in a face to face format. Face to face interviewing enabled us to establish a personal rapport with the participants, capture visual clues and generate more detailed responses from them regarding their subjective experiences of the COVID-19 crisis. Almost half of the interviewees wrapped up the conversation with their personal

[34] Andrew Sayer, *Realism and social science* (London: Sage, 2000): 31–33.

[35] Georgia Zozeta-Miliopoulou and Ilias Kapareliotis, "The toll of success: Female leaders in the 'women friendly' Greek advertising agencies," *Gender, Work and Organisation* (2021): 114.

[36] Jenny K. Rodrigeuz, Evangelina Holvino, Joyce K. Fletcher and Stella. M. Nkomo, "The theory and praxis of intersectionality in work and organisations: Where do we go from here?" *Gender, Work and Organisation* 2, no. 3 (2016): 214.

stories, lengthy comments and observations which enabled us to capture a number of new themes from these narratives.

Our sampling strategy was rooted in maximum variation purposive sampling,[37] which helped us to bring forth a range of diverse perspectives on the crisis. The first five respondents were identified through the authors' professional network. The second author is a doctor and a researcher who has been working in the region for the last thirty years. She was able to use her network within the medical profession and the community at large to recruit the initial participants for the research project. We then employed "snowballing" technique to identify the next set of respondents We asked each respondent for recommendations to identify and reach out to other women belonging to households in informal employment. This approach proved to be very useful and enabled us to recruit participants from a range of occupational categories and socio-economic groups in Punjab. The participants were drawn from different age groups, occupation entities, caste groups,[38] education levels and socio-economic status, as reflected by average monthly family income before the crisis. A summary of the interview participants is presented in Table 2.1.

An interview schedule was designed to explore the participants' experiences of the pandemic. This schedule was informed by literature and covered topics ranging from employment and income, to food security, health concerns, reproductive health and mobility during the lockdown period. The interview questions were finalised after 5 pilot interviews were conducted. After the pilot, we added two more questions to our schedule. Informed consent was taken from the participants and all interviews were anonymised to protect the identity of the respondents.

[37] Yvona S. Lincoln and Egon G. Guba, *Naturalistic inquiry* (New York: Sage, 1985): 3–5.

[38] Eleven of our interview respondents comprised of SC women. These were not purposely chosen by the researcher, but may be reflective of the socio-economic structure of the Punjabi economy. Punjab has the highest proportion of Scheduled Caste (SC) communities. They constitute 28% of Punjab's population at present (Census of India, 2011). Poverty in Punjab is concentrated disproportionately among the SC population in both rural and urban areas. On the basis of estimates of monthly per capita consumption expenditure (MPCE), 27.2% of the SC population in rural areas and 35.3% of the population in urban areas in Punjab are estimated to be below the poverty line, as compared to only 1.5% for the general population (NSSO, 2017–18).

Table 2.1 Summary of interview participants

Respondent	*Age (Y)*	*Caste*	*Religion*	*Education*	*Profession*	*Household size*	*Average monthly family income (INR)*
R1	56	SC	Sikh	Class 8	Caregiver	4	18,000
R2	40	OBC	Hindu	Class 10	Beautician	4	15,000
R3	28	SC	Sikh	BA	Receptionist	7	25,000
R4	33	General	Sikh	Class 12 with diploma	Homemaker	3	20,000
R5	31	SC	Sikh	Class 12	Homemaker	6	18,000
R6	20	SC	Hindu	Class 10	Beautician	4	20,000
R7	50	SC	Sikh	Illiterate	Domestic worker	6	5000
R8	25	SC	Sikh	Bachelor in Computer Application	Data entry operator	5	22,000
R9	38	General	Muslim	Class 10	Runs grocery shop with husband	8	60,000
RIO	24	OBC	Sikh	Class 12 with diploma	Tutor in stitching school run by an NGO	2	17,000
RI1	41	General	Hindu	Class 12	Receptionist	5	15,000
RI2	23	SC	Sikh	Elementary Teacher Training	Unemployed	6	40,000
RI3	21	General	Hindu	Class 8	Homemaker	5	15,000
R14	35	OBC	Hindu	Illiterate	Domestic worker	5	10,000
R15	22	OBC	Sikh	Class 10	Homemaker	5	25,000
RIG	27	OBC	Sikh	Class 12 with diploma in computers	Unemployed	4	12,000
RI7	24	General	Hindu	Class 10	Homemaker	4	10,000
RI8	29	SC	Sikh	Illiterate	Domestic worker	5	17,000

(continued)

Table 2.1 (continued)

Respondent	*Age (Y)*	*Caste*	*Religion*	*Education*	*Profession*	*Household size*	*Average monthly family income (INR)*
R19	48	General	Hindu	Class 10	Theatre/TV actor	2	50,000
R20	35	OBC	Hindu	Illiterate	Domestic worker	5	15,000
R2I	25	OBC	Hindu	Illiterate	Construction worker		12,000
R22	27	General	Sikh	MA	Unemployed	2	30,000
R23	26	General	Hindu	MBA	Sales representative	1	20,000
R24	42	SC	Sikh	Class 10	Tailor	7	11,500
R25	17	SC	Hindu	Class 5	House maid	5	10,000
R26	24	General	Muslim	BA and Computer course	Homemaker and helps husband in work	3	15,000
R27	31	OBC	Sikh	Class 10	Homemaker	7	8000
R28	42	General	Hindu	Class 12	Homemaker	7	7500
R29	20	General	Hindu	Class 5	Homemaker	2	5000
R30	33	ST	Sikh	Illiterate	labour at village functions	5	18,000
R3I	30	General	Muslim	Class 8	Homemaker	6	20,000
R32	37	SC	Sikh	Class 5	Domestic worker	7	37,000
R33	31	General	Hindu	MA	Librarian	4	35,000
R34	36	General	Hindu	BA	Office secretary	6	50,000

SC = Scheduled Castes; ST = Scheduled Tribes; OBC = Other Backward Castes; Mean age = 31.5 years; Average family income INR 20,823.5

Semi-structured interviews were adopted in the study to facilitate in-depth exploration of the respondent's experiences of the pandemic and to allow flexibility and space for both the interviewer and interviewee.[39] Interviewees were encouraged to elaborate on how they framed

[39] Alan Bryman and Emma Bell, "Breaking down the quantitative/qualitative divide," in *Business Research Methods*, ed. Alan Bryman and Emma Bell (New York: Oxford University Press, 2003): 465–478.

and understood the events surrounding the lockdown, and the coping mechanisms adopted by them. The interview questions were divided into two main parts. In the first part, we gathered general demographic information related to the interviewees and in the second part of the interview we asked ten open ended questions covering their employment, income and wages, forms of government and private assistance available to them, household food security, health concerns, reproductive health and mobility. The semi-structured format also enabled us to extend the conversation by asking probing/follow up questions to seek clarification, and overcome any initial resistance or vagueness. Interviews generally lasted for 30–45 minutes.

The interviews were conducted in Punjabi and recorded. Some running notes were also made while the interview was being conducted. They were then transcribed and translated into English. We used thematic analysis for our study of the interview data and employed systematic coding and categorization to explore a range of textual information to identity trends, patterns and nature of relationships.[40] As a first step, we read through the data several times to achieve immersion and obtain a sense of the whole. Open-coding was used to determine what was represented in the text, and give that phenomenon a name.[41] Codes were grouped into categories and subcategories to develop the initial coding frame and set rules. After the initial coding frame was developed, we provided clear descriptions of each category and set rules determining when and what data should be included under a category. The codes were then examined, reorganised, categories and subcategories were clearly defined, and all transcripts were recoded using the final codes to establish consistency.

To ensure the reliability and trustworthiness of our findings we instituted member checks[42] whereby two participants from the study were asked to check whether the findings resonated with them, and changes

[40] Michael Quinn Patton, *Qualitative research and evaluation methods* (Newbury Park, CA: Sage, 2015): 26–27.

[41] W. Cresswell John and Vicki L. Plano Clark, *Designing and conducting mixed method research* (Thousand Oaks, CA: Sage): 11–12.

[42] Ibid., 37.

in interpretations were made based on their suggestions. We also instituted peer examination[43] and asked another academic to comment on the plausibility of the results.

Key Findings and Discussion

From our analysis, we were able to unearth five gender specific pathways through which the pandemic impacted the lives of women belonging to households in informal employment in Punjab. These comprise of (a) Poverty-Related Stresses and Livelihood Challenges (b) Heightened Food Insecurity (c) Restrictions on Mobility (d) Unwanted Pregnancies and disruption of routine health services (e) Social Ostracisation.

In this section we discuss these pathways in detail, along with their linkages to pre-existing social structures and mechanisms from a gendered perspective.

(a) **Poverty-related stresses and livelihood challenges**

A number of the respondents in the study reported that they experienced severe economic stresses and income losses during the lockdown period.

Respondent (14) an unlettered, SC women working as a domestic worker before the lockdown period said:

> *I used to work as a domestic help in Mohali, but my employers asked me not to come for work during the lockdown. I was not given any wages either. My husband worked as a daily wage porter in the grain market. He too has not earned anything in the past two months. We have 3 children, one of whom is disabled, things have been extremely difficult for us.* (Respondent 14)

For women like respondent 14, caste entities intersected with the precarity of informal employment during the lock down period and translated into complete loss of income and livelihoods, as well as heightened social discrimination. Similar sentiments were also echoed by respondent 32. She was a 37 year old SC women who had been doing cooking and

[43] Sharan B. Merriam, "Qualitative research: Designing, implementing, and publishing a study," in *Handbook of research on scholarly publishing and research methods*, ed. Victor Wang (Hershey, PA: IG Global, 2015): 125–140.

cleaning work all her life. She had very education and no work experience other than domestic work.

> *I tried to enter the main gate of the locality, where I worked as a maid to get my salary but was not allowed to come in. My husband was a gardener in the same house. He also lost his income during the past two months. We could not get any wages during the month of March when we were in desperate need of cash.* (Respondent 32)

These narratives illustrate how the social distancing and quarantine norms amid the COVID-19 crisis in India propagated social exclusion as well as caste and class bias in society. Indian society is characterised by a rigid hierarchy of class and caste structures. Within such a social structure, these poor, low caste women began to be seen as carriers of the virus. Social distancing norms were employed as an excuse by their employers to humiliate and shun them without any consideration for their economic suffering. Similar findings on increased prevalence of caste-based discrimination amid the covid-19 crisis have been reported by Arora and Majumder[44] who conducted an empirical study on the plight of migrant women workers in India's capital, New Delhi.

The accounts of our respondents also suggest that in the absence of any regulations governing informal employment, their economic precarity was solely conditioned by their employer's prerogatives. For instance Respondent 7, a 50 year old SC woman had been working as a cook and a cleaner for the past thirty years. But unlike respondents 14 and 32 her employer needed her services during the lockdown period. He thus got an essential services pass made for her and this enabled her to continue working during the lockdown. Only three of the interviewees reported that they had received any wages during the crisis (Respondent 22,[45] Respondent 33 and Respondent 34). The Government of India had appealed to employers to pay full wages to permanent and contractual employees

[44] Shubhda Arora and Mrinmoy Majumder, "Where is my home? Gendered precarity and the experience of COVID-19 among women migrant workers from Delhi and National Capital Region, India," *Gender, Work and Organization* (2021): 13.

[45] This respondent received full wages because she had contracted the coronavirus infection from her employer's daughter, when she had gone to receive her at the airport.

during this period.[46] However, this appeal has not been backed by any legal guarantees and was solely dependent on the largess of the individual employers.

The Central Government had also announced that it would transfer cash transfers of INR 500 per month to poor women for the next three months under the *Pradhan Mantri Jan Dhan Yojna* (PMJDY). However, none of our respondents said that they had received any form of income support from the government during this period. This may be attributed to the large scale exclusion errors in the PMJDY scheme. These have been highlighted by the Financial Inclusion Insights Survey (2018), conducted by the Yale Centre for Economic Growth. This survey revealed that only 21 per cent poor women in India hold a PMJDY account, payment failures in this scheme range between 3–7 and 33% of these accounts are inoperative.[47] Without any cushion of income security or social protection available to these workers, the large scale exclusion errors and poor implementation of this limited form of income protection scheme added on to their existing income vulnerabilities and offered them little in the way of income protection.

Our interviews reveal that another section of women who were disproportionately impacted by the crisis comprised of female headed households. These women have been referred to as "poorest of poor" in literature.[48] For these women, the economic constraints induced by the pandemic mapped on to their precarious position as the sole breadwinner of the family and caring responsibilities for other members of the family. These factors created a unique constellation of disadvantages for this group of women amid the lockdown. These disadvantages reveal themselves in our participant's narratives.

Respondent 2, a 40 year old a self-taught beautician had started her home-based saloon four year when her husband suffered from an accident

[46] "COVID-19 government order tracker," GOI, 2020, accessed June 1, 2020, https://covid-india.in.

[47] Erica Field et al., "On her own account: How strengthening women's financial control impacts labor supply and gender norms." Yale Centre for Economic Growth, 2019, accessed May 12, 2019, https://elischolar.library.yale.edu/egcenter-discussion-paper-series/1076.

[48] Naila Kabeer, "Gender, poverty, and inequality: A brief history of feminist contributions in the field of international development," *Gender & Development* 23, no. 2 (2015): 203.

and became disabled. She described the precarity of their situation during the lockdown as:

> *My husband is handicapped. I have been working as a home based beautician and running the house by myself for the past 4 years. My daughter is 18 and used to do private tuitions for younger children. Her income also dried up, we have just manged with savings and some borrowings from relatives.* (Respondent 2)

Respondent 24, a 42 year old matriculate had acquired training as a seamstress as her husband's ill health prevented him from being in regular work. She had been the sole earner in her family for the past decade. She describes how the pandemic led to heightened economic uncertainty as well as increased psychological stresses.

> *The work I got before the pandemic was completed in the earlier days of lock down. I got paid for it. Later there were no orders and no payments. I stitched masks for people known to me but no payments were made to me which causes me a great deal of stress and anxiety. My husband suffers from chronic arthritis and cannot work. He remains very depressed.* (Respondent 24)

Our findings also show that the income deprivations faced by women in informal employment were not uniform, and differed according to the respondent's educational profile and occupational entities. Some of these women were able to employ their training and previous work experience to seek alternative forms of employment that came up in the lockdown period. For instance, Respondent 1 who was employed as a caregiver to two bed ridden individuals before the lockdown was able to find work as a cleaner in a private nursing home in early May. Respondent 10 who had a diploma in tailoring started working from home on a part time basis and taking orders for making scrubs and masks for hospital workers. However, most of the interviewees were either illiterate or had very low levels of education. They also did not have any alternative skill sets, other than the work they were doing prior to the lockdown. Consequently, these women experienced dire economic stress in this period with closure of economic activity and no form of social protection.

Another major theme which emerged from our analysis is with respect to coping strategies adopted by women to mitigate the financial impacts of the COVID-19 pandemic. The economic stresses induced by the pandemic intersected with the prevailing income insecurity rooted in informal employment and forced these women to liquidate the meagre amount of savings and assets they had. For instance, respondent 20, a 35 year old OBC women working as a domestic worker had been saving up for her daughter's wedding for the last couple of years. She expressed her anguish as:

> *We had saved money for elder daughter's wedding. All that money was spent during the lockdown.* (Respondent 20)

Respondent 20, a young 20 year old SC women had been supporting her widowed father, a car mechanic at a local garage and two younger brothers by working as a beautician in a local beauty parlour. She lost her job during the pandemic. Consequently, the family could no longer afford to send the boys to school.

> *My brothers studied in Class 8th and 10th before the lockdown. They may not be able to go back to school now. The elder one is looking for a job now that the lockdown has been lifted.* (Respondent 6)

Narratives from other respondents revealed that the economic stresses during the lockdown period had not only robbed them of their immediate income, but also threatened their long run income earning capacities. Respondent 19, a 48 year old women who had been working as a theatre and TV artist for the past 30 years. She had started an acting school just the previous and now feared that she would have to close down.

> *I have not been able to pay rent for the premises during the past three months. It is increasingly uncertain when we will be able to restart the classes or how many students would turn up for these. It is quite likely that the number of students will be drastically cut down. In that case we will have to shut down.*

Other interviewees (Respondent 7 and Respondent 32) who worked as domestic cleaners before the lockdown feared that they may not be re-employed as average household incomes of their previous employers had been drastically reduced during the lockdown. Respondent 10, a tailor and Respondent 24, a beautician also expressed anxiety and said that the quantum of work available to them might not pick up for the months following the lockdown period Respondent 4 and 19 who drew their income from theatre and regional cinema expressed similar concerns.

Thus, our findings revealed that unsustainable employment coupled with the lack of any form of social protection threatens to erode the economic autonomy of many women in informal employment, along with their long term earning capacity and vertical mobility. The livelihood concerns of our interviewees echo the findings put forth by Deshpande.[49] She estimated that women who were employed in the pre-lockdown period are 23.5 percentage points less likely to be employed in the post-lockdown phase compared to men. She attributes this to fact that women are over-represented in sectors which face extended periods of uncertainty and threat of permanent closure. These include restaurants, hotels, beauty salons and retail centres. While the work performed by these women is essential to meet the everyday needs of a large section of the society, they were regarded as nowhere in the system in the COVID-19 policy prerogatives.

Heightened Food Insecurity at the Household Level

The second major impact of the lockdown emerged with respect to heightened food insecurity among poor and marginalised households owing to the income and employment losses during the lockdown period. 26 of the 34 women interviewed in the study said that they did not have any money to purchase food during this time. While food insecurity and hunger affected poor households as a whole, the insights derived from our interviewees revealed that women carried additional burden of household food insecurity due to their social conditioning and sacrificed their food consumption in favour of others member of the household.

Respondent 31, a 30 year old mother of four young children lamented:

> *We used up our savings in the first week. We could not afford to buy milk for the children after the first week. I tried to give some vegetables to the children. As for myself, I have only been putting salt on dry roti and somehow surviving for the past one month.* (Respondent 31)

[49] Ashwini Deshpande, "What does work from home mean for women?" *Economic and Political Weekly* 55, no. 21 (2020): 7.

Our findings mirror those of other empirical studies which highlight that women are disproportionately impacted by household food security during economic crises.[50,51] There was the absence of effective rationing and food provision for these marginalised households during the lock-down period. The Government of Punjab has a food distribution scheme, *Atta Dal Scheme*[52] where in free rations are provided to poor SC house-holds in rural areas through fair price shops. However, the experience of some respondents suggests that even this food distribution scheme was not operative during the lockdown. Respondent 7, a 50 year old SC woman described the difficulties that she had to go through to access the meagre amount of subsidised food in order to feed her family of six.

> *We normally receive free rations from the local ration shop under government scheme. The shop was shut during the lockdown. We had to pressurise for the shop to open through the local panchayat. The distribution of the ration is highly arbitrary and we do not get the full amount. We were only given wheat, no lentils and sugar.* (Respondent 7)

The only form of food provisions available to these households was through NGOs and religious organisations.

> *We had no money to buy food. People from Gurdwara used to come in the morning to distribute langur. In the afternoon some other people[NGO] used to come to give us some food.*
>
> *In the evening no one came and we had to go hungry. Sometimes people in the nearby houses would give something to children. But we had a very hard time.* (Respondent 15)

As the quote reveals, these community-based organisations helped to alle-viate some of the suffering, hunger and starvation faced by these resource poor women amid the lockdown. However, they could not be a substitute

[50] Karen Bell, "Bread and roses: A gender perspective on environmental justice and public health," *International Journal of Environmental Research and Public Health* 13, no. 10 (2016): 1005.

[51] Erin C. Lentz, "Complicating narratives of women's food and nutrition insecurity: Domestic violence in rural Bangladesh," *World Development* 104 (2018): 275.

[52] According to the provisions of this scheme, SC households in rural areas of Punjab are provided 35 kgs of rice/wheat, along with ½ kg pulses, 1 kg sugar and 100 gm tea per month through free price ration shops (Government of Punjab, 2020).

for effective state provisioning of rations. These organisations are limited in size, capacity and institutional structures. During the lockdown period they were also constrained by the rapidly changing rules and norms in the lockdown period.

> *NGO People used to come in a van to distribute food twice a day. Then, there were three coronavirus cases in our area and it became a containment zone. There was police all around. They did not let the food van inside. We had to go without food for two days. After that people from Gurdwara came and gave us food for rest of the two weeks.* (Respondent 19)

These narratives point out to the apathy of the Government towards basic survival needs of poor households. While there were strict restrictions on movement of people, no mechanisms were put in place to ensure that food provisions were available to these households in the interim period in a sustained way. The heightened nutritional vulnerabilities created for women amid the lockdown may have grave implications for their health and nutrition. Women in Punjab suffered from poor nutritional status even before the coronavirus crisis. National Family Health Survey[53] data reveals that 54% of women in the state suffer from anaemia. There also persists pronounced intra-household gender discrimination in food consumption among poor households in Punjab.[54] Food-based vulnerabilities are likely to be intensified for these poor women as the economic deprivation created by the covid-19 crisis intersects with the absence of effective rationing systems in the lockdown period.

(b) **Restrictions on mobility**

During the lockdown period, all forms of public transport in the state were completely shut down. Literature shows that women are more dependent on public transport and the absence of safe and reliable means of public transport heightens their social exclusion.[55,56] Public transport

[53] NFHS-4. 2015–16. *National family health survey* (Mumbai: Ministry of Health and Family Welfare Government of India, 2017): 31–33.

[54] Ibid., 13.

[55] Ibid., 48.

[56] Kerry Hamilton and Linda Jenkins, "A gender audit for public transport: A new policy tool in the tackling of social exclusion," *Urban Studies* 37 (2000): 1797.

is also a central fulcrum of women's participation in the economy. 58% of women in India depend on public transport to get to work.[57]

Our field work demonstrated that the blanket ban on public transport affected women through a number of channels. Essential services workers found it extremely difficult to go to work.

> *Since there was no transport I had to walk 15 kms to work every day. If I came with my husband on scooter, the police would stop us on the way and not allow us to pass through. So I preferred to walk.* (Respondent 7)

Respondent 8, a 25 year old data entry operator in the National Health Mission (NHM), a government department who had been employed for only a few months prior to the pandemic narrated her plight:

> *I am an out sourced employee with National Health Mission. I am not entitled to leave. My office is located in Chandigarh, while I live 40 kms away. Prior to the lockdown I changed to two buses to get to work. During the lockdown my office was open but I could not go to work because no transport was available. I have been marked absent and not given any salary since April. I am fearful that I might do the jobs.*

On top of intensification of income-based vulnerabilities, absence of public transport also reduced access to routine healthcare as well as maternal health care services, especially so for resource poor women who did not have private means of transport to reach health centres. Some respondents also reported how they found it extremely difficult to access maternal health services and routine health care, due to the absence of public transport. Respondent 13, a 21 year old women who was expecting her first child described her harrowing ordeal during the lockdown period.

> *I was in the early stages of pregnancy. I could not go to the hospital since there was no transport. I suffered from severe cramps and spotting for 20 days. When I went to the doctor after the lockdown, she said I have had a miscarriage.* (Respondent 13)

Respondent 18, a native of a small village with only basic health facilities described how her 60 year old mother in law's health deteriorated during

[57] ITDP, *Women and transport in Indian cities* (New Delhi: Institute for Transportation and Development Policy, 2017): 57.

the lockdown period because they do not go to go to the hospital in the nearby city in the absence of public transport.

> *We have a health center in our village. But they did not have blood pressure medicines for my mother in law. We could not go to the hospital as no buses were available.* (Respondent 18)

Thus, we can infer that the restrictions on public transport during the lockdown had not taken account of the gender, as well as class dimensions of this policy prerogative. The lack of public transport not only lead to increased economic stresses for women, but also put their health and well-being in peril. This poorly thought out policy prerogative magnified the existing class bias in mobility and access to essential medical services. While public health facilities were operational during the lockdown period, there had been little planning behind how people would access these essential services or how essential workers would commute to work.

(c) **Unwanted Pregnancies and disruption of routine health services**

In a recent study the United Nations Population Fund (UNFPA) has projected that India would record the highest number of births in the nine months since COVID-19 was declared a pandemic, with 20.1 million additional babies.[58] These additional births would be attributed to disruption to reproductive health services in the country. The experiences of our interviewees demonstrated that amid the COVID-19 pandemic women were losing their ability to plan their families. This loss of autonomy over reproductive decisions may translate into serious economic and health impacts on women's life. This emerged through our respondent's narratives. While India protected abortion as an essential service during the coronavirus lockdown; with no transport services, limited healthcare and restrictions on movement, women lost control over their ability to plan families.

[58] "Impact of the COVID-19 pandemic on family planning and ending gender-based violence, female genital mutilation and child marriage," UNFPA, 2020, accessed May 19, 2020, https://www.unfpa.org/sites/default/files/resource-pdf/COVID-19_impact_brief_for_UNFPA_24_April_2020_1.pdf.

Respondent 12, a 23 year old newly married women, who aspires to become a primary school teacher described how she had an unplanned pregnancy during the lockdown due to constraints on mobility and lack of access to contraceptives.

> *I have finished Elementary Teacher's Training (ETT) course and was applying for jobs for the past few months. I got pregnant during the lockdown because I could not get access to contraception pills. It is an unwanted pregnancy.* (Respondent 12)

Respondent 16, a 27 year old mother of one also had a similar story to tell and bemoaned how the lockdown pregnancy would delay her going back to paid employment.

> *I was working as a computer operator before marriage. I have a one year old daughter and I was hoping to get back to work now. I fell pregnant during the lockdown, because we could not access any contraceptives. I would have to stay at home now for next few years because it would be difficult to take care of two small children.* (Respondent 16)

Feminist scholars have argued that women face a "reproductive tax" as their reproductive role in society prevents or delays their entry in the labour force. This impacts their professional progression and lifetime income.[59] These narratives reveal how restrictions on mobility during the lockdown further undermined women's autonomy regarding their reproductive choices, and led to additional constraints on their professional choices.

These unplanned pregnancies may also adversely impact the health and nutritional well-being of women from low income families, who already have multiple children. For instance, Respondent 31, a mother to 4 children said:

> *I used to get Antara injection from the dispensary every 3 months. I could not get the injection during the lockdown period, and fell pregnant again. My husband is a sole earner, he used to make decent money from denting and painting work but lost all work during the lockdown. We found it very difficult to manage food and rations. It will be quite hard to manage another child.*

[59] Ibid., 46.

Previous studies show that women's limited autonomy over their reproductive choices is a key barrier to improvements in their reproductive health outcomes.[60,61] Even though Punjab is a relatively rich state, it did not have very favourable indicators of maternal health pre-COVID-19 crisis as well. Despite the continued focus on maternal care in recent years, only 30.7% pregnant women receive full antenatal care.[62] These vulnerabilities experienced by expecting mothers are likely to increase in the post-COVID-19 period, with the spate of unplanned pregnancies, additional births, and disruption to reproductive health services.

The pandemic also had an impact on the delivery and quality of routine healthcare services, as hospitals were over-run with covid-19 patients and access to routine healthcare remained severely disrupted. Several respondents dissatisfaction with the health services that they could access during the lockdown and complained that there was no routine examination.

For instance Respondent 27, a 31 year old mother of three belonged to an economically poor household who could not afford private health services. Yet, she was deeply disappointed with the kind of treatment she received for her daughter at a public health facility.

> *My 3 year old daughter became unwell. We went to community health centre in Banur to get her checked. They shut the doors and did not see her. From a distance, they just asked questions about the problem and threw a pack of paracetamol at us.* (Respondent 27)

Even before the coronavirus crisis, Punjab has very low levels of utilisation of public health facilities at only 14.5%. Official government data also shows that 37.1% people in Punjab do not visit public health services because they regard the quality of services to be poor (National Sample Survey Organisation).[63] During the coronavirus pandemic, private healthcare facilities are operating on a very limited scale. Considering the financial vulnerability of low-income households during this period, it is

[60] Le Kien and My Nguyen, "Shedding light on maternal education and child health in development countries," *World Development* (2020): 105005.

[61] V.S. Saravanan, "Contestations and negotiations of urban health in India: A situated political approach," *World Development* 104 (2018): 377.

[62] Ibid., 50.

[63] NSSO, *Key indicators of social consumption in India: Health* (New Delhi: Ministry of Statistics and Programme Implementation, 2017–18): 58.

important that the quality of healthcare for non-COVID patients in public hospitals is maintained at a competent level to restore public confidence. These public health services may be especially important for women, given their particular needs for maternal and reproductive health services.

(d) **Social Ostracisation**

In India the spread of coronavirus has also led to rise in societal prejudices and increased incidence of Islamophobia. In April 2020, a religious congregation held by a conservative sect, *Tablighi Jamaat* was blamed one third of India's coronavirus cases on this gathering.[64] This incident spawned tremendous hatred against the Muslim community. Some bigoted news channels, went as far as saying that the Muslim community is waging a "corona *jihad*" against India After this incident, there were several of reports of ordinary Muslim men being beaten up and lynched, and their businesses being boycotted across the country. Some of our respondents also suffered from this form of prejudice during the crisis.

Respondent 9, a Muslim woman who ran a small grocery store with her husband described how their religious identity intersected with the economic constraints induced by the crisis and magnified their economic and social hardships.

> *We run a grocery shop in the village, and were supplying rations through home delivery during the lockdown. After my brother in law went out for some work for two days, he was branded a Tabhligi and our entire family was quarantined for 3 weeks. We have nothing to do with the Tabhlighi Jamaat We had already stocked up rations for home deliveries when we were quarantined. We suffered heavy losses. We have been treated like criminals.* (Respondent 9)

Another respondent, a 30 year old mother of four children was facing drastic loss in her already meagre way during the lockdown. She perceived that she was being systematically excluded from government's rationing scheme owing to her religious identity.

> *We are Muslims. So we don't get any free rations under the Atta Dal scheme of the government.* (Respondent 31).

64 Ibid., 44.

In a similar vein Respondent 9 remarked that they did not eve dare to venture out to buy medicines during the lockdown, because they feared that the police might jail them. The experience of these respondents showed that the religious-based discrimination they faced during the crisis has led to extreme psychological distress and eroded their trust in the government machinery. Our findings mirror other quantitative studies which suggest that social stigmatisation faced by Muslims resulted in increased economic distress faced by them as well.[65]

There have also been reports of Coronavirus patients facing social stigmatisation, and discrimination. Two of our respondents, who contracted the coronavirus shared similar concerns. Respondent 23, a newly engaged 26 year old woman described how she had hid her disease from her family due to fear of social ostracisation.

> *I live alone in the city. I did not even tell my parents that I had contracted the disease, even though I was in hospital for three weeks. I am engaged to be married in October. I fear that my engagement would be called off in case anyone gets to know of my illness.* (Respondent 23).

Similar anxieties were reported by Respondent 22, a 27 year old woman who was newly married at the time.

> *I got married in November last year. My parents-in-law did not approve of our marriage. When I got sick with coronavirus in April, we did not tell anyone. I was in hospital for two weeks. I have still not recovered fully and am being tested for TB now. I am anxious that someone will come to know of my disease.* (Respondent 22)

The accounts of these respondents how the patriarchal structures in Indian society and social prejudices are interact with each other to condition women's subjective experiences of the covid-19 crisis. Women who suffered from this disease not only faced health challenges, but addition fear, stress and anxiety due to the social stigma attached to the disease.

[65] Sonalde Desai, Neerad Deshmukh, and Santanu Parmanik, "Precarity in a time of uncertainty: Gendered employment patterns during the COVID-19 lockdown in India," *Feminist Economics* 27, no. 1 (2021): 171.

Conclusion

This paper brought forth the voices of women engaged in informal employment to contribute to the debates surrounding the socio-economic impacts of the COVID-19 crisis in its varied forms. Most discussion on the impact of the COVID-19 crisis is based on secondary data and analysis of macroeconomic indicators such as loss in growth rates, dip in employment figures or loss in consumer confidence. Grounded voices are often missing in these discourses. This paper foregrounds these voices through field-based interviews with 34 resource poor women, belonging to households engaged in informal employment. While there are multiple dimensions of the Covid-19-related crisis for the lives of these women, we clustered them into five main categories. Each of these categories represents a unique pathway and illuminates how the pandemic exacerbated their gendered experiences of everyday life at home and work. Our empirical investigation was framed by an intersectionality lens which enabled us to uncover the different forms of intersectional vulnerabilities which are heaped on to women in their daily lives and create a "matrix of domination" not only due to their gender, but also their caste, class and religion entities. This was reflected in the subjective experiences of different interviewees in the course of the fieldwork. We also saw how some sub-group of women within informal employment faced additional burdens due to their position as female headed households, their caring responsibilities within the households, their reproductive roles as well as their caste and religious identities. These additional burdens intersected with the economic duress induced by the COVID-19 crisis and translated into new forms of disempowerment for these women.

Our empirical analysis also uncovered how these additional forms of deprivations were essentially rooted in the absence of a gendered policy response towards the crisis. The lived experiences of our interviewees reveal that even the meagre forms of income support and food aid available to these women were poorly targeted. In the absence of any social protection cover and insurance, these poorly targeted schemes compounded their economic insecurity during the lockdown period. The other facets of women's poverty such as gendered dependence on public transport were not even considered in these policy prerogatives. This apathy created additional forms of disempowerment for women through heightened job insecurity, loss of income and erosion of assets as well as reduced access to maternal and routine medical services. Such shortsightedness in policy implementation threatens to reverse the limited gains made on women's empowerment in India. As the covid-19 pandemic continues to ravage through India there is an urgent need to implement well targeted income support measures for women workers in vulnerable forms of employment and address their differential economic and social needs in the planning process.

One limitation of this study is that it was conducted in the early period of the COVID-19 pandemic and the lockdown imposed in India. It would be instructive to conduct a follow up study in the subsequent period when the lockdown restrictions were gradually eased, but economic activity remained slow, and unemployment was at an unprecedented level. It would be insightful to compare the coping mechanisms and strategies adopted by resource poor households and women, as the pandemic continued for an extended time period.

References

Agarwal, Bina. "'Bargaining' and gender relations: Within and beyond the household." *Feminist Economics* 3, no. 1 (1997): 1–51.

Arora, Shubhda, and Majumder, Mrinmoy. "Where is my home? Gendered precarity and the experience of COVID-19 among women migrant workers from Delhi and National Capital Region, India." *Gender, Work and Organization* (2021): 1–14.

Baruah, Bipasha. "Earning their keep and keeping what they earn: A critique of organizing strategies for South Asian women in the informal sector." *Gender, Work and Organization* 11, no. 6 (2004): 605–626.

BBC. "Coronavirus lockdown: The Indian migrants dying to get home." BBC 2020. Accessed June 10, 2020. https://www.bbc.co.uk/news/world-asia-india-52672764.

Bell Karen. "Bread and roses: A gender perspective on environmental justice and public health." *International Journal of Environmental Research and Public Health* 13, no. 10 (2016): 1005–1020.

Bessell, Sharan. "The individual deprivation measure: Measuring poverty as if gender and inequality matter." *Gender & Development* 23, no. 2 (2015): 223–240.

Bryman, Alan, and Bell, Emma. "Breaking down the quantitative/qualitative divide." In *Business research methods*, edited by Alan Bryman and Emma Bell, 465–478. New York: Oxford University Press, 2003.

Butler, Judith. *Frames of war: When life is grievable*. London: Verso Publications, 2009.

Census of India. *General population tables and primary census abstracts; Punjab Part 2A and Part 2 B. Series 17*. New Delhi: Government of India, 2011.

Chagar, Rajni. "Protection or obstruction? Women and precarious work in India." *Canadian Journal of Development Studies* 30, no. 3–4 (2011): 591–614.

Chant, Svlyia. "Exploring the 'feminization of poverty' in relation to women's work and home-based enterprise in slums of the global south." *International Journal of Gender and Entrepreneurship* 6, no. 3 (2014): 296–316.

Chant, Sylvia. "Women, girls, and world poverty: Empowerment, equality or essentialism?" *International Development Planning Review* 38, no. 1 (2016): 1–24.

CMIE. *Unemployment in India*. New Delhi: Centre for Monitoring of Indian Economy. Accessed May 30, 2020. https://unemploymentinindia.cmie.com.

Collins, Patricia Hill. *Black feminist thought: Knowledge, consciousness, and the politics of empowerment*. Boston, MA: Unwin Hyman, 1990.

Cresswell, John W., and Clark, Vicki L. Plano. *Designing and conducting mixed method research*. Thousand Oaks, CA: Sage, 2011.

deHoop, Thomas, Van Kampen, Luuk, Linssen, Rik, and Van Eerdewijk, Anaika. "Women's autonomy and subjective well-being: How gender norms shape the impact of self-help groups in Odisha, India." *Feminist Economics* 20, no. 3 (2014): 103–135.

Desai, Sonalde, Deshmukh, Neerad, and Parmanik, Santanu. "Precarity in a time of uncertainty: Gendered employment patterns during the COVID-19 lockdown in India." *Feminist Economics* 27, no. 1 (2021): 152–172.

Deshpande, Ashwani. "What does work from home mean for women?" *Economic and Political Weekly* 55, no. 21 (2020): 1–7.

Duflo, Esther. "Grandmothers and granddaughters: Old-age pensions and intra-household allocation in South Africa." *World Bank Economic Review* 17 (2003): 1–25.

Field, Erica, Pande, Rohini, Rigol, Natalia, Schaner, Simone, and Moore, Charity T. "On her own account: How strengthening women's financial control impacts labor supply and gender norms." Yale Centre for Economic Growth. Accessed May 12, 2020. https://elischolar.library.yale.edu/egcenter-discussion-paper-series/1076.

GOI. "COVID-19 government order tracker." GOI. 2020. Accessed June 1, 2020. https://covid-india.in.

Government of Punjab. *Statistical abstract of Punjab*. Chandigarh: Economic and Statistical Organisation, 2020.

Hale, Thomas, Angrist, Noam, Goldszmidt, Rafael, Kira, Beatriz, Petherick, Anna, Phillips, Toby, and Webster, Samuel. "Variation in government responses to COVID-19." Blavatnik School of Government Working 2020.

Accessed May 20, 2020. https://www.bsg.ox.ac.uk/research/research-projects/covid-19-government-response-tracker.
Hamilton, Kerry, and Jenkins, Linda. "A Gender audit for public transport: A new policy tool in the tackling of social exclusion." *Urban Studies* 37 (2012): 1793–1800.
Harriss, John. "Antinomies of empowerment: Observations on civil society, politics and urban governance in India." *Economic and Political Weekly* 42, no. 26 (2007): 2716–2724.
Harris-White, Barbara. "Rethinking institutions: Innovation and institutional change in India's informal economy." *Modern Asian Studies* 51, no. 6 (2018): 1727–1755.
Hill, Elizabeth. "Women in the Indian informal economy: Collective strategies for work life improvement and development." *Work, Employment and Society* 15, no. 3 (2001): 443–464.
ILO. *Women and men in the informal economy: A statistical picture.* Geneva: ILO, 2018.
ITDP. *Women and transport in Indian cities.* New Delhi: Institute for Transportation and Development Policy, 2017.
Kabeer, Naila. "Gender, poverty, and inequality: A brief history of feminist contributions in the field of international development." *Gender & Development* 23, no. 2 (2015): 189–205.
Kabeer, Naila, Milward, Kirsty, and Sudarshan, Ratna. "Organising women workers in the informal economy." *Gender & Development* 21, no. 2 (2013): 249–263.
Kabeer, Naila, Razavi, Shahra, and van der Meulen Rodgers Yana. "Feminist economic perspectives on the COVID-19 pandemic." *Feminist Economics* 27, no. 1–2 (2021): 1–29.
Kesar, Surbhi, Abraham, Rosa, Lahoti, Rahul, Nath, Paaritosh, and Basole, Amit. "Pandemic, informality and vulnerability: Impact of COVID-19 on livelihoods in India." *Canadian Journal of Development Studies* 42, no. 1–2 (2021): 145–164.
Le, Kien, and Nguyen, My. "Shedding light on maternal education and child health in development countries." *World Development* (2020): 105005
Lentz, Erin C. "Complicating narratives of women's food and nutrition insecurity: Domestic violence in rural Bangladesh." *World Development* 104 (2018): 271–280.
Lincoln, Yvona S., and Guba, Egon G. *Naturalistic inquiry.* New York: Sage, 1985.
Mangubhai, Jayshree P., and Capraro, Chiara. "'Leave no one behind' and the challenge of intersectionality: Christian aid's experience of working with single and Dalit women in India." *Gender & Development* 23 no. 2 (2015): 261–277.

Merriam, Sharan B. "Qualitative research: Designing, implementing, and publishing a study." In *Handbook of research on scholarly publishing and research methods*, edited by Victor Wang, 125–140. Hershey, PA: IG Global, 2015.

Mileti, Dennis S. *Disasters by design: A reassessment of natural hazards in the United States*. Joseph Henry: Washington, DC, 1999.

Ministry of Statistics and Programme Implementation "Periodic Labour Force Survey (2018–19)." Ministry of Statistics and Programme Implementation, 2018–19. Accessed June 6, 2020. http://mospi.nic.in/Periodic-Labour-Surveys.

NFHS-4. 2015–16. *National family health survey*. Mumbai: Ministry of Health and Family Welfare Government of India, 2017.

NSSO. 2017–18. *Key indicators of social consumption in India: Health*. New Delhi: Ministry of Statistics and Programme Implementation (MOSPI), 2018.

Pattenden, Jonathan. "A neoliberalisation of civil society? Self-help groups and the labouring class poor in rural South India." *The Journal of Peasant Studies* 37, no. 3 (2010): 485–512.

Patton, Michael Quinn. *Qualitative research and evaluation methods*. Newbury Park, CA: Sage, 2015.

Rodrigeuz, Jenny K., Holvino, Evangelina, Fletch, Joyce K., and Nkomo, Stella M. "The theory and praxis of intersectionality in work and organisations: Where do we go from here?" *Gender, Work and Organisation* 2, no. 3 (2016): 210–222.

Salleh, Ariel. "Green economics or green Utopia: The salience of reproductive labour post Rio+20." *Journal of World Systems Research* 18, no. 2 (2012): 138–145.

Sanyal, Kalyan. *Rethinking capitalist development: Primitive accumulation, governmentality and post colonial capitalism*. New Delhi: Routledge, 2007.

Saravanan, V.S. "Contestations and negotiations of urban health in India: A situated political approach." *World Development* 104 (2018): 375–387.

Sayer, Andrew. *Realism and social science*. London: Sage, 2000.

Sen, Amartya. *Inequality reexamined*. Cambridge, MA: Harvard University Press, 1992.

Singh, Nadia. "Gender, intra-household discrimination and cash transfer schemes: The case of Indian Punjab." *Economies* (2019): 75.

Ulrichs, Martina. "Informality, women and social protection identifying barriers to provide effective coverage." *ODI Working Paper*, April 2016, London ODI, 2016.

UNFPA. "Impact of the COVID-19 pandemic on family planning and ending gender-based violence, female genital mutilation and child marriage." UNFPA, 2020. Accessed May 19, 2020. https://www.unfpa.org/sites/

default/files/resource-pdf/COVID-19_impact_brief_for_UNFPA_24_April_2020_1.pdf.

Usha, V.T. *Kerala's gendered response to the pandemic.* New Delhi: Global South and Rosa Luxemburg Institute, 2021.

Wenham, Clare, Smith, Julia, and Morgan, Rosemary. "Covid-19: The gendered impacts of the outbreak." *Lancet* 395, no. 10227 (2020): 846–848.

Zozeta-Miliopoulou, Georgia, and Kapareliotis, Ilias. "The toll of success: Female leaders in the 'women friendly' Greek advertising agencies." *Gender, Work and Organisation* (2021): 1–125.

CHAPTER 3

When Hammer Misses the Nail: Health Aspirations and Internal Migration in India

Kundan Mishra

List of Abbreviations

NGO	Non-governmental Organization
NRHF	National Rural Health Framework
NURF	National Urban Health Framework

Introduction

India went into its first lockdown during the COVID-19 pandemic on March 24, 2020 as a measure to limit interpersonal interaction and limit the spread of coronavirus (BBC 2020). There are 450 million internal migrants in India who constitute 90% of the country's workforce

K. Mishra (✉)
University of Massachusetts Boston, Ottawa, ON, Canada
e-mail: kundan.mishra001@umb.edu

S. Hewamanne and S. Yadav (eds.), *The Political Economy of Post-COVID Life and Work in the Global South: Pandemic and Precarity*, International Political Economy Series,
https://doi.org/10.1007/978-3-030-93228-2_3

employed primarily in the informal sector. The migrant workers emerged as the face of COVID-19 pandemic and its devastating impact on individuals and families. Along with the unemployment caused by the lockdown, an estimated 130 million migrants embarked on a historical and in some cases fatal journey back home (Dandekar and Ghai 2020). The coronavirus crisis “made visible a large workforce who experience precarity of work and often live hand to mouth” (Patel 2020).

However, policymakers and strategies to restore “normal” life after the pandemic, continue to ignore the precarity of migrant labour in India. The plans for a better prepared nakedness continue to fall back on health infrastructure. The chief economist of State Bank of India, a nationalized bank, suggested “to build a 500-bed hospital in 250 districts at a cost of Rs 60,000 crore over the next two years” as a plan to turn this “crisis to an opportunity” (Press Trust of India 2020). While these arguments draw attention to much needed demands of healthcare, they keep concerns around specific vulnerabilities of migrants at bay.

With the ongoing failure of the state in protecting migrant workers during this crisis, the agency of migrant individuals and households gains further significance. The Government of India stated that they do not have any data on the number of migrants or their deaths due to the COVID-19 pandemic. Even during the lockdown special provisions like trains and buses partly sponsored by the state came way after the migrants were finding their own way home. By the time of writing this chapter, 8733 people had lost their lives on railway tracks in India, most of whom are assumed to be migrant workers on their way home (Press Trust of India 2021). The state only recently declared that migrant workers stuck in cities will have access to subsidized food although the politics of this measure continues to pan out (Kumar 2021). Meanwhile, the Prime Minister of India in his national address asked migrant workers to be patient and not leave their cities, while relief measures were being worked out (India Today 2021). With the unreliable response of the state, the role of the agency of migrant individuals and households in migration decisions gains even further significance. The capabilities approach offers a unique framework that can be operationalized to understand the agency of individuals and groups, and reveal unique impacts of prolonged poverty.

The capabilities approach proposes that vulnerabilities specific to vulnerable populations can be understood through the interaction between group and individual capabilities, and in this case, specifically their health capabilities. The capabilities approach is an "incomplete theory" or a framework proposed by Sen and developed by numerous scholars across disciplines like law, human rights, poverty assessment and education (Alkire 2016; Burchi and De Muro 2016; P. Anand and Dowding 2009; Nussbaum and Sen 1993). Sen (1999) proposes that a human life comprises states of being and doing called functionings. The real opportunities of individuals, also called freedoms, to realize these functionings are called capabilities. Thus functionings and capabilities are closely related. Sen (1999, 75) notes that "Functioning is the various things that a person values being or doing" that "reflect her actual *achievements*". He proceeds to define capability as "the alternative combination of functionings that are feasible for her to achieve". He also adds that "Capability is thus a kind of freedom…to achieve functioning combinations(or less formally put, the freedom to achieve alternative lifestyles)".

Ruger (2006) captures this application of capabilities approach through interrelated concepts of healthcare quality, health agency and health norms. In this framework public policy aims to maximize an individual's choice or enhance her agency regarding the functioning of being healthy (Ruger 2007). Aspirations of health among vulnerable populations—in this case, migrant workers- are key expressions of their agency.

Across the world, the efficacy and insufficiency of testing measures became the central point of COVID-19 response. Even in India, testing infrastructure has attracted most attention in discussions for migrants' health. PPE kits, availability of sanitizers, nasopharyngeal swabs have become household terms. The enthusiasm of experts towards health infrastructure is also shared by state and non-state actors, including philanthropic organizations.

However, the promise of health infrastructure as the primary strategy needs further investigation and raises a question—if we build, will they come? It does not have a straightforward response, as evidenced in previous experiences with health crises. The campaign against diseases like polio, leprosy and tuberculosis for example indicates that the presence of sufficient infrastructure is only half the solution. The local social and cultural norms play a critical role in the success of any healthcare measure.

In this chapter, I focus on the agency of migrants through aspirations of health in a rural household. The health security of a household depends on the prioritization of the health needs of household members.

However, migrants from Nuapada district in Odisha live under prolonged periods of risk. As this chapter shows, this compromises their ability to imagine a healthy future. Based on household surveys and interviews with respondents, this chapter outlines the role of a household's health aspirations in their migration decisions. With Nuapada, Odisha as a case study, this chapter argues that the COVID-19 crisis represents migrant precarity as much as it represents a health crisis.

The Capabilities Approach, Health and Agency

The capabilities approach developed by Sen provides an agency-based framework to understand internal and external barriers towards improving the well-being of vulnerable populations. Sen (1999) proposes that a human life comprises states of being and doing called functionings. The real opportunities of individuals, also called freedoms, to realize these functionings are called capabilities. Thus functionings and capabilities are closely related. Sen (1999, 75) notes that "Functioning is the various things that a person values being or doing" that "reflect her actual achievements".

Sen (1999, 19) is categorical in presenting agency of an individual "as a member of the public and as a participant in economic, social and political actions". This definition enables the assessment of an individual's achievement in terms of her own values and objectives "towards a life that she has a reason to value". In this evolving debate, however, there is still an unanswered question that emanates from the capabilities approach. What is the place of good health in an individual's idea of a life that "they have a reason to value"?

The capabilities approach found a unique integration with healthcare ambitions across the globe. More recently, debates around universal healthcare have become more aware of behavioural and social barriers towards universal access to healthcare. The next section answers the question, what is the role of health aspirations in internal migration? This question holds a descriptive as well as prescriptive value. Understanding the health aspirations of internal migrants is at the foundation of the paradoxical migrant exodus during national lockdown in India. Second, as we consider resilience towards the ongoing COVID-19 crisis and future pandemics, understanding the agency of migrants—and other vulnerable populations—will be as critical as building new infrastructure.

Appadurai (2004), in one of the primary texts on the "capacity to aspire", points to the "futuristic" aspect of aspirations that drives the development of individuals and communities. The relationship between aspirations and well-being is based on the shared "future oriented logic" (Appadurai 2004). Among the different views on aspirations, Ray (2006) defines aspirations as "social grounding of individual desires". The "social grounding" upholds that aspirations do not appear in isolation and are "always formed in interaction and the thick of social life". Notably, aspirations may facilitate the mobilization of resources required to change the conditions of poverty (S. Ibrahim 2011b; Conradie and Robeyns 2013).

However, the capability to aspire is not uniform and is expectedly dependent on material, physical and psychological conditions of individuals and communities. Thus, materially rich communities are expected to have higher aspirations than materially poor communities (Appadurai 2004). The deficit of aspirations is a direct reflection of the capability to aspire which locates the aspirations of an individual or a community to a "supple horizon of hopes and wants" which may be unavailable under conditions of poverty (Appadurai 2004, 82).

Notably, scholars have indicated that the psychological effects of poverty may impair investment by the poor in their own well-being and human development (Ray 2006, 2016; Bryan et al. 2014). Theoretical explanations propose that the capacity of aspire plays a central role in directing us towards the future we want. People with social or economic privilege may explore the future more frequently and more realistically than those disadvantaged by poverty. So while poor people do aspire, "poverty is a diminishing of the circumstances in which these practices occur" (Appadurai 2004, 69). Meanwhile, the relationship between poverty and aspirations is not unidirectional. Although, poverty is a failure of aspirations, a deprivation in the capability to aspire and poverty may sustain each other to form a trap (Rigg et al. 2018; Ray 2006).

Another aspect of the capacity to aspire is that aspirations are "always formed in interaction and in the thick of social life" (Appadurai 2004, 67). Aspirations do not exist as "consumer preferences" and are informed by "experience and observation". Ray (2006) defines aspirations as a "social grounding of individual desires" informed by group interaction and group dynamics. The interaction between an individual and surrounding groups also implies that aspirations are exposed to biases of social norms of race, class, caste and gender in these groups.

The literature on aspirations frequently discusses the challenge of capturing aspirations while maintaining a conceptual distinction from other synonymous terms like priorities, ambition and preferences (Appadurai 2004; Ray 2006; Alkire 2002). As such, aspirations are frequently conceptualized with a time boundary and a commitment of resources. This becomes further complicated when the revealed preference is influenced by the local context and norms of gender, class and caste.

If aspirations do reflect the agency of individuals, how are we to understand its influence on migration decisions? How is an aspiration that is "largely invisible in nature" to be observed? (Appadurai 2004, 67). The next section discusses methodological challenges involved in the operationalization and measurement of aspirations relevant to this project.

Measuring Aspirations

This chapter adds to a growing scholarship that generates evidence to understand the theoretical relationship between aspirations and poverty. Appadurai (2001, 2004) found that organizations in slums of Mumbai were using the capacity to aspire to navigate political alliances, resource mobilization and securing land tenure for slum dwellers. By utilizing skills of people living the slums Alliance, a group of three NGOs, could relate "long-term visions of dignity, health, and sanitary self-sufficiency to its short-term capacities for handling contractors, builders, suppliers, engineers, and banks in Mumbai" (Appadurai 2004, 73).

Through a feedback loop between general principles and specific goals, the poor could aspire for "their own ideas of the good life" (Appadurai 2004, 77). This capacity to aspire also helped them navigate networks, political relationships and resources to realize these aspirations.

Ray (2006, 2016) found in a quantitative economic model that different groups respond differently to the aspirational gap defined as "the difference between socially generated aspirations and the current socio-economic level that the individual enjoys". Ray (2016) found that higher income levels of Muslims, a minority in India, rendered them more vulnerable to communal violence, while higher income levels of Hindus, a majority, reduced their vulnerability. Ray's findings are grounded in a theory that aspirations and conflict are interrelated and this relationship is different for majority and minority groups. When the minority group has more resources, majority groups want a share to fulfil their socially generated aspirations. However, when majority groups have more resources, there is a decline in violent conflict as it might affect their source of income and future.

Ibrahim (2011b) found that among Egyptian youth poverty resulted in aspiration failure as a downward spiral caused by cumulative failure to realize aspirations. In poor families, aspirations failure was also intergenerational where "the failure of many parents in poor communities to fulfil the aspirations of their children" (S. Ibrahim 2011b, 18) passed on to the next generation.

Bernard and Taffesse (2012, 2014) have studied the aspirations of individuals and families in rural Ethiopia found that aspirations and future-oriented behaviour could change through innovative solutions. They screened documentaries among rural communities where people from similar backgrounds "tell stories about their lives" and "describe how they improved their socio-economic position from being poor or of average socio-economic position in their communities to being relatively successful". The households that participated in this screening "changed aspirations, as well as future-oriented behavior, namely saving, use of credit and investment in education, six months after the screening". Further, the educational attainment of girls in these households also went up compared to the control group, even though girl education was not a theme in the documentaries.

The empirical studies discussed above illustrate an evolving field of understanding aspirations. Evidently, aspirations are operationalized differently in all these studies. Appadurai (2001, 2004) uses better sanitation and residential facilities in slums as an aspiration, whereas Ray (2016) locates aspirations in relative higher income among competing groups. Ibrahim (2011a) looks at unfulfilled aspirations among Egyptian youth. Bernard and Taffesse (2014) capture it as a comparison between ideal and realistic assessment of income, wealth, social status and children's educational attainment. The literature on aspirations is growing through applications at different scales and in different contexts.

Migration and Health Aspirations

The migration crisis in India exposed the scale of precarious working conditions of migrants in India. This crisis brought forward the tension in migration scholarship on three fronts.

First, there is a lot of emphasis on migration as a way out of poverty. One set of scholarship presents evidence of linear links between migration, remittance, human capital investment and improvement in the well-being of migrants. The claims to benefits of migration clearly do not extend as strongly to healthcare as they do to education and livelihoods diversification, for example. The scholarship on precarity and modern slavery continues to highlight structural barriers towards improvement in healthcare of migrants in India.

Second, the scholarship on determinants of migration closely mirrors the assumptions of trickle down socio-economic change among migrants. However, this scholarship has not provided appropriate space to the agency of migrants. In this scholarship, migrants are carriers of economic development, receivers of external changes, respondents of wage differentials but hardly the decisionmakers. This missing piece in the scholarship is instrumental in understanding the links between remittance and improvement in well-being of migrants.

Third, a limited understanding of the agency of migrants has also prevented an accurate picture of the conditions under which this agency is compromised. Appadurai (2004), in one of the primary texts on the "capacity to aspire", points to the "futuristic" aspect of aspirations that drives the development of individuals and communities as a "navigational capacity". The relationship between aspirations and well-being is based on the shared "future oriented logic" (Appadurai 2004). Among the different views on aspirations, Ray (2006) defines aspirations as "social grounding of individual desires". The "social grounding" upholds that aspirations do not appear in isolation and are "always formed in interaction and the thick of social life". Notably, aspirations may facilitate mobilization of resources required to change the conditions of poverty (Ibrahim 2011a; Conradie and Robeyns 2013).

However, the capability to aspire is not uniform and is expectedly dependent on material, physical and psychological conditions of individuals and communities. Thus, materially rich communities are expected to have higher aspirations than materially poor communities (Appadurai 2004). The deficit of aspirations is a direct reflection of the capability to aspire which locates the aspirations of an individual or a community to a "supple horizon of hopes and wants" which may be unavailable under conditions of poverty (Appadurai 2004, 82).

People with social or economic privilege may explore the future more frequently and more realistically than those disadvantaged by poverty. So while poor people do aspire, "poverty is a diminishing of the circumstances in which these practices occur" (Appadurai 2004, 69).

Meanwhile, the relationship between poverty and aspirations is not unidirectional. Although poverty may result from a failure of aspirations, a deprivation in the capability to aspire and poverty may sustain each other to form a trap (Rigg et al. 2014; Ray 2006).

Considering how aspirations reflect the agency of individuals, it is critical to understand its influence on migration decisions. This requires unique methods to observe aspirations that are "largely invisible in nature" (Appadurai 2004, 67). The next section discusses a methodological approach involved in the operationalization and measurement of aspirations relevant to this project.

India and Public Health—Between Method and Madness

The public health system in India consists of a sophisticated architecture which includes medical research, drug approval, and medical treatment institutions. The National Rural Health Framework (NHRF) and National Urban Health Framework (NURF) continue to be the foundation of public health access for citizens. The NHRF is organized from the village level to the block level responding to escalating medical complexities and facilities for the rural population. Meanwhile, the NURF is focussed on improving access to medical facilities for urban residents, particularly, urban poor.

The NHRF and NURF, in spite of an extensive health system, have consistently been inaccessible for migrants. Among the complex set of factors that may affect the access to public health in India, two factors are particularly important to the discussions on agency of migrants. First, the access to public health welfare schemes is frequently tied to the place of residence of an individual. For many migrant workers, the place of work rarely becomes their place or residence as they keep their homes and their families back in their rural homes. For seasonal migrants in India and many other agricultural societies, it is very common for individuals and families to migrate during the agricultural lean season to find employment.

Once the agricultural lean season comes to an end, they move back to their rural homes. In some cases, even if they spend more time away from their rural home in a year, their place of residence continues to be their village. This discrepancy between the place of residence and official documentation compromises the access of rural–urban migrants to social safety nets in general. Second, with limited access to the public food distribution system in destination areas, the risk of malnutrition further compounds the health insecurity of migrants and their families. A focus on building up health infrastructure side steps such interrelated risks to health security that are specific to migrants.

The Parliamentary report on Management of COVID-19 Pandemic and Related Issues (Rajya Sabha Secretariat 2020, 32) noted that migrant workers were among the "worst affected" due to the pandemic and were impacted by

> loss of livelihoods and incomes, loss of access to health infrastructure, food and shelter, loss of social interactions, mental health issues, anxieties on account of the uncertainty of Pandemic and loss of personal mobility, lack of infrastructure support for education at home and likelihood of interruption in education and dropouts, physiological and psychological impacts on children/young people, stress on account of staying together in cramped and dingy houses, inter-generational conflicts, domestic abuse and alcoholism, inadequate food, lack of nutrition, lack of access to PDS, interruption in long term treatments, expensive treatments, migrants forced to return home walking long distances by foot, creation of a culture of fear, etc.

The apathy of the state towards migrant labour is further evident in remarks of Home Secretary to the Committee recorded in the same report as

> ...All the States cooperated very well and managed them in camps or their places of stay, and their food requirements were also managed well. Their health, hygiene and all were also taken care of. Of course, when the lockdown got extended for a little longer period, the labour wanted to move. We had opened up activities thinking that they might go back to work. Perhaps that understanding, to a much extent, was not correct. They wanted to go back, and, then, at that point of time, it was decided that we should run trains and also buses. (Rajya Sabha Secretariat 2020, 35)

While the report does not provide any concrete measures, it does provide support to existing gaps around databases of migrant workers, better employment support, and minimum wage for migrant workers and reforms in the Inter-State Migrant Workers, 1979 Act. However, considering the vague nature of these recommendations, which essentially seek strengthening of existing labour laws, any significant improvement in the conditions of migrant workers remains imaginary.

Adjacent to the concerns around lack of health infrastructure for rural–urban migrants, the role of health aspirations of rural–urban migrants needs serious examination. Aspirations defined as "social groundings of desire" represent the idea of a life that an individual or group has "reason to value". Further, the "social groundings" of aspiration conceptually integrates social norms and practices into an idea of the future. Aspirations related to the health of family members can be powerful in prioritizing a future with better health security.

Low Health Aspirations and a Compromised Future—Rural Households in Nuapada

This section draws from fieldwork for my dissertation project on aspirations and migration decisions of rural households in Nuapada, Odisha. I used a mixed methods approach using group discussions, household surveys and personal interviews to understand aspirations of rural households in the sample. The sample for household surveys includes 507 households spread across 7 villages spread across five administrative blocks in Nuapada. While the survey captures aspirations in 27 different dimensions, this chapter focuses on health related aspirations of respondent households.

The household survey instrument used in data collection operationalizes aspirations window and aspirations gap for consistent measurement and comparability. Aspirations window comprise "lives, achievements, or ideals" in "an individual's cognitive world, her zone of 'similar', 'attainable' individuals" (Ray 2006, 2). This cognitive world is very broad and often includes role models within and outside of their households and families, popular public figures, or other households in the community. The aspirations window reflects perceived levels of deprivation of a respondent household with respect to the larger community (Stark and Bloom 1985). For this survey, however, the cognitive world of respondents is limited to respondents' ideas of their community. The respondents could identify their community in terms of their caste, class, village or any other characteristics.

The measurement of aspirations window locates aspirations of a household in relation to its immediate community. Such a comparison to immediate community reflects whether relative poverty or the lack of it shapes the aspirations of a household. In existing literature, relative poverty is frequently considered as a key motivation for rural–urban migration. An analysis of a rural households aspirations window can also be a way of verifying the relationship between relative poverty, aspirations and migration decisions of a household.

Aspirations gap is “the difference between the standard of living that’s aspired to and the standard of living that one already has” (Ray 2006, 3). To operationalize this, respondents assessed the parameter at present and at a point in future where they were leading their “good life”. The difference between these two responses would be the aspirations gap for that particular parameter. The concept of “good life” is deliberately left underspecified. A “good life” may not be in terms of more money, lifecycle changes or other personal changes.

Leaving the “good life” underspecified is an opportunity for respondents to imagine a life that “they have a reason to value” (Alkire 2008; Robeyns 2005) (Table 3.1).

a. Please respond to the following questions about your community to the best of your knowledge: What is the general level of health of girls in the community?
b. Please respond to the following questions about your household under the present conditions: How: What is the general level of your daughter’s health?

Table 3.1 Summary of status of health of girls in the community/household

Girls’ health status	*Community*	*Current HH*	*Future HH*
Always ill	99	89	91
Often ill	20	17	6
Sometimes ill	158	149	150
Mostly healthy	89	94	93
Always healthy	141	158	167
Total	507	507	507

Table 3.2 Summary of status of health of boys in the community/household

Boys' health status	*Community*	*Current HH*	*Future HH*
Always ill	58	42	48
Often ill	17	28	15
Sometimes ill	194	178	176
Mostly healthy	97	98	128
Always healthy	141	161	140
Total	507	507	507

c. Imagine you are living the "good life" that you always wanted. In this life: What is the general level of your daughter's health?

To understand the aspirations gap in the sample, households responded to the same group of indicators in Table 3.2 for a future where they are "leading a 'good life'". These responses were then compared to their assessment at present conditions. The difference for the same indicator in these two sets of responses will help us compare the significance and aspired improvement in the indicator in future.

a. Please respond to the following questions about your community to the best of your knowledge: What is the general level of health of boys in the community?
b. Please respond to the following questions about your household under the present conditions: How: What is the general level of your son's health?
c. Imagine you are living the "good life" that you always wanted. In this life: What is the general level of your son's health?

An analysis of survey responses indicates lower aspirations of health for girls' than boys in the community. The household responses for child health are better for boys than for girls. About the community, more respondent households thought that girls are "always ill" (99) than boys (58). As Table 3.1 suggests, households expect girls to have slightly poorer health than boys. In their present circumstances the sample households' assessment of their daughter's health was also poorer than their son's. Again, the number of households where girls (89) were "always ill" is more than twice as much as boys (42).

There is a clear prioritization of education for both boys and girls in households' idea of "a good life". More households leading a "good life" in the future would like their boys and girls to receive higher levels of education compared to the present levels (Table 3.2). However, a similar trend in aspirations about the health of both boys and girls is missing. In both cases, aspired future levels of health closely follow the responses for existing levels of health.

The role of health-related expenses is even further pronounced in household debt. In personal interviews, respondents noted that they frequently incur debt for health emergencies related to older parents, and children. This debt is then sustained through a debt cycle of repayment through an advance from the broker and then repaying this advance through manual labour during the agricultural lean season.

The low aspirations related to health and persistent debt cycles among seasonal migrants in Nuapada illustrate a precarity that goes beyond exploitative labour practices. The precarious life of a migrant household is not confined to the exploitative workplace but also extends to the household behaviour. The risks associated with precarity are further compounded by a compromise in the capacity to aspire. In light of lower aspirations about health and the risk of debt cycles related to health emergencies, the pronounced focus on health infrastructure is inadequate.

Conclusion

The debate on health systems is increasingly taking a turn towards understanding social determinants of health to explore innovative solutions to complex problems. A focus on improving health infrastructure must be complemented by efforts to empower migrants towards a health secure future. The analysis of health aspirations and priorities of seasonal migrants in Odisha indicates that a compromise in the agency of migrants may exacerbate their health insecurity.

A public health system is much more than just a crisis response mechanism, and a focus on infrastructure in light of the ongoing pandemic reduces it to just that. The need for better and increased infrastructure must be complemented with a focus on internal capabilities of migrants to avoid a health disaster in the future. Internal capabilities and aspirations for better health are a key component of recovery and a comprehensive health security of migrants.

The capacity to aspire is a powerful way to put resilience at the centre of health security in a post-pandemic world. A comprehensive approach towards health and well-being will be pivotal in addressing the challenges of health expenses and debt that often sustain a migration trap. Further, making health a priority for the future empowers migrants, and others, to navigate resources and support towards a resilient healthier future.

The conditions of precarity for migrant households are not defined by migration. These conditions are deep seated in their lives beyond seasonal livelihoods and rural–urban migration. Unless we understand the internal capabilities, or its lack thereof, among rural households that lead to precarity, more infrastructure would always be a "necessary but not sufficient" step. In the lack of an empowered community that places health at the centre of well-being, an increased focus on infrastructure will only be waiting for the next crisis to ravage migrants.

References

Ajay Dandekar, and Rahul Ghai. 2020. "Commentary: Migration and Reverse Migration in the Age of COVID-19." *Economic and Political Weekly* LV (19). www.epw.in.

Alkire, Sabina. 2002. *Valuing freedoms: Sen's capability approach and poverty reduction*. 1st ed. London: Oxford University Press. https://doi.org/10.1093/0199245797.001.0001.

———. 2008. "Using the Capability Approach: Prospective and Evaluative Analyses the Focal Question." In *The Capability Approach- Concepts, Measures and Applications*, edited by Flavio Comim, Mozaffar Qizilbash, and Sabina Alkire, 1st ed., 26–50. Cambridge, UK: Cambridge University Press. http://www.ophi.org.uk/wp-content/uploads/Alkire-Using-Prospective-Eval-07.pdf.

———. 2016. "Measures of Human Development: Key Concepts and Properties." 107. *OPHI Working Paper*. Oxford, UK.

Anand, Paul, and Keith Dowding. 2009. "The Development of Capability Indicators and Their Relation to Life Satisfaction." *Journal of Human Development and Capabilities* 10 (1): 125–52.

Appadurai, Arjun. 2001. "Deep Democracy: Urban Governmentality and the Horizon of Politics." 13.

———. 2004. "The Capacity to Aspire: Culture and the Terms of Recognition." In *Culture and Public Action: A Cross-Disciplinary Dialogue on Development*

Policy, edited by Michael Walton, and Vijayendra Rao. Washington, DC: World Bank Publications.
BBC. 2020. "Coronavirus: India Enters 'Total Lockdown' After Spike in Cases—BBC News." *BBC, British Broadcasting Corporation*. March 25. https://www.bbc.com/news/world-asia-india-52024239.
Bernard, Tanguy, and Alemayehu Seyoum Taffesse. 2012. "Measuring Aspirations: Discussion and Example from Ethiopia." 01190. *IFPRI Discussion Paper*. Washington, DC. https://pdfs.semanticscholar.org/52bc/89564f8399a54a2b816cf9bfbb0cc6528e12.pdf.
Bernard, Tanguy, Stefan Dercon, and Alemayehu Seyoum Taffesse. 2012b. "Beyond Fatalism: An Empirical Explora-Tion of Self-Efficacy and Aspirations Fail-Ure in Ethiopia." https://pdfs.semanticscholar.org/b019/f76a9854bd3798274c59576e12ffa93f54b5.pdf.
Bernard, Tanguy, and Alemayehu Seyoum Taffesse. 2014. "Aspirations: An Approach to Measurement with Validation Using Ethiopian Data." *Journal of African Economies* 23 (2): 189–224. https://doi.org/10.1093/jae/ejt030.
Bryan, Gharad, Ahmed Mushfiq Mobarak, and Shyamal Chowdhury. 2014. "Underinvestment in a Profitable Technology: The Case of Seasonal Migration in Bangladesh." *Econometrica* 82 (5): 1671–1748.
Burchi, Francesco, and Pasquale De Muro. 2016. "From Food Availability to Nutritional Capabilities: Advancing Food Security Analysis." *Food Policy* 60: 10–19.
Conradie, Ina, and Ingrid Robeyns. 2013. "Aspirations and Human Development Interventions." *Journal of Human Development and Capabilities* 14 (4): 559–80.
Ibrahim, Solava. 2011a. Poverty, Aspirations and Wellbeing: Afraid to Aspire and Unable to Reach a Better Life—Voices from Egypt Creating and Sharing Knowledge to Help End Poverty. https://www.manchester.ac.uk/bwpi.
——— 2011b. "Poverty, Aspirations and Wellbeing: Afraid to Aspire and Unable to Reach a Better Life—Voices from Egypt." 141. BWPI Working Paper, Machester.
Ibrahim, Solava S. 2006. "From Individual to Collective Capabilities: The Capability Approach as a Conceptual Framework for Self-Help." *Journal of Human Development* 7 (3): 397–416. https://doi.org/10.1080/14649880600815982.
India Today. 2021. "PM Modi Urges Migrant Workers to Stay Where They Are, Asks States to Avoid Lockdown | 5 Takeaways—Coronavirus Outbreak News." *India Today*. April 20. https://www.indiatoday.in/coronavirus-outbreak/story/pm-narendra-modi-speech-covid19-situation-migrant-workers-lockdown-1793217-2021-04-20.
Kumar, Vikas. 2021. "One Year on, Access to Subsidised Food Remains a Crucial Challenge for Migrant Workers." *Scroll.In*. May 8. https://scroll.in/

article/993197/one-year-on-access-to-subsidised-food-remains-a-crucial-challenge-for-migrant-workers.

Nussbaum, Martha C., and Amartya Sen. 1993. "Introduction." In *The Quality of Life*, edited by Amartya Sen, and Martha C. Nussbaum. New York.

Patel, Champa. 2020. "COVID-19: The Hidden Majority in India's Migration Crisis | Chatham House." *Chatham House*. July 13. https://www.chathamhouse.org/expert/comment/covid-19-hidden-majority-indias-migration-crisis.

Press Trust of India. 2020. "Healthcare Spends, Making India Slum-Free Should Be Government's Priority: Experts—The New Indian Express." *The New Indian Express*. July 11. https://www.newindianexpress.com/business/2020/jul/11/healthcare-spends-making-india-slum-free-should-be-governments-priority-experts-2168411.html.

———. 2021. "Lockdown 2020: Over 8,700 People Died on Railway Tracks This Year, Many of Them Migrants—India News." *India Today*. June 2. https://www.indiatoday.in/india/story/lockdown-2020-over-8-700-people-died-on-railway-tracks-this-year-many-of-them-migrants-1810142-2021-06-02.

Rajya Sabha Secretariat. 2020. "TWO HUNDRED TWENTY NINTH REPORT ON MANAGEMENT OF COVID-19 PANDEMIC AND RELATED ISSUES." Parliament of India: New Delhi.

Ray, Debraj. 2006. "Aspirations, Poverty and Economic Change." In *Understanding Poverty*, edited by Roland Bénabou, Dileep Mookherjee, and Abhijit Banerjee, 1st ed., 409–22. New York, NY: Oxford University Press. http://www.econ.nyu.edu/user/debraj/Papers/povasp01.pdf.

———. 2016. "Aspirations and the Development Treadmill." *Journal of Human Development and Capabilities* 17 (3): 309–23. https://www.nyu.edu/econ/user/debraj/Papers/HDCA2016.pdf.

Rigg, Jonathan, Buapun Promphaking, and Ann Le Mare. 2014. "Personalizing the Middle- Income Trap: An Inter-Generational Migrant View from Rural Thailand." *World Development* 59: 184–98. https://doi.org/10.1016/j.worlddev.2014.01.031.

Rigg, Jonathan, Buapun Promphaking, and Ann Le Mare. 2018. "Personalizing the Middle- Income Trap: An Inter-Generational Migrant View from Rural Thailand." Accessed February 19. https://scholarbank.nus.edu.sg/bitstream/10635/129102/1/2014-personalising_middle_income_trap-postprint.pdf.

Robeyns, Ingrid. 2005. "The Capability Approach: A Theoretical Survey." *Journal of Human Development and Capabilities* 6 (1): 93–117. https://doi.org/10.1080/146498805200034266.

Ruger, Jennifer Prah. 2006. "Toward a Theory of a Right to Health: Capability and Incompletely Theorized Agreements." *Yale Journal of Law & the Humanities* 18 (2): 3. NIH Public Access. http://www.ncbi.nlm.nih.gov/pubmed/25309105.

———. 2007. "Rethinking Equal Access: Agency, Quality, and Norms." *Global Public Health* 2 (1): 78–96. Taylor & Francis Group.

Sen, Amartya. 1999. *Introduction "Development as Freedom." Development as Freedom.* 1st ed. New York, NY: Alfred A. Knopf.

———. 2004. "Capabilities, Lists and Public Reason: Continuing the Conversation," 77–80.

Stark, Oded, and David E Bloom. 1985. "The New Economics of Labor Migration." *The American Economic Review* 75 (2): 173–78.

CHAPTER 4

Female Labor Workforce and Precarity in India's Construction Sector

Chantal Krcmar

Glossary of Acronyms

BOCW Acts:	Building and Other Construction Workers and Building and Other Construction Workers Cess Acts
HS:	Human Security
ILO:	International Labour Organisation
MGNREGA:	Mahatma Gandhi National Rural Employment Guarantee Act
MMC:	Mumbai Mobile Creches
NGOs:	Non-governmental Organizations
OBCs:	Other Backward Castes
SGBV:	Sexual and Gender Based Violence
YUVA:	Youth for Unity and Voluntary Action

C. Krcmar (✉)
University of Massachusetts Boston, Boston, MA, USA
e-mail: Chantal.Krcmar@umb.edu

S. Hewamanne and S. Yadav (eds.), *The Political Economy of Post-COVID Life and Work in the Global South: Pandemic and Precarity*, International Political Economy Series,
https://doi.org/10.1007/978-3-030-93228-2_4

Introduction

Human Security (HS), a paradigm which came out of the United Nations Development Program in 1994, was ground-breaking in the realm of International Relations. In essence, the HS paradigm is meant to shift focus from state security to individual security. Since then, critical and feminist HS scholars have levied criticisms against HS, including that it has not attended to local contexts enough and that it has been too western and liberal in its approach to analyzing and enhancing people's security. My research takes those critiques seriously. Despite their vast numbers and work-related challenges, very little is known about how Indian women construction workers experience and conceptualize Human Security—either before or during the COVID-19 crisis. Hence, my research fills a gap in HS scholarship. Utilizing a feminist grounded approach, I have sought to understand HS from the perspective of the laborers. What I found on the ground led me to see that the theoretical approaches of precarity and informality *together* shed light on the HS of Indian women construction workers—particularly during this tumultuous time of COVID-19.

While construction work is a large source of global employment, it is not a source of much security. There are 180 million construction workers worldwide, 50 million of which are in India (Srivastava and Jha 2016). Construction is the second-largest labor sector in India (second only to agricultural sector). The vast majority of Indian construction workers (97%) are informal laborers. "Informal employment is…usually defined by the absence of social protection (mainly health coverage) or the absence of a written contract" (Charmes 2012, 106). Deemed by the International Labor Organization (ILO) as one of the most dangerous jobs in the world, construction has a high number of work-related injuries and fatalities. Dangerous and un-sanitary work conditions, wage withholding, little to no compensation for medical care and no work contracts, drinkable water, safety gear or toilets, are all rampant in the construction industry. (See, for example, Barnabas et al. 2009; Rai and Sarkar 2012; Bhattacharyya and Korinek 2007). Additionally, though the government of India does not keep reliable statistics on fatalities of construction workers, journalists and NGO staff claim they are common. (See, for example, Shah 2019; Rebbapragada 2018; Jain and Matharu 2017; Express News Service 2017.)

The construction industry in India is a significant source of employment for women, as about 40% of all construction laborers on sites in India are women (Chen and Raveendran 2012). The number of women construction workers has been falling due to increased mechanization, economic slowdown, and the availability of more domestic service jobs. However, the number is still significantly larger than most other countries. In the US, for example, 9% of the construction workforce is women, according to National Association of Women in Construction—and the great majority of them work in administrative and executive positions in construction company offices. Despite their vast numbers in construction in India, women are terribly marginalized.

Women construction workers in India typically earn about half of what male construction workers earn (less than 2USD/day). They are from the Scheduled Tribes and Other Backward Castes (OBCs), and have high rates of illiteracy. (See, for example, Pandit et al. 2011.) Women construction laborers also face particular health hazards, including Sexual and Gender Based Violence (SGBV) and other illnesses and conditions. The majority of women workers are under the age of 35, and therefore of childbearing age (Srivastava 2014). They get no maternity leave and very few construction sites have childcare facilities. As a result, infants and young children are often at the construction site, too. Accounts of children being tethered to a corner of a construction site for their own safety, or dying due to accidents, highlight some of these everyday dangers.

Fieldwork in Mumbai and Navi Mumbai

A major slowdown of the Indian economy was brewing and completely spilled over when I arrived in Mumbai at the end of the summer of 2019 to start my Ph.D. fieldwork. Wages stagnated; consumer spending fell; construction, real estate, and other industries were sent reeling. The slowdown sent construction workers' livelihoods into constant question. Mumbai is a mega-city in the western Indian state of Maharashtra, located on the Arabian Sea. With an estimated population of 22 million, it is India's most populous city and it is one of the most densely populated cities in the world. While an estimated 40% of those living in Mumbai inhabit slums, and there is a notable "increase of 'new slums' in north-eastern Mumbai" (Whitehead 2014, 125) it is still considered India's business and finance capital. Navi Mumbai is a planned city to the east of Mumbai, with a population of 1.6 million. It is fast-growing with many new infrastructure projects including a new international airport and metro lines.

Seven months into my fieldwork, coronavirus hit and India went into "the world's harshest lockdown" (Daniyal 2021). In Mumbai, the epicenter of the COVID-19 crisis, the lockdown has been endlessly long, and endlessly punishing. While slight relaxations in restrictions in Mumbai have been announced over the past month, the relaxations are minimal and rules regarding lockdown are constantly changing. This public health crisis has turned into an economic crisis of mind-boggling magnitude for the laborers I have been studying. The insecurities facing informal workers, and in particular construction workers, are not new. The COVID-19 crisis, however, amplified them to a degree rarely seen before. I wrote this chapter in August 2020 during India's first wave of COVID-19. As I write these final revisions in June 2021, India is experiencing an even deadlier, and more devastating, second wave of COVID. Health experts predict that a third wave may also hit (Pillai 2021; Sinha 2021). How this continued pandemic is going to affect women construction workers is yet to be fully understood, though all indicators point toward any successive COVID-19 waves as being extremely troubling for them.

Before India went into pandemic lockdown, I conducted qualitative fieldwork consisting of observations and in-depth interviews of 32 women construction laborers, six male construction workers who were also *Naka* Leaders, eight staff members of MMC and YUVA (NGOs), and four executives of two large construction companies at *bastis* (slums), *nakas* (intersections where individuals congregate waiting to get selected for work), construction sites, offices of construction companies and NGOs. The construction workers can be grouped into two categories: (1) twenty *naka* laborers, and (2) twelve "proper company workers." I also took an extensive tour of construction sites in Navi Mumbai run by one of the companies. Since lockdown was established (and continues in Mumbai where I reside), I have done phone interviews of NGO staff, industry executives, and union organizers.

Naka laborers are daily wage earners who go to major intersections where *thekadars* (middlemen) come to choose workers for sites around the city. They are paid low daily wages; many told me stories of contractors withholding wages. None had bank accounts and almost none were compensated for medical care even if injured on the job. None have retirement savings or paid sick leave. All the *naka* laborers with whom

I spoke live in *bastis* near the intersections where they go looking for work everyday. Living in slums in and of itself creates precarity as they are un-sanitary and over-crowded. The dwellings are often constructed with tarps, sticks, and sometimes concrete, and toilet facilities and running water are at a minimum. Most of the slum dwellers with whom I spoke do not have deeds to their homes and face the threat of eviction all the time. "Proper company workers," as my participants call it, have more stable jobs in comparison to *naka* laborers. They do not have formal contracts, but they have verbal agreements to work for a company on the same site for a period of months, and often go work on another site run by that same company when they complete a project. Most of them live on the construction sites in half-built buildings or in huts they have built with tarps, sticks, and pieces of sheet metal.

Female Labor Workforce in India

Using a feminist grounded theory approach, which is bottom-up, helped me uncover the complex experiences and conceptualizations of Human Security in Mumbai and Navi Mumbai's construction industry, and laid the foundation for honoring the experiences and conceptualizations of women construction workers *as they expressed them*. A grounded theory approach is an iterative, dynamic process which, like Human Security, is people-centered. With that approach, findings in the field lead the way through the research process and guide us to theories that speak to what is happening on the ground. While "…no consensus exists on the definition of feminism," basic tenets are that feminism sees that "gender differences are differences of power…and permeate all aspects of social life"; they are "committed to making a difference…At the heart of feminism is an agency of change" and "feminist scholars recognize the close connections between activism, policy-making, and academic research" (O'Brien and Williams 2013, 283). A feminist grounded approach encourages researchers to honor the voices of those gifting us with their stories.

The theoretical constructs that I used were guideposts, but they changed and expanded as I discovered more in the field. According to Ackerley et al. (2006), "theories…become challenged in the field research process" (9) and a grounded approach is particularly open to that challenge. As we can see from ethnographers on migrants in India (Yadav 2018, 2020; Bhowmik 2016; Breman 2016; Breman et al. 2009; Shah 2006), hearing people's experiences is crucial to understanding social phenomena. This is particularly important since I am studying a marginalized group of workers in the Global South. Adrienne Rich captures this beautifully:

> In my white North American world they have tried to tell me that this woman - politicized by intersecting forces - doesn't think and reflect on her life. That her ideas are not real ideas like those of Karl Marx and Simone de Beauvoir. That her calculations, her spiritual philosophy, her gifts for law and ethics, her daily emergency political decisions are merely instinctual or conditioned reactions.
> That only certain kinds of people can make theory; that the white educated mind is capable of formulating everything; that white middle-class feminism can know for 'all women'; that only when a white mind formulates is the formulation to be taken seriously. (Rich 2003, 40)

Reviewing the scholarship on women construction workers in India reveals that the preponderance focuses on health security. In Mumbai and Navi Mumbai, lockdown was declared as a way of stemming the spread of COVID-19 and, therefore, protecting health security—but nothing was prepared to manage the economic or community fallout. Health security is certainly an important research concern, as health insecurity ran rampant among construction laborers before, and now during, the pandemic. For women workers, specifically, chronic urinary tract infections, silicosis, extreme and debilitating back pain, chronic skin rashes, and maternal health problems are very common. However, when I spoke to my participants, they mostly brushed off safety and health issues. The feature of HS which came up time and time again was economic security. Since lockdown, I have spoken on the phone with NGO staff and union organizers who have been keeping in touch with community members and providing relief services, as well.

They told me that the primary concern among construction workers is still livelihood. Even during this pandemic, economic security—not health security—figures the most substantially in their conceptualization of HS.

Precarity *and* Informality

As Yadav (2018, 2020) has shown in her ethnographic accounts of the Gonds in India, precarity and informality are useful lenses to understand the experiences of marginalized groups. I, too, have found that these two concepts help us understand Indian women construction workers' experiences and conceptualizations of HS before and during COVID-19. As Siegmann and Schiphorst (2016) argue, "it is time to bring the notions of informal and precarious work together" (111). Indeed, precarity and informality in the lives of Indian women construction workers are so intertwined that I have come to think of them as nested concepts that only *together* can illuminate their HS. As conceptual binaries are often too restrictive, so is a demand to choose only one theoretical lens through which to look at people's lived experiences. The lives of Indian women construction workers are generally precarious partly, or largely, due to being part of the informal workforce.

"The concept of precarity first emerged in French sociology and economics. In the concept's initial articulations during the 1970s, précarité described a social condition linked to poverty, that only later came to refer to 'new' employment forms of precarious work outside of the classic Fordist version of full-time permanent contracts" (Barbier 2002, as cited in Lazar and Sanchez 2019, 4). A notable criticism of precarity is its focus on the Global North. (See Munck's classic "The Precariat: a view from the South" [2013].) While much precarity scholarship focuses on precarious work, many scholars have also argued that precariousness can pertain to life conditions as well. (See, for example, Millar 2017; Kalleberg and Vallas 2018; Mosoetsa et al. 2016.) As you will see in the descriptions of my fieldwork, my participants are "precarious workers generally understood as persons not just engaged in precarious work but also enduring the necessary consequences of precariousness" (Anderson 2010, 303–304, as cited in Campbell and Price 2016, 315).

The term "informality" was coined in 1973 by Keith Hart, anthropologist, to describe what he was seeing in Ghana. Over the years, informality has mostly been utilized in Global South scholarship. The World Bank's 2016 report defines informality as "a term used to describe the collection of firms, workers, and activities that operate outside...regulatory systems." Though scholars often disagree on definitions of informality, many of them do agree that "It is time to move beyond narrow conceptualizations of the informal economy and to open up this field of enquiry by recognizing and highlighting the multitude of activities that take place under the 'umbrella' concept of the informal economy" (Morris and Polese 2015, 13). Informal labor is often mistakenly equated with illegal or temporary labor activities. In fact, many poor people labor legally in the informal sector their entire working lives. The general consensus among economists had been that the informal sector would eventually be subsumed into the formal economy; instead, the informal economy has continuously grown enormously across the globe. "Enterprises throughout the world and in many sectors of the economy have shed labor on a massive scale, retaining only a small core of regular workers and relying for the bulk of their workforce on a large periphery of casual and temporary workers" (Wells 2007, 88).

Understanding the informal economy helps us understand the formal economy. Indeed, the line between "formal" and "informal" is very blurry.

Lived Experiences of Precarity, Informality, and Human Security

To paint a picture of the precarity and informality in which my participants live, I will describe some of the women construction workers with whom I spoke one evening in a slum near the Belapur *Naka* in Navi Mumbai. Dotting a hillside, the homes in this sprawling *basti* are made of tattered bits of plastic and corrugated metal. They have water tapped in once a day from 8 to 10 a.m.; they have some community toilets; there is a stagnant creek nearby. I was told that malaria and dengue run rampant during monsoon; landslides during monsoon can also level dwellings given how stripped the hill gets every time the *basti* spreads out more. Most of these slum dwellers (250 of the 400 families) have no formal right to this property, so they are considered "encroachers." They face the constant threat of eviction. Poisonous snakes used to pose a problem, too—until people living in the *basti* learned how to catch and immobilize them. All the *naka* laborers with whom I spoke at this *basti* were the most informal types of laborers in the construction industry. By no objective measures are they living stable lives. However, each one's experiences and conceptualizations of HS were unique.

One of the women with whom I spoke had been working in construction as a day laborer for the past fifty years, and her two adult daughters now also work in construction as day laborers. She could not remember exactly at what age she started working construction, but guessed she was around ten years old. She lost her husband ten years into their young marriage, and raised their two daughters on her own. Due to her son-in-law being an alcoholic and not able to work, she now is mostly raising her grandchildren, and still working in construction—when she can get work. As she told me, "I had a lot of responsibilities and I have been working because I had to work to feed my family. There are no negative things in that. I have to do it so rather than looking at negative things, we look forward to our work and do it and get whatever we can get out of it" (interview 31 January 2020). Though her work is the most informal, and therefore very precarious, her experience and conceptualization of Human Security are that being able to feed and house her family—even though she has no extra money whatsoever—is enough.

Another woman who has been doing construction work throughout Maharashtra for the last twenty-five years and then settled in this *basti* in 2014 also clearly illustrated some of the precarious nature of their lives. She said, "There are no good things or the best things that come from this work. Whatever I earn, it goes to food and keeping my entire family fed. It's not like I could say that I worked here and I could buy something. Whatever I earned, I ate and the next day we repeat. It's like a tree where there are only three leaves; there are no opportunities, it's just the same thing" (interview 31 January 2020). Though her life circumstances are not objectively very different from the woman described above, subjectively her experience of HS is that she has no security. She made it very clear that she was dissatisfied with her work and life circumstances. Before the interview was over, she abruptly left with no explanation.

Another woman I spoke to demonstrates another kind of precarity. She migrated from rural Maharashtra and has worked as a *naka* laborer (getting anywhere between three to fifteen days of work per month) for the past five to six years. She told me that, while she cannot educate her children and has to earn simply to eat, "We have a much better life here than we had there [in our native place]. We never got paid high in the villages" (interview 31 January 2020). Her sons started working as *naka* laborers, one at 13 years old and the other at 14 years old. The NGO staff member who had accompanied me into the *basti* later told me that she engages in sex work when she cannot get construction work. According to "Street Corner Secrets: Sex, work and migration in the city of Mumbai" (Shah 2014), this is a fairly common practice. Because she compared her low income in Navi Mumbai to her even lower income in her native place, she expressed feeling more secure.

And one more woman who has not worked construction in four years due to an accident had objectively the least precarious life of all my participants from that *basti*—but still precarious relative to people not living in slums. She fractured her shoulder in a work-related accident and the contractor and employer never paid for the medical care she needed. Because her shoulder healed improperly, she now makes brooms out of coconut fiber and does occasional domestic work. Like the previous participant, she uses different types of informal jobs to help with family finances. As a widow, she lives with her adult daughter, son-in-law, and two grandchildren whom she relies on for financial support. In their home, they have a separate bathroom with a toilet which they built with a government loan. They also own two other properties in this slum and earn income from renting them to tenants. The two children, 12 and 14 years old, are enrolled in school.

I will now describe some "proper company" workers whom I interviewed. On a luxury residential high-rise construction site in Dadar (a neighborhood in Mumbai), which is run by one of India's largest construction companies, I had the opportunity to speak with women who did menial tasks on the site (carrying loads and cleaning), as well as one of the women who held the position of Safety Officer (what company officials call people in her position)/Controlling Authority (what she called herself). While most all Safety Officers are males, this woman had been in her position for eight years. She described her job as such: "My work mostly comprises of taking care of the women and acquiring more of human resource that is needed. I'm the one people go to and tell me when they need more people to work here…Also if there is some kind of casualty or accident on the site, I am the person who contacts the higher officials and lets them know and arrange for an ambulance to take them over there. Or any kind of emergency that happens, I'm the one to take care of it on this location" (interview 26 November 2019). When I asked her what security looks like to her, she answered, "What I think is also really good is that they [those who run the company] think of us. What I think of as *suraksha* (security) is what they are giving us now so what they are thinking for us is also very nice" (interview 26 November 2019). Being treated with respect was important to her sense of security—as was also the case with other workers with whom I spoke. "Proper company" workers and *naka* laborers told me that they do not plan for the future. Human Security, for them, is a day by day affair.

To further demonstrate the ways in which Indian women construction workers conceptualize and experience Human Security, and how COVID-19 likely will impact that, I will now discuss a major theme that surfaced in my interviews with many of the *naka* laborers and "proper company" workers: working to enhance their security. Time and time again, the women with whom I spoke told me that was their priority. And now COVID-19 has severely curtailed their preferred means of achieving HS. Once lockdown was established, and India essentially shut down, construction workers (along with most daily wage earners) lost their jobs. With the loss of work came loss of income. Most had no savings to fall back on, and most did not receive wages from their employers (even though it is Maharashtra law to do so). Most began to face severe hunger and other hardships born of having no source of income. Many took arduous and dangerous long journeys back to their native places as a means of survival. Others stayed in Mumbai and Navi Mumbai to wait out the crisis. And through it all, government measures to "help" those affected were insufficient, at best.

Precarity and informality were on the rise (Lewchuk 2017) before the pandemic hit, and now there is a dramatic spike in both. All construction projects literally ground to a halt overnight when the central government announced the lockdown four hours before it was implemented. An estimated 80,000,000 Indians (mostly daily wage earners) went back to their native places in the months since lockdown. With the exception of one of the women whom I interviewed before lockdown, all of them told me they had originally left their native places due to lack of work and income. To them, migrating to an urban center was a means of financial survival. And then many of them migrated back to native places as a means of coping with the pandemic. When they went back, they too often did not find any or enough work. The Mahatma Gandhi National Rural Employment Guarantee Act of 2005 (MGNREGA), a rural work program, was supposed to help return migrants earn income. However, many locales ran out of work within the first two months (Jebaraj July 2020; Swamy May 2020; Shrinidhi and Gururaja June 2020). Very few people found work through MGNREGA in April 2020, largely due to confusing messages from the central government about whether or not people were allowed to work on MGNREGA projects during lockdown (Agarwal May 2020; Jebaraj April 2020). As of the final revisions of this chapter (June 2021), again fewer people were employed by MGNREGA projects due to the second wave of COVID-19 (Mukherjee 2021).

Even four months after lockdown began in Mumbai (the time of the writing of this chapter), construction work has only returned minimally. I have learned from one of my YUVA contacts that *Naka* Laborers are not getting much work. Only a small percentage that normally goes to *nakas* to look for work (He estimates 10%.) is going now because of restrictions on groups congregating. And that even of those, few are picked up for work on construction projects. He said that of the *naka* laborers and their families who are still in Mumbai and Navi Mumbai, most are relying on government rations of 5 kg of staples and whatever charity they receive from NGOs. And from an industry executive, I have learned that "proper company" laborers are also not fully returning to work. He told me that his construction sites are operating at 30–40% worker capacity (phone interview, June 2020). Even when the company sends scouts back to the villages and offers bonuses and higher wages, few are accepting their offer. As NGO staff and union organizers have told me, migrant workers were so mistreated when lockdown was established that they do not trust that government or employers will treat them properly for the remainder of this COVID crisis.

The Limits of Government to Minimize Precarity of Construction Workers: The Building and Other Construction Workers Act Before and during COVID-19

During my fieldwork, the Building and Other Construction Workers Act and the Building and Other Construction Workers Cess Act (BOCW Acts) emerged as the piece of legislation most relevant (or irrelevant) for construction workers' HS. Extremely weak implementation of social security laws designed for construction workers *long before* COVID-19 is one of the main reasons for the precarity of construction workers *before and during* COVID-19. Challenges with the BOCW Act are a clear illustration that "...many of the struggles that precarious workers engage in are focused on gaining visibility, recognition, and legal standing" (Mosoetsa et al. 2016, 6). Implementation of the Act has had trouble from its inception. As Subhash Bhatnagar, one of the chief architects of the BOCW Acts, explained, "I started coordinating in 1986 and we got this law enacted in 1996...In 2006, ten years after the law was enacted, it came to be implemented only partially in 6 states in the country out of 36 states [29 states and 7 union territories, to be exact]. So we moved the Supreme Court. After moving the Supreme Court, it took six years for the law to get implemented or tripartite boards to be built up in all 36 states in India, then it took another six years until 2018 for the final verdict from the Supreme Court of what is wrong with implementation and what can be corrected…" (interview 31 March 2020).

Designed to offer schemes such as scholarships for children of construction workers, coverage of medical care, affordable housing, and other entitlements, the BOCW Act was created to enhance security of construction workers in India. It has, however, failed to do so. Most construction workers with whom I spoke (with the exception of two) had never even heard of the BOCW Acts. Most of my participants told me they had almost no support from their employers or from the government. They relied on self-sufficiency and self-reliance to get through financial, medical, and other struggles. One of the women with whom I spoke at the *basti* near Nerul *Naka* encapsulated what almost every construct worker I spoke with expressed about lack of support, in particular from the government. She said, "There's never been any external support for any sort of health or children's education or family well-being. Whatever we need, the onus is on us. Again at times you get work and at times you don't; only when you work hard and you get it [work] it's as simple as that" (interview, 10 January 2020). And when I asked a group of a half dozen *Naka* Leaders at Nerul *Naka*, "Is there any governmental social support?" without hesitation and emphatically, they answered, "No" (interview, 10 January 2020). (*Naka* Leaders are construction workers groomed by YUVA to help raise awareness about rights and entitlements amongst workers.)

Mirroring what I heard in interviews with construction workers, Subhash Bhatnagar spent a good deal of time on the phone with me during lockdown lamenting how little difference the BOCW Acts have made on the ground. To pay for its schemes, the BOCW Acts call for each state to set up welfare boards and collect cess (tax) from construction companies which have employed more than ten construction workers in the preceding 12 months. The cess paid by the company is supposed to be 1–2% of the cost of construction of each project. Most state boards, however, are not functioning as intended. Maharashtra's state board has spent only 6.8% of the cess funds on workers (Banerjee and Raibagi 2019). Bhatnagar told me, "Maharashtra is so bad because it has the highest amount of money collected, more than Karnataka, but the least amount of money being spent properly" (interview 31 March 2020). The Maharashtra government claims 90% of all construction workers in the state are registered with the BOCW welfare boards (staff at TOI 2018). NGO staff and union officials I spoke to scoff at that assertion. YUVA's survey during the early stages of the pandemic found that "5.29% [of construction workers in Mumbai and Navi Mumbai] reported being registered with the…BOCW Welfare Board" (YUVA, June 2020, 2). The vast majority of my participants were not registered with the state board. As Bhatnagar estimated, 10% [in Maharashtra] are registered, and even just 5% in many other states. During the COVID-19 crisis, the Maharashtra government has promised to give 2000 INR as cash relief to construction workers registered with the welfare board, but so few are registered. In short, Maharashtra has been, and continues to be, a "low registration and low expenditure" state (Roy and Naik 2017, 12).

My fieldwork revealed that there are multiple hurdles to registration with state boards.

From the moment I started talking to staff of YUVA, I was told over and over again how challenging registration is. To be registered as a construction worker with the board, one needs to have proof that one has done such work for 90 days. To get that proof requires a construction company official to furnish such proof for the worker. As the YUVA field staff manager told me, "Some contractors, some laborers from the city they work on six *nakas*…sometimes contractors will say 'I don't know him or her, so how can I give [proof of work]?'" (interview 25 September 2019). Most *naka* laborers work at a variety of sites over any given period of time, so even though they work for 90 days, it may not be for one employer. Additionally, the vast majority of them have been picked up for work by a *thekadar* (middleman) so they often do not even know who their employer is. Just to demonstrate how complicated registration is, the field manager also told me, "Now municipality of the state government, means Labor Department, has circulated a circular that says municipality commissioner has to authorize a person who can sign that 90 day [work] certificate. But that authorized person has to go on that labor market and see that yeah she's there, he's there with biometrics and she or he has to stand on that market, *naka* and they will file that form and then they will process for 90 days" (interview 25 September 2019). The chain of labor is so convoluted in the construction industry; therefore, responsibility is easily shirked.

Indeed, Subhash Bhatnagar told me that one regret he has about the design of the BOCW Acts is the way registration is legislated. He told me, "There is one provision which we were wanting which is not there…In the law, the registration of construction establishment is a must; the payment of cess is a must. But workers' registration is optional; that is, workers can register if they want to. And our workers are most uneducated, illiterate so how would they know about the law and why would they get registered? The government deliberately left this provision out — maybe deliberately on the advice of the builders — not to make it compulsory for the workers. That is why we are having the biggest problem...Even from the court [Supreme Court] we could not get them to rule to make it compulsory" (interview, 31 March 2020).

Not only do union organizers, NGO staff, and construction workers make it obvious that the BOCW Acts have been poorly implemented, industry officials do too. A manager of one of India's most prestigious and profitable construction companies told me that the safety and health measures they take on their work sites have little to do with government regulations, and more to do with a personal value that comes from the top management, as well as their desire to reduce employee turn-over and impress foreign investors. When we met at the company headquarters in Mumbai, he explained, "They [the government] are mostly a neutral bystander. I have yet to find an example where they come and facilitate us in a positive way. Not a single example. Either they are neutral bystanders or sometimes a hindrance" (interview 8 November 2019). He went on to say that there are "very few inspections by the [government] authorities...They come to site; it's not that they don't. But it's not in the way it should happen. We have 100 plus sites so they come to ten sites. That really won't help the cause. If a police authority, for example, visits a locality that is notorious once a year, what's the point of going?" (interview 8 November 2019).

The impotency of the BOCW Acts has been made abundantly clear during the COVID- 19 crisis. All the cess money held by the state welfare boards could have been spent for relief efforts for construction workers when nationwide lockdown was established, but it was not.

Using the idleness of the BOCW welfare board in Delhi during COVID-19 as a prime example, Bhatnagar told me: "Delhi government has 10 lakh workers to take care of. We have 3200 crore rupees [approximately 42,593,122 USD] with the construction workers board for their welfare, which means 32,000 rupees per ten workers. But they have given money only to 40,000 workers. That's not even 4% which is a small amount and the rest of the 96% workers they are not giving anything. We are asking them [the welfare board] again and again and we are asking others to ask them but there is no impact. We also cannot physically reach them, so they are enjoying it.

It's a very bad situation and we can't get answers" (interview, 17 April 2020). YUVA's interim report "Access to Entitlements and Relief: Among the urban poor in the Mumbai Metropolitan Region during COVID-19" (2020) details the profoundly weak reach of assistance to the poor during the pandemic. For example, 37% of their respondents could not access free grain rations, and 93% of households were not able to access free cooking fuel to which they were entitled (2).

My observations during lockdown in Mumbai dramatically illustrated some of YUVA's findings. An apartment building adjacent to the building in which I live in Mumbai was being renovated. Yet the work did not cease until the lockdown made it absolutely impossible for workers to continue. So the twelve laborers (all men) were stuck living in the gutted building for the first six weeks of lockdown. Upon asking, I came to know that their employer paid them enough money to get basic food supplies, but not their wages to which they were entitled by Maharashtra law. Those who supported families back in their villages were unable to continue doing so. Hence, lack of worker supports during COVID impacts not only their Human Security, but that of their families as well.

Conclusion

My fieldwork on women construction workers in Mumbai and Navi Mumbai—especially, but not only, during the COVID-19 crisis—shines a spotlight on their experiences and conceptualizations of Human Security. The conceptual lenses of informality and precarity *taken together* help guide this analysis. My findings show us the need for expansive understandings of both informality and precarity. A feminist grounded theory approach is the key to honoring the women workers' own expressions and experiences, and complex realities as they unfolded. To them, Human Security is mainly economic security. What my participants want is the opportunity to work to support themselves and their families. By and large, they do not want to rely on government support, and government schemes are terribly insufficient anyway.

COVID-19 has made Indian women construction workers' attempts to secure their lives much more precarious. But given the tenacity that I saw on construction sites, at *nakas* and in *bastis*, the women will forge on. What remains to be seen, as the COVID-19 crisis continues and then is past us, is exactly how they will.

Bibliography

Ackerly, Brooke A., Maria Stern, and Jacqui True, eds. *Feminist Methodologies for International Relations*. Cambridge University Press, 2006.

Agarwal, Kabir. "COVID-19 Lockdown: In April, MGNREGA Work Crashed to Lowest in 7 Years", *The Wire*, 1 May 2020. https://thewire.in/labour/covid-19-lockdown-mgnrega

Banerjee, Abhivyakti, and Kashyap Raibagi. "Why Construction Workers Missed Government Welfare Benefits For 23 Years", *India Spend*, 20 April 2019. https://www.indiaspend.com/why-construction-workers-missed-government-welfare-benefits-for-23-years/

Barnabas, Annette, D. Joseph Anbarasu, and Paul S. Clifford. "A Study on the Empowerment of Women Construction Workers as Masons in Tamil Nadu, India." *Journal of International Women's Studies* 11, no. 2 (2009): 121–141.

Bhattacharyya, Sanghita K, and Kim Korinek. "Opportunities and Vulnerabilities of Female Migrants in Construction Work in India." *Asian and Pacific Migration Journal* 16, no. 4 (2007): 511–531.

Bhowmik, Sharit Kumar. "Tribal Labour in the Tea Plantations of West Bengal: Problems of Migration and Settlement." *First Citizens: Studies on Adivasis, Tribals and Indigenous Peoples in India* (2016): 207–227.

Breman, Jan. "A Bogus Concept? [Review of: G. Standing (2011) The Precariat: The New Dangerous Class]." *New Left Review* 84 (2013): 130–138.

Breman, Jan. "At Work in the Informal Economy of India: A Perspective from the Bottom Up (OIP)", *OUP Catalogue*, 2016.

Breman, Jan, Isabelle Guérin, and Aseem Prakash. *India's Unfree Workforce of Bondage Old and New*, 2009.

Campbell, Iain, and Robin Price. "Precarious Work and Precarious Workers: Towards an Improved Conceptualisation." *The Economic and Labour Relations Review* 27, no. 3 (2016): 314–332.

Charmes, Jacques. "The Informal Economy Worldwide: Trends and Characteristics." Margin: The *Journal of Applied Economic Research* 6, no. 2 (2012): 103–132.

Chen, Martha Alter, and Govindan Raveendran. "Urban Employment in India: Recent Trends and Patterns." *Margin: The Journal of Applied Economic Research* 6, no. 2 (2012): 159–179.

Daniyal, S. The Pandemic in Data: Not Only are India's Poor Eating Less, They are Eating Less Nutritious Food. *Scroll.in*, June 2021. https://www.im4change.org/latest-news-updates/the-pandemic-in-data-not-only-are-india-s-poor-eating-less-they-are-eating-less-nutritious-food-shoaib-daniyal.html

Express News Service. "Accidents at Workplaces in India 'Under Reported'; 38 Per Day in Construction Sector: Study", *The Indian Express*, 21 November 2017. https://indianexpress.com/article/india/accidents-at-workplaces-in-india-under-reported-38-per-day-in-construction-sector-study-4947079/

Hart, Keith. "Informal Income Opportunities and Urban Employment in Ghana." *The journal of Modern African studies* 11, no. 1 (1973): 61–89.
Jain, Sreenivasan, and Sonal Matharu. "Fatal Heights: The Untold Deaths of India's Construction Workers", *NDTV*, 5 August 2017. https://www.ndtv.com/india-news/fatal-heights-the-untold-deaths-of-indias-construction-workers-1733974
Jebaraj, Priscilla. "Coronavirus Lockdown | Only 30 Lakh Found MGNREGA Work in April." *The Hindu*, 30 April 2020. https://www.thehindu.com/news/national/coronavirus-lockdown-only-30-lakh-found-mgnrega-work-in-april/article31467548.ece
Jebaraj, Priscilla. "Amid Demand Surge, 1.4 Lakh Families have Reached Annual MGNREGA Work Limit", *The Hindu,* 30 April 2020. https://www.thehindu.com/news/national/amid-demand-surge-14-lakh-families-have-reached-annual-mgnrega-work-limit/article32006305.ece
Kalleberg, Arne L., and Steven P. Vallas. "Probing Precarious Work: Theory, Research, and Politics." *Research in the Sociology of Work* 31, no. 1 (2018): 1–30.
Lazar, Sian, and Andrew Sanchez. "Understanding Labour Politics in an Age of Precarity." *Dialectical Anthropology* 43, no. 1 (2019): 3–14.
Lewchuk, Wayne. "Precarious Jobs: Where Are They, and How Do They Affect Well-being?" *The Economic and Labour Relations Review* 28, no. 3 (2017): 402–419.
Millar, Kathleen M. "Toward a Critical Politics of Precarity." *Sociology Compass* 11, no. 6 (2017): e12483.
Morris, Jeremy, and Abel Polese, eds. *Informal Economies in Post-Socialist Spaces: Practices, Institutions and Networks*. Springer, 2015.
Mosoetsa, Sarah, Joel Stillerman, and Chris Tilly. "Precarious Labor, South and North: An introduction." *International Labor and Working Class History* 89 (2016): 5.
Mukherjee, Sanjeeb. "Demand for MGNREGA Work Slumps 26% in May Amid Covid-19 Pandemic", *Business Standard*, 2 June 2021. https://www.business-standard.com/article/economy-policy/demand-for-mgnrega-work-slumps-26-in-may-amid-covid-19-pandemic-121060200040_1.html.
Munck, Ronaldo. "The Precariat: A View from the South." *Third World Quarterly* 34, no. 5 (2013): 747–762.
O'brien, Robert, and Marc Williams. *Global Political Economy: Evolution and Dynamics*. Macmillan, 2013.
Pandit, Niraj, Ashish Trivedi, and Das Bidisha. "A Study of Maternal and Child Health Issues Among Migratory Construction Workers." *Planning* 46, no. 56 (2011): 66.

Pillai, A. Marthanda. "Covid-19: How to Stave off the Third wave?", *The Times of India*, June 2021. https://timesofindia.indiatimes.com/city/kochi/how-to-stave-off-the-third-wave/articleshow/83454157.cms

Rai, Anu, and Ashish Sarkar. "Workplace Culture & Status of Women Construction Labourers; A case study in Kolkata, West Bengal." *Indian Journal of Spatial Science* 3, no. 2 (2012): 44–54.

Rebbapragada, Pallavi. "No Country for Construction Workers: Two Decades After First Legislation, Fight for Compensation and Identification Goes On", *Firstpost,* October 2018. https://www.firstpost.com/india/no-country-for-construction-workers-two-decades-after-first-legislation-fight-for-compensation-and-identification-goes-on-5432901.html.

Rich, Adrienne. "Notes Towards a Politics of Location." *Feminist Postcolonial Theory: A Reader* (2003): 29–42.

Roy, Shamindra Nath, and Manish Mukta Naik. "Migrants in Construction Work: Evaluating their Welfare Framework." *Centre for Policy Research Policy Brief* (2017): 1–16.

Shah, Alpa. "The Labour of Love: Seasonal Migration from Jharkhand to the Brick Kilns of Other States in India." *Contributions to Indian Sociology* 40, no. 1 (2006): 91–118.

Shah, Rajiv. "India's 80% Construction Sites "unsafe", Deaths 20 Times Higher than Those in Britain", *Counterview*, 12 May 2019. https://www.counterview.net/2019/05/indias-80-construction-sites-unsafe.html

Shah, Svati P. *Street Corner Secrets: Sex, Work, and Migration in the City of Mumbai*. Duke University Press, 2014.

Shrinidhi R, Gururaja, B.R., Gavali, Raju. "Coronavirus Lockdown: MGNREGA Provides Relief, not Enough to Counter the Crisis", *The Deccan Herald*, 14 June 2020. https://www.deccanherald.com/specials/insight/coronavirus-lockdown-mgnrega-provides-relief-not-enough-to-counter-the-crisis-849263.html

Siegmann, Karin Astrid, and Freek Schiphorst. "Understanding the Globalizing Precariat: From Informal Sector to Precarious Work." *Progress in Development Studies* 16, no. 2 (2016): 111–123.

Sinha, Amitabh. "Explained: What is a Wave in a Pandemic, and Will India See a Third Wave of Covid-19?", *Indian Express*, 14 June 2021. https://indianexpress.com/article/explained/india-coronavirus-third-wave-covid-vaccines-oxygen-supply-7322145/

Srivastava, Ravi. "Documenting the Lack of Labour Rights in India's Construction Sector", Centre for Development Policy and Research, School of Oriental and African Studies at University of London, *Development Viewpoint*, 80. (2014). https://www.soas.ac.uk/cdpr/publications/dv/file93806.pdf

Srivastava, R., and Ajit Jha. "Capital and Labour Standards in the Organised Construction Industry in India." London: CDPR, SOAS. Accessed December 16 (2016): 2016.

Staff, "53,000 Construction Labourers in Maharashtra, 90% Registered: Govt." *Times of India*, 4 October 2018. https://timesofindia.indiatimes.com/city/mumbai/53000-construction-labourers-in-maharashtra-90-registered-govt/articleshow/66061703.cms

Swamy, Rakshita. "Additional Allocation for MGNREGA Must Be Supplemented with Steps to Make it More Effective", *The Indian Express*, 22 May 2020. https://indianexpress.com/article/opinion/columns/india-lockdown-rural-distress-coronavirus-a-moment-to-revive-mgnrega-6421558/

Wells, Jill. "Informality in the Construction Sector in Developing Countries." *Construction Management and Economics* 25, no. 1 (2007): 87–93.

Wells, Jill. "Informal Construction Activity in Developing Countries." In *New Perspectives on Construction in Developing Countries*, pp. 186–202. Routledge, 2012.

Whitehead, Judy. "Flexible Labor/Flexible Housing: The Rescaling of Mumbai into a Global Financial Center and the Fate of Its Working Class." *Blood and Fire: Toward a Global Anthropology of Labor*, ed. Sharryn Kasmir, and August Carbonella (2014): 123–167.

Yadav, Smita. *Precarious Labour and Informal Economy: Work, Anarchy, and Society in an Indian Village*. Springer, 2018.

Yadav, Smita. "Precarity as a Coping Strategy of the Gonds: A Study of Insecure and Long-Distance Seasonal Migration in Central India." *Indian Journal of Human Development* 14, no. 1 (2020): 7–22.

YUVA. "Access to Entitlements and Relief: Among the Urban Poor in the Mumbai Metropolitan Region During COVID-19" (interim report), June 2020.

CHAPTER 5

Diminishing Constructions: The Work of Exposure in Pandemic Times

Adam Sargent

Across the world, the coronavirus pandemic has brought the concept of exposure to the forefront of our everyday and political awareness. The air that we breathe in and out, the surfaces that we touch, and the spaces that we share have all become sites of anxious reflection and intervention. These concerns have become especially pressing in the realm of work, where the necessity of earning a livelihood forces workers to cede varying levels of control over whom they come in contact with and how. Pernicious outbreaks in slaughterhouses—even in countries with relatively low numbers of cases such as Australia (Bucci 2020)—make visible the minute politics of production that rely on closely packed worker bodies labouring in temperature-controlled conditions. Grocery store workers have found themselves at the forefront of the pandemic and the anxieties

A. Sargent (✉)
Western Sydney University, Sydney, NSW, Australia
e-mail: A.Sargent@westernsydney.edu.au

S. Hewamanne and S. Yadav (eds.), *The Political Economy of Post-COVID Life and Work in the Global South: Pandemic and Precarity*, International Political Economy Series,
https://doi.org/10.1007/978-3-030-93228-2_5

it incites as they work overtime in crowded stores, disinfecting surfaces and attempting to limit their physical contact with customers. Struggles have emerged as workers—including many immigrant workers newly minted as "essential"—struggle for protective equipment, health care, and the right to work remotely.

These struggles highlight the relationship between work and exposure. The pandemic has revealed the ways that bodies come into contact with each other and their environments over the course of securing a livelihood, and these points of contact are far from uniform. They turn not only on the particular arrangements of one's work—the proximity of others, the surfaces one must touch—but also on the employment relationship. The pandemic also reveals a different sort of exposure: gig workers struggle against their employers to extract even minimal amounts of protective equipment or health coverage while hospitals struggle alongside their employees in order to provide them with requisite barriers between healthcare workers and their patients. Workers classified as permanent qualify for various governmental relief schemes that afford the ability to not work, while those who cannot lay claim to such stable forms of employment are increasingly squeezed between the need for income and the dangers of exposure. In the pandemic, not having the social infrastructure of formal employment itself operates as a modality of exposure.

In India, this double exposure was acutely visible in the thousands of migrant workers leaving cities ahead of local and national lockdowns (Sarmin 2020; Naik 2021). The most dramatic of these mass departures occurred on the 24th of March when Prime Minister Modi declared a nationwide lockdown four hours before it took effect (Ray and Subramanian 2020). The sudden stoppage of work destroyed the informal relations of credit, debt, and labour from which millions of migrant workers make their livelihood. Without these safety nets, workers had no choice but to retreat to their villages. These journeys subjected workers to extreme heat, exhaustion, and hunger. Upon returning to their villages, they were often treated as vectors of exposure to the novel coronavirus and were excluded or even attacked (Chatterjee 2020; see Chowdhury 2020 for similar phenomena in Bangladesh). Mere months later, many of these workers were enticed to return to the very cities they left as companies and governments realized the significance of their labour (Sharma et al. 2020). This pattern has repeated itself over the course of India's devastating second wave (Naik 2021).

These exposures in India and beyond demonstrate how the coronavirus has made the vulnerabilities of working bodies and their uneven distribution into an urgent and global issue. Exposure to COVID-19 is a condition forced upon the poor. Those with the means to do so invest in sanitizers and protective masks, rely on delivery services, and work from home. In afflicting predominantly poor and migrant workers, the pandemic does not depart from but rather intensifies older inequalities of gender, race, and class that manifest in more mundane forms of exposure. From the build-up of minerals and detritus from industrial zones to the leaching of chemicals into office buildings and homes, our late industrial lives and livelihoods are saturated with dangerous, if often unperceived, environmental exposures. Scholars studying these environmental conditions have usefully drawn our attention to complex politics of such exposures as they come to diminish the lives of structurally marginalized communities even as this diminishment is erased or made illegible (Murphy 2006, 2013; Agard-Jones 2013; Graeter 2017; Blanchette 2019). The exposures that the coronavirus has made into urgent political questions for workers travel along routes carved out by systemic inequalities that subject some populations and not others to environments rife with deleterious materials.

In the this chapter, I draw on these accounts to analyse the politics of exposure in the Indian construction industry. This analysis demonstrates the ways in which the dangerous exposures that characterize work on construction sites come to define workers even as they diminish them. In this view, exposure operates in a dialectical fashion, producing worker selves even as it destroys their bodies. The ethnographic material that I draw on was collected between 2011 and 2015 across several construction sites in and around Delhi. While this fieldwork occurred long before the coronavirus pandemic, it offers crucial insights into the ways that migrant workers orient to, make sense of, and intervene in the material exposures they face in their work. Material exposures—to dust, heat, and rust among others—diminish worker bodies by destroying their lungs, hands, and eyes. They also, workers claimed, built capacities within workers that made workers uniquely fit, and unfit, for certain kinds of work. Exposure, then, should not be seen as a simple case of risk or a question of how often one encounters dangerous materials. Rather, exposure emerges out of a complex interplay of forces in which workers are treated as expendable even as they must be specialized, a dynamic that seems to characterize migrant workers more generally. This nuanced understanding of exposure and its effects provides a framework from which to interrogate the ways that the pandemic is reshaping the politics of migrant labour in India and elsewhere.

Diminishment

"Our life is like this sir. We build from the bottom to the top, and we fall from the top to the bottom." With this poetic phrase Niraj, a twenty-eight-year-old bar bender from Bihar, summed up the lives of construction workers. The imagery is particularly poignant because at the time Niraj made this comment, he was helping to lift large pieces of steel rebar up to the sixth floor of what would ultimately be an eight-story apartment complex in Gurgaon. To lift the rebar into place, Niraj and the other bar benders stood on the open edge of alternating floors so that they could pass the long pieces of rebar up from the ground. They would eventually reach the sixth floor, which consisted of an unsteady patchwork of wooden panels that would be used as a base for pouring the cement floor. Moving the rebar up the side of the building in this way was dangerous because there were no rails of any sort around the edge of each floor; any slip or false step could send a worker toppling over the edge.

Niraj's comment was more than a reflection on the immediate danger of lifting the rebar. He offered the comment as a response to a question I often asked when explaining my presence on construction sites: "what are your lives like?" (*āp logon kī zindagī kaisī hain?*). In this context, Niraj's comment describes the exploitation of construction work in India, where workers toil to build high- rise apartment complexes and other infrastructure for middle-class urbanites only to be excluded from the fruits of their labours. Construction brought migrant workers like Niraj to the spaces of a newly affluent India only to cast them away when the buildings were completed.

I received similar responses from other construction workers when I asked this general question. Workers would respond that their life was "very bad" (*bahut kharāb*), consisting of only "work, eat, and sleep" (*bas kām, khānā, aur sonā*). Many described their work as "only for filling the belly" (*pait badhne ke liye*), framing it as something done merely to survive. Here, workers articulated a vision of the construction site and construction work as a space of exploitation, necessity, and toil. Workers engaged in this toil in order to feed themselves and provide for their families, but their time on construction sites was a time of suffering. The workers that I spoke to were often dismissive of direct questions about how they learned their trade or the skills involved in it. They would usually explain that they just started doing the work and after some time learned the trade. On one occasion, I pressed a bar bender on what the most difficult part of his trade was and he responded in a somewhat dismissive tone that "there isn't anything special in this" (*is mein koi khās nahīn*).

Worker visions of the site as a space of suffering identify a crucial dynamic in India's construction industry that is structured by the intertwining of informal and formal economic relations. The industry is notorious for skirting labour laws, high incidents of injury, and unsafe living conditions. In the context of public events such as the 2010 Commonwealth Games hosted by Delhi, construction site conditions have become the source of journalistic exposés (Han 2012) and even more formal investigations (Srivastava et al. 2010; PUDR Team 2009). For the most part, however, exploitative conditions in the industry remain an open secret, and the implementation of workers' rights remains minimal (although see Agarwala 2006 for a counter example). The persistence of such conditions in the industry is directly linked to the wide use of subcontractors who recruit workers, usually migrants, through networks of caste, kin, and village residence. Although the particular arrangements that subcontractors make with workers can vary widely, they are almost always made verbally and often involve ongoing loans that tie workers to subcontractors in relations of debt (Lerche et al. 2017; Prasad-Aleyamma 2017). While construction firms often provide space, housing materials, and basic infrastructure (e.g., water, electricity, latrines) for living on the site, subcontractors provide workers with money for food, cooking gas, and other essentials.

The mediation of these subcontractors makes enforcing labour laws difficult as it is unclear who a worker's employer is, and construction firms can easily pass responsibility for living and working conditions onto subcontractors (Lerche et al. 2017; Pang 2019). The informal worker–subcontractor relationships are often characterized as holdovers that will wither away as India adopts modern business practices. However, these labour mediators provide precisely the kinds of cheap and flexible labour that large construction firms require. The informality of these subcontracting relations is a critical support to formal real estate development rather than a holdover (Sargent 2019). Construction firms themselves may be formally registered, publicly traded companies that stringently follow labour laws even as they employ, and thus reproduce, informal labour delivered via exploitative patronage relations.

One result of this blending of formal and informal economic relations is that workers are rarely provided with sufficient protective equipment or even basic hygienic housing. A large construction site in Delhi where I conducted fieldwork was well regarded for having good work practices. While most workers were provided with hard hats and safety shoes, more specialized equipment was absent. Stone masons who encounter large amounts of stone dust as they cut tiles into shape were never provided with masks; masons and laborers who handled caustic materials such as cement did so without the benefit of gloves; welders operated their torches with little more than sunglasses to protect their eyes. Beyond trade-specific exposures, the summer months bring increased exposure to mosquitos and the attendant risk of malaria and dengue. The effects of these exposures are starkly reflected in medical reporting on morbidity rates among construction workers where silicosis, skin diseases, musculoskeletal damage, and fevers are prominent (Tiwary and Gangopadhyay 2011; Parida and Ray 2012).

The persistence of these conditions is enabled by the blending of formal and informal employment, but it also turns on the politics of exposure more generally. As an analytic lens, exposure highlights the permeable border between bodies and environments, helping scholars trace the movements of pesticides from plantations, ports, or factories to bodies, homes, and communities where they disrupt everything from mundane tasks such as walking and shopping to the reproduction of families (Graeter 2017; Murphy 2013; Fortun 2001; Cielemęcka and Åsberg 2019). The politics of exposure link the intimate contours of bodies to larger political and economic systems that bring particular groups into contact with dangerous chemicals while protecting others from them (Agard-Jones 2013). The silicosis of stone masons or the early blindness of welders are bodily signs that point to and are produced by the political economy of the construction industry in which informal subcontractors supply cheap and flexible migrant labour to construction sites. However, these signs of exposure have long temporalities. Silicosis emerges in stone masons only after years of breathing in particulates of marble, granite, and sandstone, just as musculoskeletal degeneration attests to long years of carrying heavy materials. These long temporalities further complicate questions of accountability for the environmental violence perpetrated on worker bodies (Murphy 2013; Agard-Jones 2013).

Productive Exposures?

Recognizing the destructive force of construction environments and the uneven distribution of this violence onto the bodies of poor migrant workers is essential, but it does not tell the whole story of exposure's effects. The materials to which construction workers were exposed not only diminished their lives through disease and injury but also reshaped capacities and even selves in generative ways. That is, exposure to materials made workers into particular types of people even as it injured them. In this section, I demonstrate how such transformations occurred in conjunction with worker discourses on habituation to the materials of their chosen trades. The very same workers who would initially describe work as mere toil for filling the belly would, at other times, describe the ways in which they had become fit to the materials that they encountered in this work. This process was not seen as one of diminishment but rather as one of becoming a particularly skilled sort of worker, something that was fiercely defended on the site. In the case of the construction industry, exposure must be understood not only as diminishment but rather as a complex, but no less violent, process of fitting types of people to types of work (Sargent 2020).

Although the construction workers I knew were reticent to speak of their work explicitly as a set of complex practices, they would regularly speak among themselves and with me about the physical ailments and transformations their bodies had undergone as a result of taking up a certain trade. Stone masons would comment on the marble dust kicked up by their saws, bar benders would complain about burns from handling rebar that had been left sitting in the hot sun, and welders spoke of the painfully bright light given off by their welding torches. As workers encountered the essential materials of their trade—stone dust, hot rebar, intense light—their bodies were shaped in particular ways. Workers spoke of this process as one of habit or *ādat*.[1] Unlike the English term, *adat* as used by the workers I knew focused attention on repeated encounters with the various materials of one's trade. This repeated exposure resulted

[1] For ease of reading, I have only included diacritics in the first use of Hindi.

in a sort of fit between a worker's bodily capacities and the materials they regularly encountered. Bodily ruptures such as cuts or blisters were often pointed to and discussed as signs of a lack of *adat* indexing a mismatch between the work environment and the worker's embodied self.

Many of these elements of *adat* became clear in a conversation I had with a stone mason I will call Satish. Satish had come to the construction site with a group of stone masons from Bihar. As we sat on the unfinished floor of what would one day be a lecture hall, Satish explained the concept of *adat* to me using the example of some welders who were working on the ceiling near us.

> Like you for example, right?... Now he- like he is welding If you do it you will get shocked by the current but for those people it's become *adat* so this doesn't happen, it doesn't even make a difference And, like if one day you did welding then your eyes will go bad, the whole day tears will keep coming out of your eyes then it will become your *adat* and there won't be any problem.

Welding machines draw substantial electrical currents and thus are liable to shock the user. Yet Satish implied that the welders' bodies had become immune to the electrical currents in a way that my body, for example, was not. Satish's focus throughout was on quintessential exposures of a welder's work, namely the intense light and electricity as opposed to other sensory qualities that welding might have in common with other forms of work. The cultivation of *Adat* consisted of specific bodily modes of interacting with the material environment. Satish did not seem to be simply saying that welders did not shock themselves because they knew how to operate their equipment, although this is no doubt also part of what he referenced. He said that they do not get shocked—"this doesn't happen"––but also that "it doesn't even make a difference," which suggests that the welder's body had become immune to electrical shock. This focus on material exposures was amplified in the next phrase where Satish focused on the intense light of the welding torch. Satish noted that my eyes were not attuned to the intense light of the welding torch, hence my tears. *Adat* was achieved through repeated exposure to the materials of one's trade and was depicted in the movement from a state of bodily rupture—tearing eyes or cut fingers—to one of compatibility: "there won't be any problem" (*koi dikkat hi nahin*).

Adat not only focused on material exposures but also assigned these materials an agentive force in reconfiguring worker bodies. Before Satish began explaining *adat* as such, we had been talking about his own trade, stone masonry. Our conversation was punctuated by the noise of his circular saw and the thumps of a wooden hammer that Satish was using as he fit floor tiles together. As he worked on the tiles, he would run the saw down the edge of each one to grind down the edges and ensure a tight fit between tiles. The saw kicked up plumes of dust consisting of small pieces of marble stone. While Satish would sometimes hold a plastic tube filled with water mere inches from the spinning saw blade in an effort to keep the dust down, he and his colleagues were always covered in stone dust by the end of the day.

In between bouts of cutting, I asked Satish if the stone dust did not bother him. He told me that it had when he started, but now the dust had become his *adat*. As he went on to narrate, stone dust played a crucial role in the advancement of a worker from an unskilled helper to a skilled mason (*mistrī*). Satish noted that when a stone mason helper begins, they only carry tiles to the area where the mason is working, meaning that they stay far away from the saw and the stone dust. As the helper progresses, they begin to assist the mason in cutting by holding the straight edge while the mason cuts. This brings the helper closer to the dust until ultimately, they become masons who are exposed to the most stone dust. This process of progressive exposure helped form the stone mason into a particular type of worker.

Satish's account of *adat* here depicts stone dust as what Jane Bennett would call "vibrant matter" (2010). Bennett calls attention to the ways in which matter is not simply the inert backdrop to human actions; rather, it should be seen as an active force itself, enabling, thwarting, and otherwise transforming human plans. New materialist accounts that follow Bennett stress the ways that the vibrant actions of materials exceed and exist beyond discourse and signification (Coole and Frost 2010). The goal here is to render the agency of matter itself analytically visible not only in the sense of acting back on human intentions but in pursuing separate ends. From this perspective, work is not so much the interaction between a subject and an object, but rather an active shaping of workers by a material world with its own trajectories and capacities.

This approach usefully focuses our attention on the force of materials, allowing us to see these encounters not as laid over the top of socioeconomic realities such as class, but rather as generative of different subjects.

However, there is a tendency to treat matter in a decontextualized way that writes out the possibility of human interventions in their encounters with vibrant matter. The force of matter here is depicted as being beyond and beneath the realm of language and meaning, yet this results in an account that tends to presume material exposure as an unmediated space of encounter. Such an account, however, would miss the work that the construction workers I interviewed engaged in not only when they encountered materials but also when they spoke about and reflected on such encounters.

Rajesh, a stone mason helper who had just started working with Satish, would often complain to me of the stone dust getting caught in his lungs but also of the weight of the marble tiles that he had to carry. On one occasion, he showed me his hands rubbed raw by a long day of carrying heavy, wet tiles. Looking at his hands, he complained that they were still "soft" but that as he kept working, his hands would become "tight." Similarly, welders told me that the intense light of the torch made their eyes "strong." But these comments do not simply reflect a reality of agentive materials shaping human bodies. Rather, construction workers actively picked out sensory experiences—breathing dust, staring at intense light, rubbing fingers against metal—and assigned them value. Crucially, they also erased other alternatives. The silicosis, skin disease, and blindness that appear in medical reports disappear under the image of lungs that can handle stone dust, tight hands, and strong eyes. The point here is not that one account is more, or less, objective than the other. Rather, what is at stake is the way that materials act in conjunction with workers' articulations of their work. This is not to say that they are not in tension, just that the effects of exposure are always mediated. The exposures of work include the practices of narrating such exposures.

Here we might note that trade worker claims to *adat* draw on longstanding models of South Asian personhood grounded on what Cecilia Busby has called the "fluid and permeable body boundary" of the self (1997, 269). As Sarah Lamb puts it, this permeable boundary means that "parts of other people, places, and things become part of one's own body and person" (Lamb 2000, 39; see also Marriott 1991). To make a particular trade one's *adat* was to become a particular type of person, namely one whose bodily capacities were fit to that trade. The transformational entanglements of *adat* include discursive practices rather than being opposed to them. Part of making *adat* was complaining about the effects of new work on one's body and narrating crucial elements of work. In complaining about not having *adat* and in enumerating its qualities, workers shaped the heterogeneous materials experienced during work. The discourse of *adat* among trade workers should be understood as an important way in which workers sought to control and make sense of the experience and value of work (Sargent 2020).

Language was not the only way that workers intervened in the transformative forces of materials. Workers also refused to do forms of work that were outside of their *adat* and claimed that doing so was dangerous and could result in injury. Such refusals could draw the ire of construction site managers or engineers who occasionally tried to order workers to do tasks that fell outside their *adat*. By refusing to do tasks considered outside of one's *adat*, workers attempted to shape the materials that their work exposed them to. In this sense, worker practices of refusing certain tasks are akin to the practices that other workers engage in by eating particular foods at certain times to balance out the environmental exposures of their work (Kantor 2019; Walters 2016; Solomon 2016). Materials play an active role here, transforming bodies in particular ways, but not in an unmediated way. Rather, it is in the interplay between an unruly material environment and the construals and interventions of workers that the effects of exposure take place. Discourses of *adat* and refusals of certain tasks are different modalities in which workers attempted to guide the transformative forces of exposure.

At stake in these attempts to shape exposure's effects are issues of health and bodies, but also types of people. As a trade became one's *adat*, workers became not only skilled workers but also bar benders, stone masons, or welders. Repeated exposure to the materials of their trade produced certain bodily capacities—to handle stone dust, to be able to stare into intense light—that made one the type of person who was fit to a particular kind of work. To do work that was outside one's *adat* was not only to risk bodily injury but also, by virtue of exposing oneself to other materials, to risk becoming a different type of person. It is in this sense that exposures on the construction site were generative, but this is not to say that they were not also destructive. That stone masons may have been able to handle stone dust does not mean they would not also develop silicosis; that welders' eyes become strong does not preclude their going blind. Rather, the politics of exposure operates through the entwining of diminishment and generativity. Workers' comments that there is "nothing special" in their work and that they have built up particular capacities do not reflect conflicting perspectives as much as they capture the complex politics of exposure. In the Indian construction industry, this is a politics that simultaneously subjects particular groups of workers to encounter with harmful materials and recuperates workers' own construals of and interventions into these encounters. The person types that are generated by exposure are uniquely fit to capitalist development as it unfolds in India.

Conclusion: Corona Exposures

We began by noting how the Coronavirus pandemic has made questions of exposure urgent, yet exposure to COVID-19 is not often spoken of in the same terms as exposures to environmental pollutants. COVID-19 is spoken of in terms of infection and contagion even as the pandemic causes us to more carefully monitor the environments we pass through. This distinction is important, and it is not my aim to conflate environmental and viral exposures. COVID-19 interacts with and moves through bodies in ways that stone dust, light, and exhaustion do not. The virus reproduces itself within bodies and moves to new hosts through shared air or surfaces. We need not engage in a particular form of work to be subjected to the pathogen's debilitating effects. Nevertheless, it has become increasingly clear that the violence of COVID-19 is not evenly distributed but rather routed along familiar lines of inequality shaped around class, gender, and race. In India and elsewhere, the uneven effects of the pandemic are often interpreted as COVID-19 spotlighting, or "accentuating" social inequality (Kapoor and Yadav 2020). This is an important insight, but by way of conclusion I would like to suggest that we might be able to push this insight further by analysing the pandemic through the politics of exposure developed here. While the pandemic has made questions of exposure more urgent, it is also the case that the politics of exposure may illuminate the pandemic.

We might start by noting that it is often the very same populations that are subjected to environmental pollutants who have been hit the hardest by the pandemic, from poor Black and Latinx communities in the post-industrial US (Lerner 2020) to urban slum-dwellers in Mumbai and Delhi (Biswas 2020). It is not only the case, then, that structural inequalities make it harder to seek treatment, but also that groups subjected to polluted environments are also increasingly exposed to COVID-19 as well. Exposure points back to the systemic processes that bring certain bodies and not others into contact with toxic materials. These processes can do this for multiple materials at once. Thus, the blended structure of formality and informality that delivers cheap workers to Indian construction sites without protective equipment or access to clean living conditions also routes the path of COVID-19. These workers are essential to the construction industry and by extension the Indian economy, yet they are essential as cheap, unprotected workers. As a form of exposure then COVID-19 is yet another detrimental material exposure that has been shaped by the requirements of capitalist development.

Just as the encounters described in this chapter entangled destructive and generative elements, framing COVID-19 through the politics of exposure may help us take a more nuanced view of the destruction the pandemic continues to cause. My point here is not that infected patients are made into different sorts of people. Rather, I would suggest that as with construction workers in India, we should look for the ways that active engagement with and orientation to harmful materials becomes part of the politics of exposure. The effects of exposure are complex and mediated not only by physical facts of contact but also by the ways in which people come to know about and represent such exposures. Worker discourses of *adat* erased the diminishing effects of construction materials under the image of the hardened hands and strong eyes of a skilled worker, even as their labours on the construction site transformed them into people uniquely fit to encounters with dangerous construction materials and, increasingly, COVID-19. At stake in combatting the violence of coronavirus exposures is not only the uneven distribution of contact with deleterious materials but also the ways that the very modes of orienting to and intervening in these exposures may reproduce and naturalize its damages.

References

Agard-Jones, Vanessa. 2013. "Bodies in the System." *Small Axe: A Caribbean Journal of Criticism* 17 (3): 182–92.

Agarwala, Rina. 2006. "From Work to Welfare." *Critical Asian Studies* 38 (4): 419–44.

Bennett, Jane. 2010. *Vibrant Matter: A Political Ecology of Things*. Duke University Press.

Biswas, Soutik. 2020. "India Coronavirus: 'More Than Half of Mumbai Slum-Dwellers Had Covid- 19.'" *BBC News*, July 29, 2020. https://www.bbc.com/news/world-asia-india-53576653.

Blanchette, Alex. 2019. "Living Waste and the Labor of Toxic Health on American Factory Farms." *Medical Anthropology Quarterly* 33 (1): 80–100.

Bucci, Nino. 2020. "Meatworks and Coronavirus: The 'Domino Effect' from Victoria's Abattoirs Pushing COVID-19 Case Numbers Higher." *ABC News*, July 26, 2020. https://www.abc.net.au/news/2020-07-26/coronavirus-covid-19-meatworks-abattoirs-victoria/12490178.

Busby, Cecilia. 1997. "Permeable and Partible Persons: A Comparative Analysis of Gender and Body in South India and Melanesia." *The Journal of the Royal Anthropological Institute* 3 (2): 261–78.

Chatterjee, Patralekha. 2020. "The Pandemic Exposes India's Apathy Toward Migrant Workers." *The Atlantic*, April 12, 2020. https://www.theatlantic.com/ideas/archive/2020/04/the-pandemic-exposes-indias-two-worlds/609838/.

Chowdhury, Nusrat S. 2020. "Crowd, Contagion, Corona." Covid-19, Fieldsights. May 8. https://culanth.org/fieldsights/crowd-contagion-corona.

Cielemęcka, Olga, and Cecilia Åsberg. 2019. "Introduction: Toxic Embodiment and Feminist Environmental Humanities." *Environmental Humanities* 11 (1): 101–7.

Coole, Diana H., and Samantha Frost. 2010. *New Materialisms: Ontology, Agency, and Politics*. Durham: Duke University Press.

Fortun, Kim. 2001. *Advocacy After Bhopal: Environmentalism, Disaster, and New Global Orders*. Chicago: The University of Chicago Press.

Graeter, Stefanie. 2017. "To Revive an Abundant Life: Catholic Science and Neoextractivist Politics in Peru's Mantaro Valley." *Cultural Anthropology* 32 (1): 117–48.

Han, Phil. 2012. "Hard Evidence of Child Labor at 2010 Commonwealth Games." CNN. 2012. http://www.cnn.com/2010/WORLD/asiapcf/09/23/commonwealth.games.child.labor/.

Kantor, Hayden S. 2019. "A Body Set between Hot and Cold: Everyday Sensory Labor and Attunement in an Indian Village." *Food, Culture and Society* 22 (2): 237–52.

Kapoor, Amit, and Chirag Yadav. 2020. "View: How Coronavirus Accentuates Inequality." *The Economic Times*, June 11, 2020. https://economictimes.indiatimes.com/news/economy/indicators/view-how-coronavirus-accentuates-inequality/articleshow/76309452.cms.

Lamb, Sarah. 2000. *White Saris and Sweet Mangoes: Aging, Gender, and Body in North India*. Berkeley: University of California Press.

Lerche, Jens, Alessandra Mezzadri, Dae-oup Chang, Pun Ngai, Lu Huilin, Liu Aiyu, and Ravi Srivastava. 2017. "The Triple Absence of Labour Rights: Triangular Labour Relatioins and Informalisation in the Construction and Garment Sectors in Delhi and Shanghai." Working paper 32/17, Centre for Development Policy and Research, SOAS, University of London.

Lerner, Sharon. 2020. "What Racism Smells Like: Ravaged by COVID-19, Polluted Communities Demand Justice." *The Intercept*, August 8, 2020. https://theintercept.com/2020/08/08/coronavirus-pollution-environmental-justice-racism/.

Marriott, McKim. 1991. "On 'Constructing an Indian Ethnosociology'." *Contributions to Indian Sociology* 25 (2): 295–308.

Murphy, Michelle. 2006. *Sick Building Syndrome and the Problem of Uncertainty*. Durham: Duke University Press.

———. 2013. "Chemical Infrastructures of the St. Clair River." In *Toxicants, Health and Regulation Since 1945*, edited by Soraya Boudia and Nathalie Jas, 103–15. London: Pickering and Chatto.

Naik, Mukta. 2021. "As the Pandemic's Second Wave Rages, Migrants Trudge Home Again." *The Indian Express*, May 1, 2021. https://indianexpress.com/article/opinion/columns/as-the-pandemics-second-wave-rages-migrants-trudge-home-again-7297303/.

Pang, Irene. 2019. "The Legal Construction of Precarity: Lessons from the Construction Sectors in Beijing and Delhi." *Critical Sociology* 45 (4–5): 549–64.

Parida, Ratri, and Pradip Kumar Ray. 2012. "Study and Analysis of Occupational Risk Factors for Ergonomic Design of Construction Worksystems." *Work* 41: 3788–94.

Prasad-Aleyamma, Mythri. 2017. "The Cultural Politics of Wages: Ethnography of Construction Work in Kochi, India." *Contributions to Indian Sociology* 51 (2): 163–93.

PUDR Team. 2009. "Violation of Workers' Rights at the Commonwealth Games Construction Site." *Economic & Political Weekly* 44 (24): 10–12.

Ray, Debraj, and S. Subramanian. 2020. "India's Lockdown: An Interim Report." *Indian Economic Review* 55 (1): 31–79.

Sargent, Adam. 2019. "Moral Economies of Remuneration: Wages, Piece-Rates, and Contracts on a Delhi Construction Site." *Anthropological Quarterly* 92 (3): 757–85.

———. 2020. "Working Against Labor: Struggles for Self in the Indian Construction Industry." *Anthropology of Work Review* 41 (2): 76–85.

Sarmin, Utsa. 2020. "Hunger, Humiliation, and Death: Perils of Migrant Workers in the Time of COVID-19." In *Borders of an Epidemic: COVID-19 and Migrant Workers*, edited by Ranabir Smaddar. Kolkata: Mahanirban Calcutta Research Group.

Sharma, N., F. Malik, S. Sachin, and S. Aparasu. 2020. "Reverse Migration, Dip in Output Spell Tough Times for Industries." *Hindustan Times*, January 19, 2020. https://www.hindustantimes.com/india-news/reverse-migration-dip-in-output-spell-toughtimes-for-industries/story-oQghUEqzs8bNt2XXwXFdOM.html.

Solomon, Harris. 2016. *Metabolic Living: Food, Fat, and the Absorption of Illness in India*. Durham: Duke University Press.
Srivastava, R. D., A. K. Singh, Arundhati Ghose, and Lakshmidhar Mishra. 2010. "Report of the Committee Constituted by the Hon'ble High Court of Delhi in WP (Civil) No. 524/2010 in Peoples Union for Democratic Rights and Others Vs. Union of India on Working and Living Conditions of Workers in Commonwealth Games Construction Sites." New Delhi: Delhi High Court.
Tiwary, Guddi, and P. K. Gangopadhyay. 2011. "A Review on the Occupational Health and Social Security of Unorganized Workers in the Construction Industry." *Indian Journal of Occupational and Environmental Medicine* 15 (1): 18–24.
Walters, Kimberly. 2016. "The Stickiness of Sex Work: Pleasure, Habit, and Intersubstantiality in South India." *Signs* 42 (1): 99–121.

CHAPTER 6

Women Workers at the Forefront of COVID-19: A Roadmap for Recovery and Resilience in India

Jashodhara Dasgupta and Kanika Jha Kingra

Abbreviations

SEWA:	Self Employed Women's Association
SC:	Scheduled Caste
OBC:	Other Backward Castes
PMJDY:	Pradhan Mantri Jan Dhan Yojna

The authors are part of the Feminist Policy Collective (FPC), which is a voluntary group of gender equality advocates and feminist economists in India, committed to transforming policy and the financing agenda towards achieving women's rights and gender justice. This paper also benefited from substantial technical inputs given by Subhalakshmi Nandi.

J. Dasgupta (✉)
Uttarakhand, India

S. Hewamanne and S. Yadav (eds.), *The Political Economy of Post-COVID Life and Work in the Global South: Pandemic and Precarity*, International Political Economy Series,
https://doi.org/10.1007/978-3-030-93228-2_6

NHM: National Health Mission
UNFPA: United Nations Population Fund

Introduction

Context

As the world continues to grapple with the COVID-19 pandemic and its impacts, it is becoming abundantly clear that future preparations for health resilience need serious rethinking. The model that many countries have followed thus far relied upon lowered investments in social protection and public health services (Kim et al. 2019), banking heavily on unpaid and underpaid care work by women to fill in the gaps. The pandemic has exposed the flaws of this model in India, triggering enormous stress on an under-resourced public health system, overstretched essential workers and women struggling with enhanced burdens of household care work.

In March 2021 India witnessed a second wave of the pandemic triggered by a rapidly spreading variant of the virus that wreaked havoc across the country, including rural areas which were not adversely impacted in the previous year. This wave further paralysed an already weak public health system leading India to seek international aid and medical oxygen supplies and medicines from other countries. While India is still recovering from the aftermath of this wave, efforts are underway to develop a plan for recovery and for making communities more resilient. It is becoming increasingly imperative to explore longer-term solutions that are responsive to the myriad needs of women and girls who have been disproportionately impacted by this crisis.

Since March 2020, India has confronted the inadequacy of its short-sighted economic outlook that disregarded public investments in the care sectors and relied on the private sector; reminding us of the urgent need to strengthen public services. With peripheral public health facilities barely functioning, the community-based frontline workers were hurriedly marshalled for the crucial tasks of door-to-door surveillance, quarantine

---

K. J. Kingra
Gurugram, India

tracking and public health awareness. When India announced its vaccination drive in January 2021, several community-based frontline health and nutrition workers were additionally tasked with getting households vaccinated. They face stigma and violence, prompted by misinformation and myths associated with the vaccinations.

This paper describes the context of community-based frontline health and child development workers in India, examining how the COVID-19 pandemic is impacting their lives and work. Notionally, the state is the employer that has appointed these women workers; but by labelling them 'volunteers' and retaining them in informal working arrangements, the state has erased its own obligations around fair wages and social security.

Conceptual Framing

The term frontline worker is generally used in the health sector to indicate the medically trained staff who come in direct contact with those seeking healthcare within clinical settings, and is often used to refer to midwives, nurses and doctors. In this paper we use the term Community-Based Front-Line Worker (CB-FLW) to refer to those women employed within government schemes and given the direct responsibility of implementing programmes and providing services within community settings, notably the Accredited Social Health Activist (ASHA) workers and their Facilitators who work to implement the National Health Mission (NHM) and the Anganwadi Workers (AWW) and Helpers who work for the Integrated Child Development Scheme (ICDS). We have chosen to avoid the term 'community health worker/community child development worker' owing to the inherent ambiguity of the term that sees them as community agents fulfilling the agenda of the state machinery and yet deprived of formal benefits of state employment (Schaaf et al. 2020: 8; Ved et al. 2019: 7).

We attempt a feminist analysis of the situation, basing our analysis on the frameworks proposed by Dewan (2019), King et al. (2020) and Wichterich (2020) to interrogate how women's economic activity effortlessly segues into community voluntarism as an extension of her unpaid care work within the household. Commenting upon the decreasing participation of women in the paid workforce, Dewan underlines that the precarious nature of women's economic activity is a consequence of complicity of the state, market, community and household that reinforces entrenched gender norms (Dewan 2019). Drawing the connection to health systems, King et al. (2020) have analyzed how the economic arrangements, policy frameworks and market forces that determine the distribution of paid and unpaid labour across society are powerful structural determinants of health. Wichterich (2020) emphasizes that the care economy in the overall political and economic context of deepening privatization, corporatization and neo-liberalization leads to a reliance on the lowest end of the health hierarchy. She uses the notion of 'extractivism' to mark the intensified commodification and exploitation of the resource labour in social reproduction for the purpose of managing crises situations without burdening the state or the health industry with additional costs and responsibilities (Wichterich 2020).

This inequitable division of paid and unpaid labour aligns with pervasive and entrenched gender norms that define women as caregivers—nurturing, self-sacrificing and caring (King et al. 2020) while simultaneously reducing their capacity to be in formal full-time economic activity. Gender norms also define who and what is valued, with the consistent undervaluing of many female-dominated occupations. The underfunded and neglected domain of care work has been exposed by the COVID-19 pandemic, highlighting the importance of recognizing the value of paid and unpaid care provision. Redressing the underpayment and poor employment conditions of many female-dominated occupations, particularly those that provide paid care including health care is vital for protecting their rights and ensuring dignified work for female workers in these sectors (King et al. 2020). We propose pathways for a post-COVID economic recovery plan that could address the multiple axes of disadvantage faced by these women as well as put in place robust decentralized mechanisms for primary health care and social protection in anticipation of future shocks.

Background

Under-Resourced and Gendered Public Systems

Despite an overarching commitment to universal health coverage under the Sustainable Development Goals (SDGs), less than half of the world's population has access to essential health services as per latest global estimates. India continues to invest much lower than expected in the health sector: as per 2021–2022 budget estimates, the Government of

India's health budget is a meagre 0.35 per cent of the Gross Domestic Product (GDP), and only 2.21 per cent of the entire Union Budget, which has marginally reduced from the previous year (CBGA 2021). The Indian government's strategy as per the National Health Policy (2017) is to move away from 'provisioning' to 'purchasing'; which raises many concerns about the lack of equity in health services.

Unsurprisingly, the public health system in India faces an absolute crisis of availability and distribution of health workers; which has been exacerbated through systematic disinvestment in strengthening the health system and its workforce. Although there are over 3.1 million people employed in the health workforce within India, more than half of these, over 56 per cent, are not qualified (Karan et al. 2021). The ratio of nurses to doctors should ideally be 4:1, however a recent estimate puts the ratio at 1.7:1, or less than two nurses per doctor, which is a significant imbalance in the human resource mix (Karan et al. 2021: 9). In actual numbers, the availability of qualified allopathic doctors, nurses and midwives per 10,000 population are around one quarter of the World Health Organization (WHO) benchmark. More than 46.4 per cent of health workers are women, but among doctors, women constitute only 29 per cent (Karan et al. 2021). Women health workers in the public sector include auxiliary-nurse midwives, over 200,000 of whom work in the health sub-centres and 'Health and Wellness Centres' as well as over 80,000 nurses who work in primary health centres (MoHFW 2019).

More than 65 per cent doctors and more than half the nurses and midwives in the country work in the private sector (Karan et al. 2021). Out of all qualified health workers, nearly two-thirds were located in urban areas, even though the urban population is only one-third of the total population of the country. The burden of publicly provided care in the rural areas thereby lies on the shoulders of a band of community women, the Community-Based Front-Line Workers (CB-FLWs), who provide the last-mile delivery of health and nutrition services while remaining the most vulnerable and unprotected workers (Addati et al. 2018). The crucial roles of health and nutrition care work in the community are managed by these 'part-time volunteers': Accredited Social Health Activists (ASHAs) working as community health workers, and the older cadre of Anganwadi Workers (AWW) and Anganwadi Helpers (AWH or *Sahayikas*), cadres of community workers for child development services who run community centres for supplementary nutrition and part-daycare for children. They number almost 1 million ASHAs and 2.8 million AWWs and AWHs.

This shifting of the burden on to precarious informal labourers undermines hopes for recognition of women's care work and women's economic empowerment. Formal labour force participation for women has been declining consistently over the last few decades, while sectors in which women's participation is seen to increase is in the services sector—mainly in health and education. At least 1 million of this recent growth in jobs has been due to the increase in the ASHAs. However, this growth in service sector jobs is characterized by informality and precarity: more than 94 per cent of the women in India continue to be in informal and unprotected jobs, earning much less than even minimum wage. While the data on women's labour force participation is unable to accurately capture women's contribution to economic activity in India, the nation-wide lockdown in 2020 has hit women much harder than men, as recent estimates point to the fact that permanent job losses for women due to COVID-19 related lockdown and distress could be as high as 47 per cent of employed women while the corresponding estimate for men was only 7 per cent (APU 2021).

In the global South, especially in countries like India, with very little job creation in the economy, high levels of unemployment and the operation of unequal gender norms: it is often the most marginalized women who are forced to take up these scheme-based jobs. Traditionally, nursing labour, similar to paid domestic work, was offered by women located on the margins of Hindu Brahmanical society, partly because nursing was caste-based corporeal labour that included dealing with blood and bodily fluids (Panchali Ray quoted in Roy 2020). Often coming from very poor households and disregarded communities like *Dalits* and *Adivasis*, these women have been instrumental in not just improving crucial maternal and child health indicators but collecting important data that underpins the healthcare system (Rao and Tewari 2020).

Recruited from communities themselves, mostly from deprived households, meant a kind of positive discrimination of low caste and lower-class women (Wichterich 2020). Nonetheless, the assumption that poor women can set aside time for 'volunteer' work is deeply problematic, as are the structural barriers that often prevent their progression in the health workforce (Ved et al. 2019: 8). Duggal's analysis of Census data brings the caste character of the hierarchy within the health profession (Duggal 2014). From the early days of colonial concepts of nursing in

India, in addition to gender, the intersection with caste, class, ethnicity and religion were decisive for status issues (Wichterich 2020). The fact that many ASHA workers come from poor families, have low educational qualifications and are the lowest paid makes it easy to consign them to the bottom of the health hierarchy.

As one ASHA worker from Andhra Pradesh observed: '*We are like worms in the eyes of our higher officials because we come from poor families and have studied only until the 10th grade. Sometimes, ASHAs struggle to maintain records. They shout at us and call us incompetent. Just because we struggle with writing sometimes, does it make our work any less important?*' (Rao and Tewari 2020).

Community-Based Frontline Workers: Concerns and Struggles

In the 2020 Global Hunger Index, India ranks 94 (Global Hunger Index 2020) out of 107 qualifying countries. Data from the fifth round of the National Family Health Survey (MoHFW 2020b) shows that while health services have improved, undernutrition among children is on the rise. In India, the Ministry of Women and Child Development has the responsibility of managing the extreme malnutrition among women, girls, children and infants. Yet the crucial task of tracking malnutrition and ensuring the supplementary nutrition reaches the most deprived has been relegated since 1975 to a group of 'part-time volunteer' women workers in the local community who are called Anganwadi Workers (AWW). The AWW and AWH work together in every hamlet to anchor nutrition monitoring programmes, delivery of supplementary nutrition, health counselling and immunization services, as well as manage early childhood education in their Anganwadi Centres.

The ASHA cadre was developed in 2005 with the start of the National Health Mission (earlier National Rural Health Mission) as a part-time woman worker from the local community with some schooling, who agreed to take responsibility for a certain number of households where she would work as a health volunteer and act as a bridge with the health system. Similar to many CHW programmes, it started with instrumentalist concerns: deploying poor women in rural areas on a volunteer basis to address family planning, maternal and child health issues (Ved et al. 2019). The unique situation of India is that these women are provided incentives for supporting institutional deliveries and providing other health services, but are not considered 'paid workers' despite working several hours each day to deliver on government programmes and meet relevant targets. Since 2005, the number of tasks to be covered by ASHAs has increased from 6 to 43 (Srivastav et al. 2020) in 2019 which is the pre-COVID era, and the incentive-based remuneration from USD 13 to USD 26 per month (*Indian Express* 2018). However, this is nowhere close to providing economic security or remunerating them for their skilled service, time and effort.

The Seventh Pay Commission proposed even unskilled labour should earn minimum wages of USD 240 (INR 17,800) per month; however, the CB-FLWs are paid way below even minimum wage levels. There are certain variations across states: ASHA workers could get an honorarium ranging between 27 and 133 USD (INR 2000–10,000) per month, but even with this meagre salary, they have to pay for travel and stationery themselves. Anganwadi workers earn between 30 and 60 USD (INR 2250–4500) and Anganwadi helpers between 20 and 30 USD (INR 1500–2250) per month (Press Information Bureau 2020a). Scheme-based work, in reality, is honorary unpaid work, not considered as employment in the public sector but a gendered community service, *sewa*. In fact, the government had even decided to replace male Village Health Guides by women community workers, thereby reinforcing a strict gender division of labour (Wichterich 2020).

There are some existing social security benefits for ASHAs, ASHA Facilitators, AWWs and AWHs in insurance schemes, although these do not exactly provide them with cash in hand. The workers in the age group of 18–50 years receive life insurance cover under the *Pradhan Mantri Jeevan Jyoti Bima Yojana* (PMJJBY) while those in the age group of 18–59 years would be covered under the *Pradhan Mantri Suraksha Bima Yojana* (PMSBY) for covering accidents. In 2017 the government announced coverage of Anganwadi workers and helpers and in 2018 this was extended to the ASHAs and their Facilitators (Press Information Bureau 2018). The AWWs and AWHs in the age group of 51–59 years would continue to be covered under the erstwhile *Anganwadi Karyakarti Bima Yojana* (AKBY) for life insurance coverage as long as they are engaged in this role (Ministry for Women and Child Development 2018).

Evidence shows that the women scheme workers, like others in the paid health workforce, continue to experience gendered barriers, such as a gender wage gap, lack of growth opportunities and the experience of violence and harassment at work (Ved et al. 2019). Despite frequent complaints by ASHAs about sexual abuse during home visits and at night while accompanying expecting women to hospitals, the state refused to protect women scheme workers by including them in the 2010 Bill on Protection of Women against Sexual Harassment (Wichterich 2020).

Recent studies have noted CB-FLW's dissatisfaction with their pay in relation to their workload and contribution, identifying negative consequences linked to the limited remuneration structure. Limitations on their movement outside the home and heavy domestic responsibilities often curtail ASHAs' ability to perform their professional role, in fact ASHAs were belittled by family members when their remuneration was delayed or when incentives were found to be extremely low (Ved et al. 2019: 6). The lack of decent working conditions, including wages, social security, freedom from violence and harassment in the world of work, has been a long-standing agenda for struggle and campaigning by women's organizations and trade unions in India.

The Anganwadi Workers and Helpers have been protesting over the years and presently appear to be the best organized group in the informal sector. Their political mobilization and demands for higher pay have gone against the narrative of selfless women invested in the wellbeing of children and their communities at the expense of themselves (Ved et al. 2019: 8). In fact, government actors express concern that ASHAs would 'underperform if guaranteed a salary, as was an ongoing challenge with Anganwadi workers' (Ved et al. 2019: 5). The Anganwadi workers have criticized voluntarism and demanded regularization and recognition as public servants and as 'real' workers (Wichterich 2020). The Anganwadi workers even marched to Parliament to demand that the government keep its promises in February 2019 (Mallick 2019), but these demands have still not been met.

ASHAs have staged a number of protests and strikes at both the state and national levels seeking increased wages and permanent government employee status (Schaaf et al. 2020: 8) They were assured of a raise by the federal government in 2018 which has not yet materialized (Majumder 2020). In the state of Haryana, ASHAs needed to protest seven months before they received a fixed salary of USD 53 per month (Rs 4000); in Andhra Pradesh, ASHAs struggled for ten years before the Chief Minister set a monthly salary of USD 133 (INR 10,000) (Rao and Tewari 2020). Recently, tens of thousands of ASHA workers have been on strike in Bihar (NewsClick 2018), and in Karnataka (*Deccan Herald* 2020).

Impact of COVID-19 on Frontline Workers

Global Evidence

COVID is the first global pandemic in recent times, but in the past two decades several viral epidemics have shown some impacts of such outbreaks on the health workers; these include severe acute respiratory syndrome (SARS) in 2003, influenza caused by the virus subtype H1N1 in 2009, Middle East respiratory syndrome (MERS) in 2012, and Ebola virus disease in West Africa between 2014 and 2016. It is estimated that in all 500 health workers lost their lives in the Ebola epidemic (NBC News 2015) with hundreds more being infected; in fact, health workers were 21–32 times more likely to be infected with Ebola than the others in Sierra Leone (Raven et al. 2018). In addition to infection, frontline health workers had to contend with denial, mistrust and even violence from affected communities (Intra Health International 2014). In addition, the psychological impact of increased workload, need for personal protection and fears of infection for themselves and their families have also been recorded. The stigma, isolation and social ostracization of frontline health works is becoming more obvious as the COVD-19 pandemic peaks.

Experience shows that women are not just disproportionately affected by the crisis, but that they take longer to recover from its health and socioeconomic fallouts. Gender analyses from different parts of the world point to the importance of addressing issues of domestic violence, sexual and reproductive health and jobs (Nature 2020). Past pandemics tell us that it is not just the risk to infection, but also the experience of violence and stigma that makes the frontline health workers among the most vulnerable in a crisis (UN Women 2020). This is more so for community health systems in the global South that are predominantly run on the shoulders of frontline workers. Hence, what has been called the 'shadow pandemic' by the United Nations Secretary-General (United Nations 2020) is not just one relating to violence in the domestic sphere, but possibly a challenge for women in the world of work and in their public service as health workers.

Global data on COVID-19 shows that while women are infected slightly less than men (49 per cent women as compared to 51 per cent men), when it comes to the incidence of COVID-19 in health workers, women are more affected. In the early months of the pandemic 75 per cent of health workers in Spain affected by COVID-19 were women, and this figure was 73 per cent in the United States (UN Women 2020). This is not very surprising since the global health workforce is about 70 per cent female, with a 28 per cent gender wage gap (Gender in Humanitarian Action 2020). While there is no consolidated sex-disaggregated data available for India on COVID-19 prevalence among CB-FLWs, we can assume the trends might be similar. For instance, from media coverage we know that as of July 2020, over 15,000 frontline healthcare workers have tested positive for COVID-19 (Sharma 2020).

Unfair Conditions of Work for CB-FLWs

As the pandemic started peaking in India around March 2020, health systems across the country were struggling with the rising COVID-19 positive cases. While the poor health infrastructure was laid bare in India's biggest cities, health and welfare system inefficiencies were worse in smaller cities and rural areas. Access to even basic health services that were not linked to COVID-19 treatment were severely disrupted (Rukmini 2020). It is estimated that an additional one million unsafe abortions, an additional 650,000 unintended pregnancies and 2600 maternal deaths in India have occurred on account of gaps in access to basic healthcare and maternal services for women (Marie Stopes International 2021).

During the COVID pandemic, the Centre's plan has relied heavily on the fieldwork of CB-FLWs such as ASHA, ANM and Anganwadi workers. In addition to care-giving work, it assigned the task of primary data collection to them, which formed the basis of field research on the COVID pandemic in India. ASHA workers have been deployed to conduct house-to-house visits to curb the pandemic. They are to report symptomatic cases, then carry out contact tracing, maintain documentation, monitor the situation and create awareness about the pandemic in the community. They are responsible for coordinating various aspects of surveillance, tracing and monitoring of incoming migrants, recording travel histories and referring them for testing and local quarantine facilities or public health centres. Additionally, since January 2021 CB-FLWs are responsible for going door-to-door to mobilize individuals to get vaccinated, spread awareness and dispel misinformation about vaccines, register eligible individuals, administer the vaccines (in this case ASHAs) where needed and escort the elderly and the disabled to vaccination centres. This is in addition to the list of existing tasks that they are already responsible for within the National Health Mission.

Earlier the ASHA workers were allotted a population of 1000 each in rural areas and 1000–2500 in urban areas. Since the pandemic, this allocation has been expanded and now they have to cover other neighbouring areas including the 'hotspots' and 'containment zones', further aggravating the risks faced by them. However, there has been only a limited increase in any kind of protection to the workers (Amnesty International India 2020). They continue to perform their duties often at great personal risk, working longer hours, facing community anger and violence. Sometimes the violence they face is linked to their lower social status as members of marginalized communities such as Dalits, as the General Secretary of the Haryana ASHA Workers' Union pointed out: '*Attacks on ASHAs from Dalit communities in Haryana especially from the landed community strongmen (is) a means to assert their caste supremacy once again*' (Rao and Tewari 2020).

As the pandemic progressed, several CB-FLW received online training on COVID protocols; however, in the early months of the pandemic several ASHA workers stated that they were deputed to field duties without adequate training or protective gear (Rao and Chowdhury 2021). The insurance scheme covering frontline health workers that was first announced in March 2020 still does not cover the cost of medical expenses in case of illness, leaving low-paid workers like ASHAs or their families vulnerable in the case of a long COVID-19 illness (Srivastav et al. 2020). Insights from the field and qualitative reports show that there were significant delays in the payouts of insurance for health workers (Rao and Chowdhury 2021).[1]

The state has downplayed their risk level, compelling them to work with almost no protective equipment and no public recognition or appreciation. The callous and differential treatment of health workers who are coming in direct contact with potentially infected persons makes the ASHA workers bitter, as one ASHA worker of the Union in Maharashtra rhetorically asked: '*Do we not risk our lives too? Are our lives not important?*' (Amnesty International India 2020). A mark of their neglect is the very limited research and in-depth understanding of the conditions

[1] On 29 March 2020, the finance minister announced an insurance cover of approximately USD 67,500 (INR 5 million) to workers performing COVID-19-related work. The insurance scheme covers the loss of life due to COVID-19, and accidental death on account of COVID-19-related duty for the next 90 days (Srivastav et al. 2020). This scheme has been extended for another year as it was slated to end by April 2021.

of work and challenges faced by community-based frontline workers, although there has been some amount of media coverage during their protests.

This situation has not been without resistance. For instance, ASHA workers in Bihar refused to work without any PPE (personal protective equipment) (Kalra 2020). After several media reports and agitations by ASHA unions highlighted the gross inadequacies in protective equipment, the Ministry of Health and Family Welfare issued some guidelines, yet continued to classify ASHA workers as 'low risk', recommending only triple layer masks and gloves for their protection.

Even with these guidelines, CB-FLWs in several areas have still not received any protective gear from the government and are making do with their own resources.

Some instances of CB-FLWs facing violence and harassment, experiencing stigma and discrimination in the community and non-payment of incentives have been reported through micro-studies and anecdotal evidence. In Haryana, the ASHA Workers Union had to stop working to protest when one of them tested positive for the virus but was neglected at the hospital. Door to door surveys and vaccination drives have created a negative association of ASHA Workers with the virus and myths have been perpetuated about vaccinations; this has led their neighbours and family members to stigmatize them as vectors, even threatening eviction and violence (Amnesty International India 2020). Yet the women soldier on doggedly, with limited access to social security and health insurance, inadequate access to higher-level healthcare facilities and staff in addition to growing hostility from the public due to misinformation.

Ironically, while the Ministry of Health and Family Welfare considers their job low risk and not deserving of protection, the ASHA workers face stigma and discrimination from their communities; as an ASHA worker in Assam shared, '*We are called 'Corona-walas' (Corona carriers) and kept at a distance by our neighbours because we are in touch with community members without proper protective gear*' (Rao and Tewari 2020). There are even reports of them being chased out by communities during routine surveys (Majumder 2020); ASHAs in Haryana and across Karnataka reported being violently attacked by community members while on COVID-19 duty. ASHA workers continue to be discriminated against and face violence as they are now responsible for spearheading the world's largest vaccination drive against COVID-19 (*Indian Express*

2021). Yet the incentives being offered to get beneficiaries vaccinated are not being paid in some states, or in some cases CB-FLWs are being paid only a meagre amount of INR 2 (USD 0.03).

In a survey conducted by BehanBox in 16 states from Kerala to Tripura, ASHA workers—who now routinely clock over twelve-hour days and are 'on call' the rest of the time—reported feeling alienated and undervalued for the disproportionate burden they now bear. As the pandemic rages, there are fears of an impending mental health crisis due to the constant anxiety and physical exhaustion suffered by ASHAs (Rao and Tewari 2020). The plight of Anganwadi workers, who were already shouldering several responsibilities, is no different. They have been going door-to-door to distribute dry rations and raise awareness in communities, with limited or no protective equipment. This further exposes them to the risk of the disease as they are also responsible for tracking and tracing suspect cases (Ministry of Health and Family Welfare 2020).

Unpaid and Underpaid Public Service

During the COVID-19 pandemic and after the subsequent lockdown measures, several ASHA workers continue to remain not only underpaid but have been delayed in their regular incentives, along with incentives that were promised as part of the COVID-19 relief packages. This is despite the Government of India announcement in April 2020 of a token incentive of USD 13.30 (INR 1000) per month for the additional tasks, to be paid to ASHAs from January to June 2020. This incentive was part of India's COVID-19 Emergency Response and Health Systems Preparedness Package. But in 2021 during the second wave, the additional incentive was made 'optional' and only extended for an additional six months (Chhabra 2021).

The central government also directed state governments to ensure that ASHAs receive their regular monthly honorarium of USD 7 (INR 2000) along with the task-based incentives for immunization and antenatal care. Yet a study by Behan Box shows that between April and May 2020, 16 state governments were not complying with the central government directive. The data shows that in most states, ASHAs did not receive a fixed monthly payment to begin with and not a single state was paying the regular incentives for activities such as immunization that were suspended during the lockdown (Rao 2020a). Some states like Haryana have not recognized scheme-based workers like ASHAs and

AWWs while announcing that the salaries of other healthcare workers would be doubled during this pandemic; neither was the announcement made for sanitation workers who are similarly at the forefront of managing the pandemic.

In March 2020, the Government of India announced social security benefits for health workers under the *Pradhan Mantri Garib Kalyan Yojana* (PMGKY). Around 2.2 million health workers, including sanitation workers (*Safai Karamcharis*) and ASHAs, would receive INR 5 million as personal accident cover during the first three months of the pandemic (Press Information Bureau 2020a; Mathew 2020). But soon after this announcement, it became clear that the insurance scheme only covered the death of the health worker, not their treatment (Yamunan 2020). In Odisha, the state government extended coverage for the families of Anganwadi workers if they succumbed to the disease (*Indian Express* 2020). An ASHA worker from Jharkhand saw the insurance cover as indicating the low value of their lives: '*An ASHAs' life has no value to the government. That is why it has put a value to our death after sending us to dangerous containment zones without adequate safety*' (Rao 2020a).

These inequalities are further exacerbated for those CB-FLWs who are from vulnerable and marginalized social groups, including Adivasis and Dalits, single women or women-headed households, those struggling to meet their daily needs. Referring to her own fear and exhaustion in the face of complete apathy from the state during the lockdown of 2020, an ASHA worker in Bihar shared, '*Almost every day it used to feel like I would die working in the field. No shops were open to buy food, there was no transport available to travel and all we got from the government was Rs 1000 for a month*' (Srivastav et al. 2020).

In June 2020, ASHA workers initiated a country-wide protest demanding that both central and state governments recognize their work as emergency services and provide protective equipment as well as an increase in honorariums (Rao 2020b). Various workers' unions across several states have been on strike and have been raising demands to ensure that their work is no longer underpaid and invisible: ASHAs in Karnataka (*The Hindu* 2020) and in Delhi are demanding enhanced compensation for the COVID-19 related surveillance activities as well as an increase in the incentive amounts they receive (Chitlangia 2020); in Maharashtra, the ASHA union affiliated with the All India Trade Union Congress (AITUC) has demanded to be paid the minimum wages for skilled workers (Amnesty International India 2020).

In August 2020 yet again, the inaction and apathy towards this cadre of community-based frontline health and nutrition and scheme-based workers triggered a two-day nation-wide strike of approximately 600,000 such workers, including ASHAs, Anganwadi workers and others working under the National Health Mission. A year later the situation is no different: once again, the ASHAs staged a nation-wide protest in May 2021, demanding the payment of remunerations and incentives that have been pending for several months in several states. Aside from the demands made previously, these workers are also protesting against the privatization of certain health and nutrition services. Demands included the formal recognition of these workers; social security and pension benefits; as well as universal health care and protective equipment (Seth Sharma 2020; Scroll 2020; *Outlook* 2020).

The workers remain bitter about the fact that successful implementation of all health outreach programmes depends on their work, yet their demands have remained unaddressed. As one of the Union functionaries said, '*It's not just with coronavirus. All big schemes, whether it's Polio or COVID, rely on scheme workers. They are the ones who finally do the work. In fact, the public health system rests on their shoulders. But when it comes to acknowledgment, they are not even recognized as employees deserving a minimum wage*' (Kalra 2020).

A Feminist Roadmap from the Global South

Building on the evidence that we have presented in this paper, we argue that the choices and decisions being made about the health system and the COVID-19 response are driven by gender norms not just within the household and community, but also within policy frameworks, institutions and structures. The female stereotyping of *sewa* or caring for others is seen as a kind of extended housework and poor women in the villages are the ideal worker volunteers (Wichterich 2020). This has rendered the CB-FLWs, already at the bottom of the social and economic ladder, even more powerless and marginalized during COVID-19, despite being at the forefront of the pandemic's response. In fact, they have been made into the shock-absorbers for an under-resourced health system.

Yet this moment of crisis can also be an opportunity for change. As we gradually look to the future pathways out of the health and socioeconomic crisis, we use our feminist analysis to propose a few policy directions that we think might have transformative potential. Our three proposals are described below:

Recognition and Representation

The first area of action should be to formalize the work of the community-based frontline health workers and acknowledge their contribution as regular employees. Most public programmes in which women are primarily engaged are not recognized as 'work': women are employed on a voluntary basis and do not possess formal contracts or eligibility for most social security benefits. In women's provision of this 'community service' we find public policy instrumentalizing the labour of these women to extend their unpaid domestic work and care-giving responsibilities into 'government work', but without any concomitant assurance of formal employment. By being 'part-time' volunteers, CB-FLWs neither get the full wages, nor do they get the associated entitlements or opportunities for growth and promotion. Despite their crucial role in last-mile public service delivery, women involved in scheme-based work are denied decent work conditions and remuneration.

As critical elements of the health workforce, it is a moral imperative and indeed a right, that these 'volunteers' should be treated as workers in the health system and in public service. An issue requiring urgent attention as a matter of justice and efficiency is the improvement of the working conditions, and representation of rights of workers in essential care services (ILO 2020). Related to this would be regular contracts, living wages for their skilled care work, social security and protection, and opportunities for growth, promotion and up-skilling.

Alongside this, there should be strong policy and institutional support to ensure that they have safe and enabling working conditions, be it freedom from violence and harassment, the access to grievance redressal mechanisms or the right to organize and demand accountability for their rights. It is strongly recommended that CB-FLWs and their unions and associations have a seat at the table where decisions are being made in health and economic policies, in order to be able to represent and voice their concerns directly.

Reimagining Macroeconomic Policies from a Feminist Lens

COVID-19 has shed light on the cracks in economic systems that have poorly prioritized investments in the care sectors, leading to shortages in health workers and exacerbating poor working conditions of essential workers. It has also provided us with the learning that strengthening of public services is a policy imperative (ILO 2020). This pandemic provides us with lessons on how we can emerge stronger from the current situation through more gender-responsive fiscal policies. India can creatively use the opportunities presented by the crisis to think ahead on how women's participation in the paid workforce can be safeguarded and expanded. At a time where economies are on the downturn, and job losses are at their highest, the government can step in to create employment at unprecedented scale, thereby providing jobs for women, through converting their unpaid and underpaid work into public employment opportunities.

The SDG target 5.4 already provides a framework for expanding gender-responsive infrastructure, social protection and public care services, and ILO (International Labour Organization) has suggested prioritizing public investment in these areas, including in rural and informal settings, to redistribute unpaid care work and free women's time. A recent UN Women brief also points to the need for more gender-responsive macroeconomic policies, labour market policies and care systems to recover from the COVID crisis (Diallo et al. 2020). A recent ILO estimate suggests that 269 million new jobs can be created by 2030 in the care economy (as compared to the number of jobs in 2015) to meet the unmet need of care; this would take GDP to 14.9 per cent (from 8.7 per cent in 2015) (Addati et al. 2018).

For India, some estimates point to the fact that there are around 7 million 'scheme workers' in the country, including the one million ASHAs under the National Health Mission, the 2.8 million Anganwadi workers and helpers under the Integrated Child Development Services (ICDS) and 2.5 million School Mid-day Meal cooks (Press Information Bureau 2020c; Sinha et al. 2021).

Given that women's participation in the formal workforce is steadily declining in India, the state could effectively ramp up the figures by officially acknowledging its own responsibility as an employer to all these women in the public sector who are performing 'care work'.

Estimates show that regularizing employment of Anganwadi workers, ASHAs and Helpers and other contractual employees in the public health and education system has the potential to create good jobs for another 3 million workers. This can be achieved by expanding public services for health, education, food and nutrition security and childcare, by filling up existing vacancies and human resource shortfalls (Sinha et al. 2021). In other words, instead of treating the care jobs in their current form as extensions of gendered care-giving and nurturing roles of women, they can hold economic value if converted into decent service sector jobs—one for which a highly skilled workforce already exists.

Recovery and Resilience

The 'care crisis' has been steadily growing over many years, but the COVID-19 pandemic has pushed it to breaking point (Diallo et al. 2020). Therefore, moving forward, prioritizing public investments in robust health and social protection systems will be vital to ensuring long-term recovery and resilience. The importance of public financing is critical in the post-COVID-19 context as emphasized in the guidance of the WHO on health system strengthening (Barroy et al. 2020). Expansion of public services on one hand, job creation on the other and strengthening of local level institutions and systems—including the rights and capacities of community-based frontline workers—are key elements for a decentralized approach for building resilience.

We know that after the Ebola pandemic in West Africa, a reduction in the health workforce due to health worker mortality led to an increase in maternal, infant and under-5 mortality (Donnell and Rick 2020). In India, critical functions carried out by community-based frontline health workers are now restricted or have been stalled due to the range of other COVID-related activities being undertaken by an already overburdened cadre of clinical and community-based workers (Srinivasan et al. 2020). Early estimates from studies show that if routine health care is disrupted and access to food is decreased, there will be a significant increase in child and maternal deaths in low-income and middle-income countries. If India's ICDS system—delivering its services through the hamlet level Anganwadis and community level Anganwadi workers—is unable to grapple with the double burden of the pandemic and growing food insecurity, years of progress will be reversed with potentially devastating results. This calls for a more proactive approach towards recognizing and formalizing India's community-based frontline workforce at the forefront of improving the nutrition outcomes of women and children who are seriously malnourished.

India needs to invest more in expanding the worker-to-population targets so that hard to reach areas, often where the most vulnerable are located, are sufficiently covered by community health workers—who are known to have the best outreach and contact at community level. The evidence on incentive-based 'piece-rate' payments system has shown that it builds skewed priorities: certain tasks for which higher incentives are offered take priority over other types of health services and activities, thus affecting comprehensive healthcare delivery (Barria et al. 2018).

This can be avoided by formalizing the work done by community health workers like ASHAs and providing decent wages and benefits, ultimately improving health and nutrition outcomes for India's population.

Conclusion

In conclusion, we aver that the health crisis is also a severe economic crisis that has drawn attention to the inequalities that already existed pre-COVID. For feminist theory and practice, we believe this is a moment of 'rebooting': a unique opportunity to recalibrate our policy approaches and do things differently. Through our analysis and discussion in this paper, we build on the learning of feminist movements in the global South in order to propose that in this 'rebooting' we can help improve the situation of women in the economy, improve conditions of work for CB-FLWs and ensure broader outcomes for longer-term resilience.

Fundamentally, we propose converting the unpaid and underpaid work of women CB-FLWs into decent work opportunities. CB-FLWs should have access to social protection measures, health benefits and decent wages for the skilled care work that they perform. They should get formal recognition as workers. We argue that this can help create a more caring society and economy, while also ensuring job creation for women in the post-COVID context. Creating employment in care jobs and in public service jobs (as we propose) will also be good for economic growth in the long run. We suggest that this policy measure will also lead to human development outcomes on health, food and nutrition security.

Most importantly, from a global South and Indian perspective, we believe that the profile of the health workforce is significantly different from the North, and therefore the implications for them have been different. Community-based women health workers at the frontlines live with gendered realities and socioeconomic disadvantages that have got further exacerbated through the crisis—with very little institutional and policy support. They are further dis-enfranchised by structural issues such as violence in their world of work and by broader compulsions of economic precarity, joblessness and an overall crisis of employment.

We draw upon Dewan's comment regarding the precarious nature of women's economic activity (Dewan 2019) to call for overhauling the entrenched gender norms that perpetuate the inequitable gender division of paid and unpaid labour and undervalue female-dominated occupations. As we have demonstrated, these pervasive gender norms confine women to underpaid work that expands unpaid household roles into undervalued community 'volunteer' service, while simultaneously reducing women's capacity to be in formal full-time economic activity. The continued refusal to pay heed to the demands of the protesting CB-FLWs reveals gendered assumptions that female workers ought to display an inherently altruistic, acquiescent and apolitical nature (Ved et al. 2019: 8). This gendered use of women's labour occurs in tandem with the erosion of the public health system and diversion of public resources into the private sector, thus illustrating the complicity of state policy, market forces, community and household in maintaining the structural determinants of health (Dewan 2019; King et al. 2020).

The underfunded and neglected domain of care work has been exposed by the COVID-19 pandemic, highlighting the importance of recognizing the value of paid and unpaid care provision. We recommend that the state acknowledge the economic contribution of women in the care economy rather than stereotype women as nurturing, self-sacrificing caregivers (King et al. 2020; Wichterich 2020). It is vital now, more than ever to redress the underpayment and poor employment conditions of occupations that provide care including health care (King et al. 2020). We call for a complete rehauling of our macroeconomic frameworks, for bold and generous fiscal policy measures to help transform the lives of millions of hardworking women who have championed the COVID-19 response at the frontlines. We call for a more caring and a more feminist approach to ensure longer-term, all-round resilience in the economy and in society.

Bibliography

Addati, L, Cattaneo, U, Esquivel, V, and Valarino, I, 2018. *Care Work and Care Jobs for the Future of Decent Work.* International Labour Organization. https://www.ilo.org/wcmsp5/groups/public/---dgreports/---dcomm/---publ/documents/publication/wcms_633166.pdf

Amnesty International India, 2020. *The Women Warriors Fighting COVID-19 at the Frontline: ASHA Workers Left Without Hope.* Amnesty International India. https://amnesty.org.in/the-women-warriors-fighting-covid-19-at-the-frontline-asha-workers-left-without-hope/

Azim Premji University, 2021. *State of Working India 2021: One Year of Covid-19.* Centre for Sustainable Employment, Azim Premji University.

Barria, S, Aye, B, Goss, J, Lappin, K, Montufar, V, and Whaites, M, 2018. *Decent Work for Community Health Workers in South Asia: A Path to Gender Equality and Sustainable Development.* International Labour Organization.

Barroy, H, Wang, D, Pescetto, C, and Kutzin, J, 2020. *How to Budget for COVID-19 Response? A Rapid Scan of Budgetary Mechanisms in Highly Affected Countries.* World Health Organization.

Centre for Budget and Governance Accountability, 2021, *Budget in the Time of the Pandemic: An Analysis of Union Budget 2021–22.* https://www.cbgaindia.org/wp-content/uploads/2021/02/Budget-in-the-Time-of-Pandemic-An-Analysis-of-Union-Budget-2021-22.pdf

Chhabra, R, 2021. ASHAs to Stage One-Day Nationwide Strike on May 24. 20 May 2021. *NewsClick.* https://www.newsclick.in/ASHAs-Stage-One-Day-Nationwide-Strike-May-24

Chitlangia, R, 2020. Asha Workers on Covid-19 Duty Demand Timely, Better Wages. 19 April 2020. *Hindustan Times.* https://www.hindustantimes.com/delhi-news/asha-workers-on-covid-19-duty-demand-timely-better-wages/story-x3g8ewZPlDzFe89ceNhu8J.html

Dewan, R, 2019. Gender Equalisation Through Feminist Finance. *Economic and Political Weekly*, 54(17), 27. April 2019. https://www.epw.in/journal/2019/17/commentary/gender-equalisation-through-feminist-finance.html

Diallo, B, Qayum, S and Staab, S, 2020. *COVID-19 and the Care Economy: Immediate Action and Structural Transformation for a Gender-Responsive Recovery.* UN Women.

Donnell, M, and Rick, S, 2020. *A Gender Lens on COVID-19: Investing in Nurses and Other Frontline Health Workers to Improve Health Systems.* Center for Global Development. https://www.cgdev.org/blog/gender-lens-covid-19-investing-nurses-and-other-frontline-health-workers-improve-health-systems

Duggal, R, 2014. *Caste Background of Health Professionals in India.* MFC Bulletin 357-360. *Medico Friend Circle 2014.* http://www.mfcindia.org/mfcpdfs/MFC357-360.pdf

Gender in Humanitarian Action, 2020. *The COVID-19 Outbreak and Gender: Key Advocacy Points from Asia and the Pacific*. Gender in Humanitarian Action Working Group.

Global Hunger Index, 2020. *Global Hunger Index by Severity*. https://www.globalhungerindex.org/ranking.html

ILO, 2020. *The COVID-19 Response: Getting Gender Equality Right for a Better Future for Women at Work*. International Labour Organization. Geneva

Indian Express, 2018. PM Modi Announces Hike in Remuneration of ASHA, Anganwadi Workers. 11 September 2018. *The Indian Express*. https://indianexpress.com/article/india/pm-modi-announces-hike-remuneration-asha-anganwadi-workers-5350480/

Indian Express, 2020. Odisha Govt to Give Rs 50 Lakh to Kin of ASHA, Anganwadi Workers Who Die of COVID-19 on Duty. 18 July 2020. *Indian Express*. https://www.newindianexpress.com/states/odisha/2020/jul/18/odisha-govt-to-give-rs-50-lakh-to-kin-of-asha-anganwadi-workers-who-die-of-covid-19-on-duty-2171422.html

Indian Express, 2021. ASHA Worker Gathering Details for Vaccination Assaulted in UP. 8 June 2021. *Indian Express*. https://indianexpress.com/article/india/asha-worker-gathering-details-for-vaccination-assaulted-in-up-7348721/

Intra Health International, 2014. Ebola Outbreak Underscores Need for Stronger Frontline Health Workforce in West Africa. https://www.intrahealth.org/news/ebola-outbreak-underscores-need-for-stronger-frontline-health-workforce-in-west-africa

Karan, A, Negandhi, H, Hussain, S, Zapata, T, Mairembam, D, De Graeve, H, Buchan, J, and Zodpey, S, 2021. Size, Composition and Distribution of Health Workforce in India: Why, and Where to Invest? *Human Resources for Health*, 19, 39 (2021). https://doi.org/10.1186/s12960-021-00575-2

Kalra, S, 2020. Why Healthcare Workers on COVID Battle Frontline Need Protection Themselves. *Citizen Matters*. April 8, 2020. https://citizenmatters.in/government-containment-strategy-role-and-vulnerability-of-asha-workers-16974

Kim, H, Novakovic, U, Carles Muntaner, C, and Michael T. Hawkes, MT, 2019. A Critical Assessment of the Ideological Underpinnings of Current Practice in Global Health and Their Historical Origins, *Global Health Action*, 12, 1. https://doi.org/10.1080/16549716.2019.1651017

King, T, Hewit, B, Crammond, B, Sutherland, G, Maheen, H, and Kavanagh, A, 2020. Reordering Gender Systems: Can COVID-19 Lead to Improved Gender Equality and Health? *The Lancet*. Published online June 19, 2020. https://doi.org/10.1016/S0140-6736(20)31418-5

Majumder, M, 2020. It''s Time to Recognise that Govt Plans Are Oblivious to the Realities of Care Workers. 29 April 2020. *The Wire*. https://thewire.in/rights/covid-19-asha-anganwadi-workers-nurses

Mallick. S, 2019. Anganwadi Workers Hit the Streets in Protest. 26 February 2019. *Down to Earth*. https://www.downtoearth.org.in/news/governance/anganwadi-workers-hit-the-streets-in-protest-63363

Marie Stopes International, 2021. *Resilience, Adaptation and Action: MSI's Response to COVID-19*. https://www.msichoices.org/media/3849/resilience-adaptation-and-action.pdf

Mathew, G, 2020. 30 Claims Under Process for Rs 50 Lakh Healthcare Workers' Insurance. 16 June 2020. *Indian Express*. https://indianexpress.com/article/business/30-claims-under-process-for-rs-50-lakh-healthcare-workers-insurance-6460832/

Ministry for Women and Child Development, 2018. *Coverage of Anganwadi workers (AWWs)/Anganwadi Helpers (AWHs) under the Pradhan Mantri Jeevan Jyoti Bima Yojana (PJJBY); Pradhan Mantri Suraksha Bima Yojana (PMSBY) and Anganwadi Karyakartri Bima Yojana (AKBY) and benefits available to them*. Ministry for Women and Child Development. https://wcd.nic.in/sites/default/files/ICDS.PDF

Ministry of Finance, 2016. *Seventh Central Pay Commission*. https://www.finmin.nic.in/seven-cpc

Ministry of Health and Family Welfare, 2019. *Rural Health Statistics 2018–19 Government of India Ministry of Health and Family Welfare Statistics Division*. https://main.mohfw.gov.in/sites/default/files/Final%20RHS%202018-19_0.pdf

Ministry of Health and Family Welfare, 2020a. *Micro Plan for Containing Local Transmission of Coronavirus Disease (COVID-19)*. https://www.mohfw.gov.in/pdf/ModelMicroplanforcontainmentoflocaltransmissionofCOVID19.pdf

Ministry of Health and Family Welfare, 2020b. *National Family Health Survey (NFHS) Survey-5*. http://rchiips.org/nfhs/factsheet_NFHS-5.shtml

MOSPI, 2019. *Periodic Labour Force Survey 2017–18, Ministry of Statistics and Programme Implementation, Government of India*. May 2019. http://www.mospi.gov.in/sites/default/files/publication_reports/Annual%20Report%2C%20PLFS%202017-18_31052019.pdf

MOSPI, 2020. *Periodic Labour Force Survey Annual Report July 2018–June 2019, Ministry of Statistics and Programme Implementation, Government of India*. http://www.mospi.gov.in/sites/default/files/press_release/Press%20Note.pdf

National Health Mission. Guidelines on Accredited Social Health Activists (ASHA). https://nhm.gov.in/images/pdf/communitisation/task-group-reports/guidelines-on-asha.pdf

NBC News, 2015. *Ebola Kills Nearly 500 Health Care Workers*. 8 January 2015. NBC News. https://www.nbcnews.com/storyline/ebola-virus-outbreak/ebola-kills-nearly-500-health-care-workers-n281801

NewsClick, 2018. *PM Modi's Announcement of Hike in the Monthly Honorarium of ASHAs and ANMs in September This Year, Remains Unfulfilled*. 10 December 2018. News Click. https://www.newsclick.in/bihar-asha-workers-go-indefinite-strike-demanding-better-wages-and-social-security

Outlook India, 2020. 10 Trade Unions Call for Nation-Wide Protest on Aug 9 Against Worker policies. 22 July 2020. *Outlook India*. https://www.outlookindia.com/newsscroll/10-trade-unions-call-for-nationwide-protest-on-aug-9-against-worker-policies/1900503/

Press Information Bureau, 2018. *Cabinet Approves ASHA Benefit Package*. September 2018. Press Information Bureau, Delhi. https://pib.gov.in/Pressreleaseshare.aspx?PRID=1546619

Press Information Bureau, 2020a. *Increase in Salaries of Anganwadi Workers*. September 2020. https://pib.gov.in/PressReleasePage.aspx?PRID=1655616

Press Information Bureau, 2020b. *Finance Minister Announces Rs 1.70 Lakh Crore relief Package Under Pradhan Mantri Garib Kalyan Yojana for the Poor to Help Them Fight the Battle Against Corona Virus*. Press Information Bureau Delhi. https://pib.gov.in/Pressreleaseshare.aspx?PRID=1608345

Press Information Bureau, 2020c. *ASHA Workers*. Press Information Bureau Delhi.

Rao, B, 2020a. Promised, Mostly Never Paid: Rs 1,000 Covid Wage to Million Health Workers. *Article 14*. June 2020 https://www.behanbox.com/promised-mostly-never-paid-rs-1000-covid-wage-to-million-health-workers/

Rao, CL, 2020b. Asha Workers to Observe 'Demands Day' on June 25. 22 June 2020. *The Hans India*. https://www.thehansindia.com/andhra-pradesh/asha-workers-to-observe-demands-day-on-june-25-629358

Rao, B and Chowdhury, SD, 2021. Female Frontline Community Healthcare Workforce in India During COVID-19. https://behanbox.com/wp-content/uploads/2021/03/APU-Report-Final.pdf

Rao, B, and Tewari, S, 2020. Anger, Distress Among India's Frontline Workers in Fight Against Covid-19. *Article 14*. June 2020. https://www.article-14.com/post/anger-distress-among-india-s-frontline-workers-in-fight-against-covid-19

Raven, J., Wurie, H., and Witter, S., 2018. Health Workers' Experiences of Coping with the Ebola epidemic in Sierra Leone's Health System: A Qualitative Study. *BMC Health Services Research*, *18*(1), 251. https://doi.org/10.1186/s12913-018-3072-3

Roy, V, 2020. Though a High-Skill Job, Nursing Remains Low-Paid and Stigmatised: Panchali Ray. *The Hindu*. 25 July 2020. https://www.thehindu.com/society/though-a-high-skill-job-nursing-remains-low-paid-and-stigmatised-panchali-ray/article32181653.ece

Rukmini S, 2020. How Covid-19 Response Disrupted Health Services in Rural India. 27 April 2020. *LiveMint*. https://www.livemint.com/news/india/how-covid-19-response-disrupted-health-services-in-rural-india-11587713155817.html

Schaaf, M, Warthin, C, Freedman, L, and Topp, SM, 2020. The Community Health Worker as Service Extender, Cultural Broker and Social Change Agent: A Critical Interpretive Synthesis of Roles, Intent and Accountability. *BMJ Global Health 2020*, 5, e002296. https://doi.org/10.1136/bmjgh-2020-002296

Scroll, 2020. Coronavirus: Around 6 Lakh ASHA Workers Launch Protest, Demand Better Pay, Health Insurance. 7 August 2020. *Scroll*. https://scroll.in/latest/969718/coronavirus-around-6-lakh-asha-workers-launch-protest-demand-better-pay-health-insurance

Seth Sharma, Y, 2020. Unpaid for Months, Anganwadi and Asha Workers to Hold Strike on August 7–8. 6 August 2020. *Economic Times*. https://economictimes.indiatimes.com/news/politics-and-nation/unpaid-for-months-anganwadi-and-asha-workers-to-hold-strike-on-august-7-8/articleshow/77390884.cms

Sharma, M, 2020. Exclusive: Over 15,000 Frontline Workers Tested Positive for Coronavirus in India. 18 July 2020. *India Today*. https://www.indiatoday.in/india/story/over-15-000-frontline-workers-tested-positive-for-coronavirus-in-india-corona-warriors-1701915-2020-07-18

Sinha, D, Ghosh, J, Gupta, M, and Gupta, V, 2021. *Generating Female Employment Through Public Employment: A Scoping Paper*. IWWAGE. New Delhi.

Srinivasan, S, Arora, R, Bhardwaj, R, Pandey, B, Kullu, A, Raykar, N, Khanuja, J, Nambiar, D, and Lewis, TN, 2020. *Understanding the Role of Indian Frontline Workers in Preventing and Managing COVID-19*. Oxford Policy Management. https://www.opml.co.uk/blog/understanding-the-role-of-indian-frontline-workers-in-preventing-and-managing-covid-19

Srivastav, N, Priya, A, Hathi, P, 2020. Our Essential Workers Need Essential Care. *Economic & Political Weekly*. August 1, 2020, 55(31), 15–16.

Suraksha, P, 2020. Asha Workers Strike for 4th Day, Demand Minimum Wage of Rs. 12,000. 14 July 2020. *Deccan Herald*. https://www.deccanherald.com/state/karnataka-districts/asha-workers-call-off-strike-after-governmentassures-july-wages-to-meet-cm-on-friday-891994.html

The Hindu, 2020. Health Activists' Strike Hits COVID-19 Work, but Govt. Claims Others Have Taken Over. 18 July 2020. *The Hindu*. https://www.thehindu.com/news/national/karnataka/health-activists-strike-hits-covid-19-work-but-govt-claims-others-have-taken-over/article32126059.ece

UN Women, 2020. *The Impact of COVID-19 on Women*. UN Women. https://reliefweb.int/sites/reliefweb.int/files/resources/policy-brief-the-impact-of-covid-19-on-women-en.pd

UN Women Data, 2020. COVID-19: Emerging Gender Data and Why It Matters. https://data.unwomen.org/resources/covid-19-emerging-gender-data-and-why-it-matters

United Nations, 2020. Secretary-General Calls Gender Violence 'Shadow Pandemic', Spotlights COVID-19 Lockdowns, in Message to College Campus Event. 3 July 2020. United Nations Press Release. https://www.un.org/press/en/2020/sgsm20160.doc.htm

Ved, R, Scott, K, Gupta, G, Ummer, O, Singh, S, Srivastava, A, and George, AS, 2019. *How Are Gender Inequalities Facing India's One Million ASHAs Being Addressed? Policy Origins and Adaptations for the World's Largest All-Female Community Health Worker Programme*. Human Resources for Health (2019), 17, 3. https://doi.org/10.1186/s12960-018-0338-0

Wenham, C, Smith, J, Davies, SE, Feng, H, Grépin, KA, Harman, S, Herten-Crabb, A, and Morgan, R, 2020. Women are most Affected by Pandemics—Lessons from Past Outbreaks. *NATURE*, 583(7815), 194–197. https://www.nature.com/articles/d41586-020-02006-z

Wichterich, C, 2020. *Who Cares About Healthcare Workers? Care Extractivism and Care Struggles in Germany and India Social Change*, 50(1), 121–140. https://doi.org/10.1177/0049085719901087

Yamunan, S, 2020. Indian Health Workers Would Have to Die Before Their Families Get Coronavirus Insurance Funds. 6 April 2020. *Scroll*. https://scroll.in/article/958206/indian-health-workers-would-have-to-die-before-their-families-get-coronavirus-insurance-funds

CHAPTER 7

Gendering Precarity in Postcolonial Sites: Health Securitization and Sexual Labor in India's Commercial Sex Trade Industry

Sudeshna Chatterjee

List of Abbreviations

AINSW	All India Network for Sex Workers
DMSC	Durbar Mahila Samanwaya Committee
FCDA	Feminist Critical Discourse Analysis
GCF	Global Fund for Children
HIV/AIDS	Human Immunodeficiency Virus, Acquired Immunodeficiency Syndrome
ICRSE	International Committee on Rights of Sex Workers in Europe
ITPA	Immoral Traffic (Prevention) Act

S. Chatterjee (✉)
University of Massachusetts Boston, Boston, MA 02124, USA
e-mail: sudeshna.chatterj001@umb.edu

S. Hewamanne and S. Yadav (eds.), *The Political Economy of Post-COVID Life and Work in the Global South: Pandemic and Precarity*, International Political Economy Series,
https://doi.org/10.1007/978-3-030-93228-2_7

NSWP	Global Network of Sex Workers Projects
SAARC	South Asian Association for Regional Cooperation
SEM	Standard Employment Model
UNAIDS	The Joint United Nations Programme on HIV/AIDS
UNODC	United Nations Office on Drugs and Crime
VAMP/Sangram	Veshya Anyay Mukti Parishad/Sasmpada Grameen Mahla Sanstha

Introduction

The COVID-19 pandemic has brought to the forefront the vulnerability of the most marginalized populations, thus exposing the faultlines in neoliberal governance. Be it immigrants in the US, domestic migrant workers in India or violence against black bodies in western democracies, the pandemic has now enthused academics to think about the role of precarity and the resultant differential distribution of resources across the world. Amidst this, sex workers have been hard hit. On April 8, 2020 UNAIDS released a press statement asserting that as already criminalized, marginalized and living in financial precarity, 'sex workers must not be left behind in the response to COVID-19' (UNAIDS 2020). Yet, sex work precarity is by no means recent phenomenon. Sex work has been, for a long time, theorized as precarious labor and sex workers as precarious bodies. Sexual labor posits the body at the center stage of neoliberal biopolitics, whereby commodification, consumption and controlling of precarious bodies go hand-in-hand with and become integral for preserving the gendered/racialized neoliberal body politic. Thus, sexually precarious bodies become the site for several legal and pathological securitization initiatives.

In this chapter, I explore how health securitization as an analytic deepens our understanding of reproductive and sexual precarity. Taking the case of commercial sex work in India, I explore how health securitization underlying the HIV/AIDS and COVID-19 governance in India deepen precarity of sexual labor by excpetionalizing it legally and pathologically. This is crucial ultimately for the constitution of the gendered neoliberal-postcolonial state and sustenance of global-sexual power relations. The chapter begins with an overview of the precarity literature and its postcolonial/feminist critiques, followed by building a theoretical framework for the health securitization analytic to study reproductive precarity in the Global South. I coined the term 'contamination-invisibility' nexus which lies at the heart of this securitization process and elucidates how sexually precarious bodies are exceptionalized by virtue of their health-centric vulnerabilities and/or their potential to threaten 'public' health, via spatial/moral segregation.

Here, the Indian case deepens understanding of sex work precarity in two ways. One, it opens up ways in which we imagine (in)security as well as precarity. Centering most debates on precarity around 'extreme' and the most obvious sites of securitization (such as camps) and emergency governance mechanisms alone is itself gendered/racialized act it as it maintains a hierarchical ordering of global precarity, where historically oppressed subjects have had to be defined in relation to only the most extreme forms of violence and its resultant impact on privileged lives, to be considered as viable subjects of security studies. Politicization of some cases comes at the expense of depoliticizing others which preserves securitization's divisive problem at the very core. The Indian case then becomes important to understand how securitization of reproductive labor precarity in the Global South sustains global power inequalities. Second, sex work in India is exceptionalized through legal securitization (categorizing the trafficking aspect as a transnational crime while maintaining security silences on the sex work dimension of sexual commerce), as well as by pathological securitization through spatial/moral segregation of sex work. The health securitization analytic here becomes important to elucidate why juridical (legal) and pathological exception[1] should not be taken as two distinct historical processes, but rather as mutually constitutive and reflective of the same logic which renders sexually precarious labor as an exception to the gendered norm and an identifiable threat to (post)colonial states and neoliberal world order.

My study draws on an interpretive research methodology, based on qualitative research data collected as part of my dissertation research in India (2016–2017) on sex work governance. I was particularly motivated by the drive to enable the articulation of lived experiences and subjectivity constructions of actors engaged in sex work governance in India. I generated data through a combination interviews, focus

[1] Viewing sex work as an exception to juridical law as well as transgressions against 'natural' social/moral codes, frequently termed as social pathology.

groups and unobtrusive research methods such as participant observation and document/policy analysis and adopted Feminist Critical Discourse Analysis (FCDA) combined with grounded theory to understand localized meaning making and non-hegemonic knowledge constructions by subjects. The unit of analysis being actors engaged in governance, I worked with a total of ten organizations which play key role in sex work governance in India, based on Kolkata, New Delhi and Sangli. These include three major groups of organizations: (a) State institutions involved in governing/regulating sex trade in India: the National Ministry of Women and Children and the West Bengal Ministry of Women and Child Welfare; (b) International, National or State level non-profits working with sex workers: Apne Aap, Sanlaap, New Light, Women's Interlink Foundation. (c) National/Local sex workers organizations: VAMP/Sangram, All India Network for Sex Workers, Durbar Mahila Committee, Sanlaap-Subah youth group. A total of 24 personal interviews and two focus groups (with parties of 4 and 10) were conducted. Out of all interviewees, 22.5% self-identified as men and 77.5% self-identified as women.

Precarious Labor and Racialized-Gendered Absences

Labor historians have long debated precarious work and its role in contemporary global capitalism. The precarity literature has shifted from defining the standard employment model (SEM)[2] being the norm under global capitalism (Bosch 1986; Clarke 1991; Castells 1996; Carnoy et al. 1997; Harvey 1999), to critically theorizing precarity, insecurity and informality as being the norm rather than the exception (Breman and Van der Linden 2014; Das and Randeria 2015; Lambert and Herod 2016; Millar 2017; Neilson and Rotisser 2008; Yadav 2018). Breman and Van der Linden's (2014) work highlights this standard employment model as a historical exception 'which had a deep impact in a limited part of the world for a relatively short period of time' (Breman and Van der Linden 2014). Similarly, Yadav's ethnographic work on India's indigenous Gonds

[2] SEM here indicates relatively secure, full-time wage labor organized around an employer's premises, and which yields extensive statutory benefits and entitlements for workers (Fudge 1997; Rodgers 1989; Vosko 1997).

elucidates the agentic potential that lies in choosing informal, precarious labor over state employment (Yadav 2018).

Studies on the Global South have historicized the standard employment model and elucidated how 'precarity is originary to capitalism' (Millar 2017), how wage labor itself might be an experience of insecurity, especially through colonial impositions in post-colonial contexts (Barchiesi 2012) and the exclusion of a wide range of work related to subsistence and reproduction driven by West's view of work as market-oriented, creating the distinction between work-home and labor-leisure and differential labor values (Komlosy 2018). Despite socialist feminists insisting that housework and emotional labor of women must be paid (Federici 1975; Malos 1975; Vogel 1995), studies on work and employment in the 1970s and 1980s (Aglietta 1979; Alchian and Demstez 1972; Doeringer and Piore 1971) continued to be largely Eurocentric and gender-blind. It was only in the later works of critical, postcolonial and feminist scholars post-1990s that the debate on informal, black/shadow/undocumented work and precarity crossed paths in academic works on Global South. These scholars began to raise questions about the ontologies of precarity, work and their relation to capitalism and labor the world over.

Gendering Precarity: Feminist Critiques

A robust body of postcolonial/feminist theorizing has elucidated the important lessons to be learnt from gendered and racialized forms of precarity in the Global South and its interactions with neoliberal institutions and practices thus upholding the realities of gendered assumptions underlying work and questioning if the standard employment model was actually a norm in Western civilizations during the so-called Golden Age of the twentieth century as it never fully included all of the western workforces such as women and migrants. The standard model was presupposed by unpaid domestic labor of women and hyper-exploitation in the colonies (Betti n.d.). Feminists argue that the standard employment model reinforced gender roles and didn't quite help reduce gender inequalities as men were still the breadwinners and women care-givers in this scheme of things (Agathangelou 2004; Butler 2004; Federici 2006; McRobbie 2011).

Federici argues that precarious labor theory has long presented itself as gender neutral, assuming "that the reorganization of production is doing away with the power relations and hierarchies that exist within the working class on the basis of rage, gender and age, and therefore it is not concerned with addressing these power relations; it does not have the theoretical and political tools to think about how to tackle them" (Federici 2006, para. 1). While precarious labor theory does pay a kind of 'lip service' to feminist analyses in its theorization of 'affective labor' as 'immaterial labor', it renders ineffective in the rich feminist work on demystifying housework, instead "suggesting that reproducing people is just a matter of making producing 'emotions', 'feelings'" (ibid., para. 6). Federici cautions that even pathbreaking works in the field such as that of Hardt and Negri (2000) ignore the feminist struggle to redefine work itself.

McRobbie carries the critique of Hardt and Negri (2000) further to assert that in addition to being gender blind, the precarity literature is stuck with 1970s jargons, in need of dire revision and represents how gender, race and ethnicity are subsumed by class, a concept modelled originally on white men. McRobbie emphasizes the need for investigating how gendered the process of feeling distress, pain and injury is when it comes to flexible work. However, while McRobbie builds a robust critique of the gender neutral/outdated feminist analyses of the precarity literature, her analysis fails to move beyond the formalized economy and doesn't quite extend to the much-needed theorization of reproductive labor in the informal economy, illicit networks and neoliberal governance (McRobbie 2011, 69).

Judith Butler defines precarity beyond the concept of the workplace. Especially in context of post 9/11 America, Butler considers precariousness as an ineradicable part of human nature, which is "a social condition from which clear political demands and principles emerge" (McNeily 2016, para. 2). Not all lives are equally precarious though all lives are defined by precariousness. Butler enthuses us to think about the differential impact of norms, social and political organizations and international institutions, which enhance precariousness of some while minimizing it for others. Hence, Butler's theorization and expansion of precarity also intersects with gender to elucidate how differential gendered performativity creates gendered states of precarity and provides a critical theoretical tool to think about the ways in which the 'human' is (re)produced in contexts of precarity. However, Butler fails to highlight the complicated and complicit neoliberal/capitalist networks of power that thrives on this differential precariousness. As Agathangelou writes "these theorists consider precarity undesirable, not so much because it is immoral but because it is part of a 'bad economy of power...and is pivotal moment of inscribing colonial expropriations in a hierarchized grid of global power" (Agathangelou 2018, 541).

This necessitates reading reproductive and sex work precarity in context of consumption- orientation, service-led industries and the free market rhetoric which underline and drive global political economy today. Sex work, defined as that which involves the exchange of sexual services, performances or products for material compensation (Weitzer 2000), has diversified and expanded in the past thirty years, under the aegis of neoliberal political economies to include: live sex shows; a variety of pornographic texts, videos and images; fetish clubs and sexual 'emporiums'; escort agencies; organized sex tours of developing countries, and many more. Western academic deliberations in the 1960s–1980s viewed any form of sexual commerce as either oppressive (dominance feminists) or agentic (sex radicals). With increasing industrialization and infusion of neoliberal ideas, prostitution came to be emphasized as 'sex work', emerging mostly within radical feminist circles in the 1970s and 1980s (Schotten 2005) and has emerged as a lucrative, globally integrated industry around the world today. This trend has been accompanied by a resulting paradox between the normative push for sex as romance (casting non-relationally bound erotic experiences as pathological) and sex as recreation (Bernstein 2008). Thus, it is safe to say that the sexual commerce industry is a child of neoliberal capitalism, merging public and private, and service sectors with the commodification of all kinds of sexual experiences (Chatterjee and Parpart 2018).

Agathangelou's The Global Political Economy of Sex: Desire, Violence and Insecurity in Mediterrenean Nation States (2004) provides a holistic insight on state complicity, capitalist technologies of power and reproductive/sexual labor. Agathangelou points out that a core concern of contemporary globalization is the international restructuring of reproduction and reproductive power. The rational economic man model underlying most studies in IPE overlooks the structural constraints and political-economic interests that shape decisions of female migrant workers. The complicity of states in enabling an active racialization of reproductive labor through 'desire economies' encompassing a range of intimate economies from migrant female domestic workers to trafficked sex workers is unmistakable. Agathangelou's intense critical-theoretical investigation into economic organizations of sex and reproduction enables an understanding of postcolonial states as objects of as well as complicit actors within contemporary global-neoliberal gendered and racialized hierarchies.

Precarity of Sex Work

I extend Aganthangelou's (2004) logic further to argue that emergent postcolonial and decolonial feminist interventions in precarity must be mindful of not just postcolonial sovereignty's inherent ties to global capitalism but also of the politics of exception and securitization through which global racilized and gendered hierarchies are sustained. Reading precairty against securitization politics is crucial here for a number of reasons. *First*, securitization theory[3] itself has focused substantially on the (de)securitization aspect (undermining socially constructed threats) to address the inherent 'us-versus-them' conflict that lies at the heart of securitization rather than juridical/legal exceptionalization[4] or "(t)he question of which legal and institutional transformations actually follow from securitization" (Hanrieder and Kreuder-Sonnen 2014, 334) and constitutes the legal, spatial and moral 'othering' of certain subjects within a political community, thus preserving, facilitating and enhancing precarity. This manifest itself through security speech acts (identifying trafficking as a 'threat' to human life, dignity, and rights as well as national-global well-being), security silences (aspects of sexual commerce being securitized viz-a-vis others) and security performances (such as institutional changes and resource allocation) (Jackson 2006). *Second*, feminist critiques highlight the gendered and racialized nature of security politics and how gender affects vulnerability distribution through securitization and exception, hence enabling us to understand how the logic of rule by exception systematically creates gendered/racialized precarity, magnified by unequal global relations (Butler 2004; Lorey 2015). Dingli and Purewal highlight how citizens of postcolonial states have to counter not just necropolitical global-sovereign power (such as the war on terror) but also face intense vulnerabilities and precarity resulting from imposition of liberalization and structural adjustment programs on these states.

[3] Securitization theory views how global issues (like migration and climate change) are socially constructed as a security threats through powerful discourses.

[4] See Agamben (1998).

They write, "gendered security logics are woven into the legacies of colonization through state power and accompanying states of exception. This requires a conceptual pulling apart of the contemporary global (dis)order of 'security' through an analysis of the foundations of this order/(dis)order and its gendered contours" (Dingli and Purewal 2018, 156).

For this to happen, we must view sexually precarious labor not just a a manifestation of the neoliberal sexual regime but also understand how sexual precarity is constituted in constant opposition to non-sexual and/or non-precarious labor. The range of reproductive economies subsumed under the umbrella of 'desire industries' must be further complicated to understand hierarchies *within* subcategories of gendered/racialized informal economies. This is not an erasure of common logics of systemic neoliberal exploitation that unite experiences of migrant domestic workers and trafficked women. Rather, it necessitates understanding how power hierarchies create differential experiences and vulnerabilities within similar ontological categories such that some forms of reproductive labor are not exceptionalized/excluded from the larger body politics, the way sexually precarious labor is.

In contemporary India, the legal exceptionalization of sex work through securitization can be seen progressing via three steps. One, conflating commercial sex work with human trafficking, in which the human trafficking aspect of sexual commerce has become the axis of any major policies to govern/regulate sex work in India and have been integral in influencing resource allocation (ITPA 1956; UN Convention against Transnational Organized Crime 2003; SAARC 2002). Second, criminalization of trafficking, whereby narratives on sex work precarity have transitioned from being defined in relation to immorality to being categorized as transnational crime along with terrorism. Third, the binary positioning of sex work vis-a-vis trafficking in governance narratives. A transnational organized crime perspective to sex work assumes a dichotomous relationship between consent-coercion; voice-silence; empowerment- oppression. This reflects clearly a binary positioning of sex work and trafficking.

Legal securitization has a powerful impact on deepening precarity for sex workers in India both explicitly and implicitly. Given the criminalization, stigmatization and discrimination of sex work, sex workers struggle for protection from legal enforcement and coercive state machinery. They "live in daily fear of being 'rescued'...when feminist rescue organizations work with the police who break into our work places and beat us, rape us and kidnap our children in order to 'save' us" (Mgbako, 2012, para. 7). Challenges arising from legal securitization also hinder sex workers' rights to access health-care and other protection services. During my field research, I found that sex workers reported precarity as being an unavoidable part of their lives, subject to violence by various actors (police, traffickers, family and even NGOs) and with no platform to seek redressal before the formation of sex workers rights organizations such as VAMP/Sangram and DMSC in early 1990s. According to a sex worker in DMSC, Kolkata:

> Before 1992, sex workers had no rights. They faced violence from the police, local goons and brothel madams. There was rampant sexual abuse of these girls, and they felt hopeless, that they weren't a part of society, that they weren't worth living...In 1995, Durbar came into being. This would help stop marginalization, discrimination and ensure the power to say no and stand up as a human. (Interviewee 18)

Moreover, the focus group discussion conducted with VAMP/Sangram identified several challenges, most of which are body-centric and health-related:

> We can identify at least seven challenges: one, no awareness about STDs, HIV. Two, Goon and police violence: women in this profession are used as disposable bodies. Three, sex without condoms or money. Fourth, lack of rights awareness. Fifth, lack of health awareness. Sixth, lack of access to healthcare facilities at hospitals. Seventh, lack of access to education for children due to untouchability. (Focus Group, VAMP/Sangraam)

Legal securitization has a deep and direct impact on the children of sex workers, where "'the children' functions...as a trump card through which discourse about commercial sex decriminalization is shifted away from women advocating on their own behalf to the invisible children about which sex workers supposedly care little" (Massey 2014). I found that several sex workers allied with anti-trafficking NGOs to protect their children from precarity. NGOs like Sanlaap, New Light and Apne Aap frequently provide day care and night shelter services for children of sex workers. Rama, a female sex worker associated with New Light in Kolkata, is supported by the NGO which serves as a day care for her children.

> I came to be associated with New Light only for my children. Will I leave it (sex work)? Can I ever? If I do, it will be for my children. (Rama, New light, 2017)

This elucidates the direct impact legal securitization has on deepening precarity for sex workers. This is further aided by pathological exception whereby health securitization becomes central to the process of securitizing sex work.

The Health Securitization Analytic for Precarity: The Contamination-Invisibility Nexus

My research on sex work governance in India[5] suggests that securitization of sex work along the axis of health governance must be read not just as one particular case of securitization but also as being inseparably and inevitably tied to the broader dynamics of securitization and excpetionalizing of sexually precarious labor as a whole. It is significant to analyze how this process of 'othering' sexual-subjects is inseparably tied to discourses around preserving the metaphorical physical and moral health of the nation-state and continuously defined in opposition to a gendered/racialized idea of the postcolonial sovereign state and its ideal citizen subjects.

Regulating the human body as a biopolitical moment is well theorized in the Foucauldian tradition as biopower or 'an explosion of numerous and diverse techniques for achieving the subjugation of bodies and the control of populations' (Foucault 1978). Thus, it becomes integral to explore how emergency and non-emergency health discourses emerge as a biopolitical moment to deepen sexual precarity. Hannah Roberts writes, 'the…danger in seeing the carrier of the disease as the threat is that it massively increases the stigma associated with the disease and can perpetuate stereotypes about different groups of people. Public health measures have historically served as a means of racial exclusion and securitizing health only serves to legitimate this kind of behavior under the guise of health security' (Roberts 2019a, b). In context of epidemic and pandemic governance, Girogio Shani reflects how one might theorize pandemics as "'invented', its political effects as experienced through the imposition of

[5] Conducted as part of my dissertation research on Sex work governance in India: agency, subjectivity and resistance in bare life.

states of emergencies, the securitization of public space, self-isolation and 'lockdowns' constitute a challenge to the norms of democratic politics and everyday life" (Shani 2020a, b, para. 2). This in turn might make one question those included within this fold of protective measures of public health emergencies and those who aren't. I will discuss governance of HIV/AIDS epidemic and the COVID-19 pandemic in conjunction with sex work governance in India to elucidate gendered/racialized logics which preserves the exceptionalization of sex work precarity.

Based on my field research, I propose that health securitization exceptionalizes sex work in India based on two modalities. One, *politics of contamination*, whereby historically marginalized populations are systematically identified as posing pathological threats to the physical, mental and moral health of the larger body politic. Politics of contamination have manifest through historical movements like the purity movement in nineteenth century, supported by social reformers, activists and feminists alike, launched a crusade against all forms of sexual commerce including prostitution and pornography by combining political reform, social hygiene, white slavery abolition and women's rights movements to restructure American/European society on the basis of family and children (Maschke 1997). Mohan Dutta throws light on the racialized logic that drives purity politics, arguing that "notions of purity that are intrinsically connected to dominant ideas of race are utilized as strategies for categorization and mapping within multicultural spaces of neoliberal governance…Prevailing perceptions of class intersect with perceptions of race in the articulation and implementation of security policies" (Dutta 2015, 183). Second, *politics of invisibility and exclusion*, whereby certain precarious groups and populations are rendered invisible from the scope of 'public' health agendas, thus adopting oversight as a strategizing tool of constituting the national body politic through exception. For instance, studies on HIV/AIDS governance in the USA (Forbes 2015) emphasize the absence of 'sex workers' as a state-identified target group for the policy, despite being highly vulnerable because the state refuses to recognize this dimension of sexual commerce in legal texts.

Exceptionalization of sex work in India through health securitization has a long history, entrenched in colonialism and hence inseparably tied to discourses on civilization, progress and development which still remain at large in several state-led narratives on sex work governance. Colonial biopower manifested itself in health securitization strategies, such as efforts to regulate venereal diseases and prevent 'immorality' (Bhandari

2010). Very much in sync with Christian ethos on purity and redemption and the global racialized discourses on white slave traffic of the times, colonial era laws in India such as the Contagious Diseases Acts (1864, 1869) and Cantonment Acts pitted sex workers into the colonial 'biomedical gaze', mandating medical examination and forbidding miscegenation. This language of morality is still visible in India's core legislation on human trafficking, the Immoral Traffic Prevention Act (ITPA, 1956). A natural corollary of securitizing health is a spatial-moral segregation which implies that zones of precarity such as brothel-based commercial sex work are often viewed as a source of contamination/multitudinous health threats to the larger body politic on one hand while being subject to policy oversight in larger 'public' health agendas, all of which serve to exceptionalized sexually precarious labor.

The moral panic surrounding sex work further contributes to health securitization. For instance, during a conversation with an NGO official from Sanlaap, she stated:

> Don't mind her silence. She is not in the right frame of mind. We also suspect she has been taking drugs and wants to push her children into prostitution too. (Interviewee 5, December 12, 2016)

This observation was made about Bina (name changed), a female sex worker associated with Sanlaap, who refused to verbally answer the questions on my questionnaire. The official complained how 'she is non-communicative and doesn't let us help her daughters', attributing irresponsible parenting to drug abuse and mental health issues which she perceived to be rampant among sex workers. She extensively spoke about how Bina had endangered her daughters' lives by refusing 'rescue' and help from Sanlaap, which she explained as aberrant behavior most likely to result from engaging in commercial sex work.

In contemporary India, exceptionalization through health securitization is further evidenced through structural-spatial segregation of commercial sex work and sex work's unique positionality in relation to other forms of informal labor. Brothels as sites of commercial sex work are spatially segregated in India's major cities. I witnessed this while conducting research in Kolkata, whereby several sex workers and nonprofit workers expressed their reservations about me as a researcher, setting foot into Sonagachi, Asia's largest brothel. My interviewees were specifically brought into NGO offices so that I may interview them 'safely'. Health securitization was also palpable in the way NGO offices were structurally arranged. There I recall noticing HIV/AIDS and protection awareness flyers on the office walls and boxes of contraception which lay scattered around the office space.

In interviews conducted with several NGOs in Kolkata, NGO officials and sex workers often highlight why precarity facing sex works was different from other informal labor practices, primarily in terms of health insecurity.

> Common problem (of informal labor) is exploitation and non-standardized income. However, in the case of prostitution, there are rigorous health hazards involved which are unique to this profession. (Official 7, Apne Aap, 2016)

> Women (sex workers) have to accept these threats in the trade…no overlapping threats with other professions. All throughout the world, prostitutes face unique challenges in this profession. It is rampant with threats to everyday living. It is psychologically hard for these women to accept their fate and hence alcohol and drug dependence is induced. Entire lifestyle changes and they are stuck until death. (Official 8, Apne Aap, 2016)

Securitizing health of sex workers thus emerges from the structural-spatial organizing of brothels, sex workers and governance actors as well as discursive organizing in terms of its relation to the informal sector as a whole. These stories clearly reflect the material and immaterial dynamics underlying sex work exceptionalization, even within the ontological category of 'informal-precarious labor'.

The Case of HIV/AIDs Securitization: Contamination based Conflictual Politics

Sex workers frequently counter severe health issues. My interviews bear testimony to the fact that health-related grievances and concerns are quite predominant in India's governance of sex work be it physical such as HIV/AIDS, STDs or psychological such as depression, anxiety and substance dependence/abuse, often leading to death. During my time at the field, I observed that several sex workers were often visibly agitated and admitted feeling helplessness, hopelessness and anxiety, especially for their children. For instance, Sakina (name changed), a 40-something old female sex worker I interviewed through Sanlaap, stated:

> My identity as a mother is most important. I am doing this (sex work) to just provide for my child. (Sakina, Sanlaap, 2016)

Yet, significant difference in narratives emerges from different actors when it comes to sex work governance and health security in India. Here, HIV/AIDS securitization becomes a ground for conflictual politics between two predominant and quite ideologically polarized approaches to sex work governance in India: anti-trafficking and sex-as-work. Organizations premised on an anti-trafficking policy stand (including non-profits and government departments) articulates intersectional concerns about sex work and public health, while sex worker activism appears to be discursively and institutionally informed and constituted by HIV/AIDS securitization in India post-1990s. More importantly, contamination politics underlies both these approaches, with albeit contrary political objectives. For the former, this politics of contamination feeds the state's 'moral panic' about sexually precarious labor and drives the justification for mainstreaming, while for the latter, it is used to consolidate collective identity based on this sexual precarity and push back against the policing and mainstreaming. For both, contamination politics goes on to frame ideas and debates about sexually precarious labor.

Legislative and policy regulations and recommendations surrounding sexual commerce elucidate a major concern for ensuring collective health. Anti-trafficking NGOs similarly work toward community health but HIV/AIDS securitization is not a formative factor but rather a byproduct of such articulations. Anti-trafficking and slavery narratives highlight the overall patrimonial concern about mental and public health repercussions to prevent 'immorality' and preserve moral health by rescuing sex workers and reintegrating them into the folds of the larger body politic. HIV/AIDS then, for these actors, must be read in context of other social pathological problems that sexual commerce raises for a society at large.

My field research on sex work governance in India elucidates how the Indian state and anti-trafficking NGOs securitize commercial sex work by emphasizing health insecurities of trafficked victims. The institutional overlap between health and various forms of gender violence is palpable in the scope/jurisdiction of the State Department of Women and Child

Development and Social Welfare, which is the ministry in-charge of anti-trafficking regulations. A high-ranking bureaucrat in the department in the state of West Bengal outlined this in the scope of her functions:

> I am in-charge of helping the minister. We look at women and child development, the various aspects of development. We don't look at health or education per se, but consider those in context of development. We concern ourselves with: i. Children in pre-school stages, child nutrition; ii. Protecting children in all situations (violence, abuse, trafficking). For women or girl children, the nutritional aspect of pregnant, lactating mothers...Pregnant mother's nutrition, along with healthcare on the ground. The whole ministry looks at violence against women (pre-birth/post birth, sexual abuse, domestic violence and anti-dowry), whole subject of women's empowerment. (Interviewee 4)

While the ministry clearly states that health per se is not a concern, it is quite clear that healthcare, especially in the context of any kind of gender-based violence is a key on the department agenda. What is noteworthy here is the intersectional understanding of women's health itself. Moving from a narrative that focuses primarily on physical health of women engaged in sexual commerce, India's policies are also cognizant of mental health ramifications of sex work. For instance, the Anti Trafficking Bill which came to be formulated in 2018 recommends the set-up of 'Protective Homes' at the Centre and states, to ensure, among others, medical services and counselling of victims.

On one hand, governance mechanisms in India seek to engage with the issue of ensuring holistic healthcare for (rescued) trafficked victims to eliminate such health threats to the larger national community, while on the other hand, state recognition of sex-as-work in policy discourses and legal texts is selectively limited to epidemic narratives around the prevention of HIV/AIDS among sex workers. Trafficked victims are constructed in opposition to 'sex worker' subjects and are discursively recognized and discussed predominantly in context of HIV/AIDS. This conditional visibility of sex workers deepens the gender binary underlying the logic of health securitization: that unconsenting trafficked victims must be rescued from an unhealthy and immoral space and agentic sex workers pose a threat to the body politic as a source of contamination. Thus, while anti-trafficking dialogues are multi-faceted and health care is a key dimension of ensuring protection to trafficked victims, any state-centric, global and national discourse on sexually precarious labor seems to gain visibility only by virtue of its significance for global public health concerns such as HIV/AIDS.

The UNODC governs only upon the anti-trafficking and transnational crime dimension of sexual commerce. Any other UN discourse recognizing 'sex workers' as a subject group primarily emerges from UNAIDS, which as the name suggests, has a predominantly epidemic centric agenda, whereby sex workers are identified as one of five 'key populations'. The UNAIDS website states:

> UNAIDS considers gay men and other men who have sex with men, sex workers, transgender people, people who inject drugs and prisoners and other incarcerated people as the five main key population groups that are particularly vulnerable to HIV and frequently lack adequate access to services. (UNAIDS 2014)

This identification of a health threat goes hand-in-hand with the narrative on vulnerability and pandemics. In identifying sex workers as one of the key populations when it comes to pandemics, governance discourses contribute to further securitization of sexual commerce as a whole. For instance, the UNAIDS states:

> Vulnerability to HIV as a result of sex work extends to women, men, and transgender people. Although the links between sex work and HIV vulnerability have been recognized since the earliest days of the epidemic, surveys indicate that sex workers have inadequate access to HIV prevention services, and it is believed that their access is even more limited for appropriate treatment, care and support. To date, the HIV response has devoted insufficient attention and resources to efforts to address HIV and sex work, with less than 1% of global funding for HIV prevention being spent on HIV and sex work4.The epidemiological data on HIV infection rates among sex workers and their clients rejects the failure to adequately respond to their human rights and public health needs. Recent studies continue to confirm that in many countries sex workers experience higher rates of HIV infection than in most other population groups. (UNAIDS 2014)

Similar concerns are echoed in a SAARC charter on HIV/AIDS. The SAARC Conventions against Trafficking (2002) on the other hand carry no mention of sex workers and equate prostitution with trafficking.

> There are significant variations in HIV epidemics between and within countries. The epidemic are concentrated in certain geographical pockets and among key population at higher risk, which include people who inject drugs, female and male sex workers and their clients, men who have sex with men and transgender people. Other vulnerable populations include migrants, prisoners, intimate partners of key populations at higher risk and people working in certain industries such as mining, construction, and transport services. (SAARC TB & HIV/AIDS Center 2017)

Securitizing sex work through HIV/AIDS contamination politics deepens precarity for sex workers. According to sex workers' organizations, many sex workers are apprehensive about accessing HIV/AIDS healthcare for fear of being branded as 'prostitutes,' especially since 13 states in India criminalize people with HIV arrested for prostitution-related charges. Sex workers also worry about alerting police who might report seeing them at healthcare clinics. These barriers inhibit their willingness to attend such clinics (Saunder et al. 2015).

While HIV/AIDS prevention and anti-trafficking programs in India often overlap, they are oftentimes at odds with each other. HIV securitization in India has also been formative in constituting and consolidating the sex workers activism movement, post-1990s, which has been historically and ideologically opposed to the anti-trafficking movement. The HIV epidemic, increased migration and HIV response have helped transform Indian sex workers from an invisible and largely insignificant group to a target of health, welfare and surveillance programs (Magar 2012). As a formative strategy, HIV/AIDS securitization has enthused sex work activists to resist and push back against the contamination politics narrative which exceptionalizes commercial sex work as a space and to reappropriate health concerns of sex workers in order to solidify sex worker subjects as a global ontological category.

My study engages with two sex workers organizations. One is Kolkata's Durbar Mahila Samanwaya Committee and the other is Sangli's VAMP/Sangram. Both these organizations are members of the All India Network of Sex Workers, are at the forefront of the sex workers movement in India demanding decriminalization of sex work and were formed in early 1990s in relation to HIV/AIDS intervention programs.

Durbar traces its origins to a 1992 vertical HIV prevention program implemented by the All India Institute of Hygiene and Public Health. Attempting to develop a 'peer based approach' to provision of health servies, dissemmentation of information and communication and condom usage, it aimed to recruit sex workers in Kolkata's Sonagachi area to spread awareness. Durbar came into being in 1995 following structural barriers that hindered the process, such as police violence, discrimination to access basic services and violence. Dr. Samarjit Jana was a founding member of the organization and till date functions as the chief advisor of the organization. In 1999, DMSC took over the implementation of HIV prevention programs to form the 'Sonagachi Project'. Similarly, VAMP/Sangram traces its roots to the global HIV/AIDS discourse. In an informational pamphlet, the VAMP/Sangram team writes:

> Ironically, it is the HIV/AIDS discourse, the location of sex workers within it, and the impact of the epidemic itself that played a catalytic role in the formation of the SANGRAM/VAMP sex workers movement. As it has evolved, the AIDS discourse in India professed that women in prostitution are at greater risk to HIV infection than other categories of women. But despite this seemingly rational view, the neglect of sex workers by HIV prevention programs—especially in the early stages of the epidemic in India—demonstrated that women in sex work were actually considered dispensable. (VAMP/Sangram 2011, 3–4)

In 1992, a NGO called Sampada Grameen Mahila Sanstha (SANGRAM) under the leadership of Meena Seshu took up the initiative to speak to women sex workers about HIV and condom use in a small town called Sangli (Maharashtra). In light of brutal violence faced by sex workers in the area on a daily basis, Sangram decided to organize a community-based organization of sex workers called the Veshya Aids Muqabla Parishad/VAMP ("struggle against AIDS") which came into being in 1996, which later changed its name to Veshya Anyay Mukti Parishad ("freedom from injustice"). This transition from 'AIDS Muqabla' (struggle against AIDS) to 'Anyay Mukti' (freedom from injustice) was 'an important marker for a collective journey that began as a struggle against AIDS but has now broadened to a movement that seeks liberation from oppression and injustice', thus clearly reflecting the formative impact of HIV/AIDS securitization in forging sex workers identities (Sangram/VAMP 2011, 5).

HIV AIDS securitizations is not reflected in organizational activism alone. Patterns of global resource allocation might be helpful to elucidate how sex workers' mobilization is closely linked to the contamination politics underlying health securitization. A study on global donors to Sex Workers Health and Rights Organizations indicates that 'there has been a significant increase in the number of NGOs supporting sex workers in most regions', due to funding derived for the purpose of leading global donors. The study conducted by Open Society Institute shows how "donors involved in HIV/AIDS prevention provide most of the funding for organizations that serve sex workers, whether or not these organizations are run by sex workers themselves. Such donors include large multilateral agencies, national and local bodies, bilateral aid agencies, private and public foundations, and, depending on the country, business and corporate donors" (Dorf 2006, 6). Bilateral aid organizations such as DFID, NORAD and ODA were the early funders for DMSC's Sonagachi Model of peer education and HIV/AIDS prevention. Today, DMSC runs 45 health clinics for brothels, street-based sex workers and their partners, 28 literacy centers, and many other services. Moreover, the Ford Foundation had the largest grants for both sex worker organizations and allied NGOs in Asia, Africa, and in the United States. Julie Dorf writes 'the Ford Foundation's directed funding in India to numerous organizations for advocacy work and for building networks of sex worker organizations is particularly noteworthy because no other donor surveyed gave grants as large over as long a time period for such work. The average Ford Foundation grant to SWHROs was over $100,000' (Dorf 2006). Moreover, the Bill and Melinda Gates Foundation in 2009 committed $338 million to India through the Avahan AIDS Initiative.

The case of HIV/AIDS securitization clearly elucidates how sex work precarity is exceptionalized through the politics of contamination. Anti-trafficking actors have often overlooked the structural barriers to ensuring health and welfare of sex workers that stems from deep-rooted stigma and discrimination against sexually precarious labor. Sex work activism, though quite contrary to anti-trafficking discourses, has been fueled and formed by the same politics of contamination. Thus, health securitization and contamination politics is instrumental in not just deepening precarity for sex workers, but also emerges as the space where (often opposing) conversations about precarious gendered subjects, neoliberal capital and agency takeplace. Irrespective of the ideological point of view, the sex workers' bodies become the site of neoliberal power contestations, resource allocation and securitizing strategies.

Invisibility: The Other Side of the Contamination Coin

While the case of sex work governance in India reflects the spatial and moral segregation resulting from metaphors of contamination, this is far from being the only approach. The most recent global COVID-19 pandemic exposes how sexually precarious labor has been rendered invisible in pandemic securitization. This kind of invisibility for sex workers is limited not just to COVID-19 but even in several instances, the securitization of HIV/AIDS. For example, in the US, sex workers themselves have been left out of the conversations, despite being recognized as one of the top key populations to be vulnerable to HIV/AIDS. And yet this absence hardly challenges the securitization narrative. By rephrasing sex workers as 'men who have sex with men', 'persons who inject drugs' and 'heterosexually active persons at increased risk of HIV', the American state securitizes the space of commercial sex work without granting visibility to sex work as a viable ontological category.

In April 2020, the UNAIDS called on countries to ensure respect and protection for sex workers' human rights (UNAIDS 2020), given how "every sex worker is struggling right now", scrambling to gain access to safety nets (Breslin 2020, para. 5). The International Committee on Rights of Sex Workers in Europe (ICRSE), a network of more than 100 sex workers organizations in Europe published a report on April 23, 2020 asking European governments to issue moratorium on raids, arrests and prosecutions as well as financial support and emergency assistance for sex workers across Europe during these exceptional times. The report further states how sex workers are rarely benefitting from pandemic response and recovery plans (ICRSE 2020). Precarity driven by invisibility has two major ramifications: one, it has a direct bearing on welfare and survival of sex workers themselves and second, it carries the possibility of hindering the effective implementation of pandemic regulation efforts. Invisibility politics underlying pandemic securitization deepens precarity of sex workers as well as the national body politic as a whole, as the fear of criminalization and discrimination incentivizes silence and suppressive, discreet behavior which might limit pandemic testing and disease control in important ways.

In India, the invisibility of precarious labor is quite palpable in the pandemic governance initiatives. India imposed one of the world's harshest lockdown strategies on March 15th amidst the global COVID pandemic. While media reports and government statements consistently wrote of horror stories of survival which India's poor, especially the domestic migrant worker population in urban cities, were countering, commercial sex workers were left out of COVID-19 relief measures from the government and in several media reports. On April 29, 2020 Chakraborty and Ramamprasad reported in *The Guardian*:

> Exclusion from government Covid-19 relief has left many reliant on private food donations, as fears raised over protection from transmission after lockdown... As non-essential economic activity has ground to a halt, the lockdown has hit millions of people working in the informal sector. The government has announced relief schemes for the poor, but women working in the sex industry are outside their ambit. In India sex work is not illegal, but several supporting activities are; maintaining brothels and soliciting customers are criminal offences... As part of the government's relief scheme for the poor, India's prime minister Narendra Modi has announced a financial package that will deposit 500 rupees (£5.30) monthly into the bank accounts of 200 million people. But those working in or trafficked into the sex industry – many of whom lack government-approved documentation to access public distribution systems and relief schemes – are not included. (Chakraborty and Ramaprasad 2020)

Feminist activists with a long record on working with sex workers in India opined similar apprehensions. For instance, the report quoted Ruchira Gupta, founder of Apne Aap Worldwide:

> They have no food, they are starving. They live in tiny, windowless rooms with no fresh air. Many don't have access to running water; sometimes, the choice is between paying water bills or topping up phones. (ibid., para. 9)

Urmi Basu, the founder of anti-trafficking NGO New Light in Kolkata identifies stigma as a key reason for this invisibility:

> Sex workers don't feature anywhere as a marginalized group. The government doesn't want to accept that there's prostitution in the country. It's the elephant in the room. (ibid., para. 17)

Several non-profit organizations have been left to pick up the mantle to provide for sex workers at this difficult time. With complete silence on this issue from national and state governments, the spokesperson of

All India Network of Sex Workers stated that this lack of a specific relief policy for sex workers meant that several sex workers, especially those based out of urban spaces, have to return back to their villages to survive. He says, "many of them have nothing to eat...The government has made some arrangements for migrant laborers, but nothing has been done [exclusively] to help sex workers" (Ghosh 2020, para. 10).

As COVID-19 related precarity hits similarly marginalized groups (undocumented migrants, people of color, LGBTQ people, etc.), policy experts foresee many others will turn to sex work to survive and just like the post-2008 recession, the economic impact of COVID-19 would 'increase the number of women and LGBTIQ people selling sexual services to compensate for income loss and reimburse debts accrued during the crisis.' Experts also foresee that similar to aftermath of the 2004 tsunami in Southern Asia and 2014 earthquake in Nepal, the pandemic will be followed by a surge in child trafficking. A report from Global fund for Children (GCF) states:

> After the coronavirus is under control, people will be jobless or underemployed, leaving them vulnerable to fake promises of better future. Families are lured by the offer of better paid work for their children in places that may be completely unknown to them. Traffickers will use this opportunity to offer some advance payment to parents or other family members. The disruption in the state and civil society institutions and child protection mechanisms put children at high risk and in a very vulnerable situation. Girls living in the red-light districts are especially at risk, as their mothers may sell them off to get out of debt. (GCF 2020)

Sex workers in India are challenging this discursive invisibility, especially rendered through a western gaze. A recent study by Yale and Harvard Medical school recommended keeping the red-light areas in 5 cities (New Delhi, Kolkata, Mumbai, Nagpur and Pune) shut to delay COVID-19 spread. This invited a vehement pushback from sex workers' collectives, activists, lawyers and decision makers 'for making scapegoats of sex workers and blaming them for the spread of COVID-19'. In a letter, they wrote:

> We strongly denounce this study for its lack of rigorous methodology and transparency, misleading assumptions about sex work, and egregious disregard for the rights of the urban poor in India. The recommendations of this study essentially invite the state to use its coercive powers – police

raids and evictions – to victimise the most marginalized of slum dwellers in the name of public health. (NWSP 2020)

Sex work activists have also highlighted that pandemic governance as a whole would rarely be effective if legally precarious subjects such as sex workers are left out of regulations. This is led to a concerted effort toward inclusion of marginalized communities in public health agenda. The absence of precarious bodies in health discourses, coupled with criminalization rarely eliminates precarity. Rather, criminalization of sex work would only encourage silence and suppression of information, as marginalized peoples often use silence as a strategy for survival (Chatterjee and Parpart 2018) and lead marginalized communities to negotiate their precarity in unique ways to ensure survival and during pandemic times, this may very possibly deepen precarity for the entire body politic. Like the ICRSE report reminds us, "instead of addressing sex work through an ideological and punitive lens... states must implement evidence and rights based policies" and that ignoring marginalized communities could prove to be detrimental to pandemic regulative efforts as a whole (ICRSE 2020).

Concluding Thoughts

If the contemporary neoliberal global economy is sustained by the exceptionalization of labor precarity, sexually precarious labor lies at the heart of this phenomenon. While precarity of 'care economies' and reproductive labor has now emerged as a robust field of feminist theorizing, it is important to take note of sexual precarity in postcolonial states, which lie at the periphery of global gendered labor networks and yet play a pivotal role in sustaining and functioning of these neoliberal hierarchies. Theorization of reproductive labor precarity must nuance that ontological category itself to understand and adequately address legal, pathological and moral exceptionalization that underlies the securitization of sex.

The case of Indian sexual commerce industry does just that. Academics and policy experts have long warned against the dangers of health securitization policies, especially in the Global South. Governance crises in India during the recent pandemic have exposed how health securitization renders some populations more vulnerable than others. It also motivates us to think about how sex workers precarity is continuously fueled by contamination and invisibility politics, such that on one hand, securitizing sexually precarious bodies lies at the roots of ensuring the survival of the national body politic which is the object of the Westphalian state, and on the other, access to health security is restricted to that very national body politic at the cost of systematic invisibility for others.

The contemporary Indian laws and policies that regulate sexual commerce, securitize and exceptionalize sexually precarious labor through the contamination-invisibility nexus. As the case of HIV/AIDS securitization elucidates, sexually precarious labor has been systematically identified as a site of contamination for the (post)colonial body politic, irrespective of the ideological position one occupies on the sex-is-work and sex-work-is-slavery spectrum.

Additionally, they have also been subject to systemic oversight on matters deemed to be of 'national' or 'global' importance, such as the COVID-19 pandemic. Deepened precarity has stemmed from and further perpetuated criminalization of sex workers, lack of access to emergency as well as non-emergency health services, invasive technologies of governance over sex workers' bodies and the broader subset of violations and discriminations quite unique to this space. This dual modality of excpetionalizing sexually precarious labor in India is mutually constitutive and elucidates how it is integrated within the colonial-global regime complex to regulate sex and sexuality in postcolonial sites.

Bibliography

Agamben, Giorgio. 1998. *Homo Sacer: Sovereign Power and Bare Life*. Stanford University Press.

Agathangelou, Anna. 2004. *The Global Political Economy of Sex: Desire, Violence and Insecurity in Mediterrenean Nation States*. Palgrave: New York.

Agathangelou, Anna. 2018. "What Suicide and Greece Tell Us About Precarity and Capitalism." *Globalizations* 16 (4): 541–558.

Aglietta, Michel.1979. *A Theory of Capitalist Regulation*. New Left Books: London.

Alchian, A. A., and H. Demsetz. 1972. "Production, Information Costs, and Economic Organization". *American Economic Review* 62 (5): 777–795.

Barchiesi, Franco. 2012. "Liberation of, Through, or from Work? Postcolonial Africa and the Problem with 'Job Creation' in the Global Crisis." *Interface* 4 (2): 230–253.

Bernstein, Elizabeth. 2008. "Sexual Commerce and the Global Flow of Bodies, Desires, and Social Policies." *Sexuality Research and Social Policy* 5 (1), 1–5.

Betti, Eloisa. n.d. "Precarious Work: Norm or Exception of Capitalism? Historicizing a Contemporary Debate: A Global Gendered Perspective." www.iwm.net. https://www.iwm.at/publications/5-junior-visiting-fellows-conferences/vol-xxxv/precarious-work/#_edn3

Bhandari, Sudhanshu. 2010. "Prostitution in Colonial India." Accessed 2017. https://www.mainstreamweekly.net/article2142.html.

Bosch, G. (1986). "Hat das Normalarbeitsverhältnis eine Zukunft?." *WSI-Mitteilungen* 39: 163–176.

Breman, Jan, and Marcel Van der Linden. 2014. "Informalizing the Economy: The Return of the Social Question at a Global Level." *Developement and Change*.

Breslin,Susannah. 2020. "A Sex Worker Reveals How The COVID-19 Pandemic Has Changed Sex Work." Forbes. Accessed July 2020. https://www.forbes.com/sites/susannahbreslin/2020/05/14/a-sex-worker-reveals-how-covid-19-has-changed-sex-work/#2dc5607f3a81.

Butler, Judith. (2004) *Precarious Lives: The Power of Mourning and Violence*. New York: Verso.

Carnoy, M., Castells, M., and Benner, C. (1997). "Labour Markets and Employment Practices in the Age of Flexibility: a Case Study of Silicon Valley." *International Labour Review* 136: 27–48.

Castells, M. (1996). *The Rise of the Network Society*. Oxford: Blackwell.

Chatterjee, Sudeshna, and Jane Parpart. 2018. "Silence as strategy in the sexual commerce industry: A case study from India." In edited by Jane Parpart, and Swati Parashar, *Silence, Gender and Power in Insecure Sites: Rethinking Feminist Security Studies and Global Political Economy*. New York: Routledge.

Chakraborty, Reshmi, and Hema Ramaprasad. 2020. "They are starving': women in India's sex industry struggle for survival." April 29. Accessed June 10, 2020. https://www.theguardian.com/global-development/2020/apr/29/they-are-starving-women-in-indias-sex-industry-struggle-for-survival.

Clarke, L. (1991). "The significance of wage forms: the example of the British construc tion industry." In *Paper given at the 13th Annual Conference of the International Working Party on Segmentation Theory*, Bremen.

Das, V., and S. Randeria. 2015. "Politics of the Urban Poor: Aesthetics, Ethics, Volatility, Precarity." *Current Anthropology* 56 (11): 3–14.

Dingli, Sophia, and Navtej Purewal. 2018. "Gendering (in)security: Interrogating Security Logics Within States of Exception." *Third World Thematics: A TWQ Journal* 3 (12): 153–163.

Doeringer P. B., and M. J. Piore. 1971. *Internal Labor Markets and Manpower Analysis*. Boston: Heath and company.

Dorf, Julie. 2006. "Sex Worker Health and Rights: Where is the Funding?" Accessed June 2, 2020. www.opensocietyfoundations.org.

Dutta, Mohan. 2015. *Neoliberal Health Organizing: Communication, Meaning, and Politics*. New York: Routledge.

Federici, Silvia, 1975. *Wages Against Housework*. London: Power of Women Collective.

Federici, Silvia. 2006. "Precarious Labor: A Feminist Viewpoint." Precarious Labor: A Feminist Viewpoint. NYC: Convention Protests, Movement and Movements, October 28th.

Forbes, Anna. 2015. "Speaking of Sex Workers: How Suppression of Research has Distorted the United States' Domestic HIV Response." *Reproductive Health Matters* 23 (45): 21–29.

Foucault, Michel. 1978. *The History of Sexuality: An Introduction*. New York: Pantheon Books.

Fudge, J. 1997. *Precarious Work and Families*. Working Paper, Toronto: Centre for Research on Work and Society, York University.

Ghosh, Syamantak. 2020. "COVID-19: Sex Workers Suffer During Social Distancing in India." April 4. Accessed June 10, 2020. https://www.dw.com/en/covid-19-sex-workers-suffer-duringsocial-distancingin-india/a-53106907.

Global Fund for Children. 2020. *Lives on the line: COVID-19 in India's red-light districts*. Accessed August 2020. https://globalfundforchildren.org/story/lives-on-the-line-covid-19-in-indias-red-light-districts/.

Hanrieder, Tine, and Christian Kreuder-Sonnen. 2014. "WHO Decides on the Exception? Securitization and Emergency Governance in Global Health." *Security Dialogue* 45 (4): 331–348.

Hardt, Michael, and Antonio Negri. 2000. *Empire*. Cambridge: Harvard University Press.

Harvey, M. (1999). "Economies of Time: A Framework for Analysing the Restructuring of Employment Relations." In *Global Trends in Flexible Labour*, edited by A. Felstead and N. Jewson, London: Macmillan, pp. 21–42.

International Committee on the Rights of Sex Workers in Europe. 2020. 100 Ngos Endorse A Statement Calling For Emergency Support To Sex Workers Amid The Covid-19 Crisis. April 23.

Jackson, Nicole J. 2006. "International Organizations, Security Dichotomies and the Trafficking of Persons and Narcotics in Post-Soviet Central Asia: A Critique of the Securitization Framework." *Security Dialogue* 37 (3): 299–317. https://doi.org/10.1177/0967010606069062.

Komlosy, Andrea. 2018. *Work: The Last 1,000 Years*. London: Verso.

Lambert, Rod, and Andrew Herod. 2016. *Neoliberal Capitalism and Precarious Work Ethnographies of Accommodation and Resistance*. Cheltenham: Edwar Elgar Publishing Limited.

Lorey, Isabelle. 2015. *States of Insecurity: Government of the Precarious*. London: Verso.

Lucchini, Lucia. 2017. "What is the role of precarity in security." July 17. Accessed May 1, 2020. https://www.e-ir.info/2017/07/17/what-is-the-role-of-precarity-in-security/.

Magar, Veronica. 2012. "Rescue and Rehabilitation: A Critical Analysis of Sex Workers' Antitrafficking Response in India." *Signs* 37 (3): 619–644.

Malos, Ellen (ed.). 1975. *The Politics of Housework*. New York: The New Clarion Press.

Maschke, Karen J. 1997. *Pornography, Sex Work, and Hate Speech*. New York: Garland Publishing, Inc.

Massey, Alana. 2014. "Keeping Sex Workers Quiet." *Jacobin Magazine* February 11 [Online]. www.jacobinmag.com/2014/11/keeping-workers-quiet/.

McNeily, Kathryn. 2016. "Livability: Notes on the Thought of Judith Butler." May 26. Accessed May 1, 2020. https://criticallegalthinking.com/2016/05/26/livability-judith-butler/.

McRobbie, Angela. 2011. "Reflections On Feminism, Immaterial Labour And The Post-Fordist Regime." January. Accessed May 1, 2020. https://www.researchgate.net/publication/233606500_Reflections_On_Feminism_Immaterial_Labour_And_The_Post-Fordist_Regime.

Mgbako, Chi. 2012. "Why the Women's Rights Movement Must Listen to Sex Workers." *Rewire News* May 22 [Online]. http://rhrealitycheck.org/article/2012/05/22/why-women%E2%80%99s-rights-movement-must-listen-to-sex-workers/.

Millar, Kathleen M. 2017. "Toward a Critical Politics of Precarity." *Sociology Compass* 11 (6): e12483. https://doi.org/10.1111/soc4.12483.

Neilson, B., and N Rossiter. 2008. "Precarity as a Political Concept, or, Fordism as Exception." Theory, *Culture and Society* 25 (7–8): 51–72.

NWSP. 2020. Yale-Harvard Study Scapegoats Sex Workers for COVID-19 Spread. Accessed August 2020. https://www.nswp.org/news/yale-harvard-study-scapegoats-sex-workers-covid-19-spread.

Roberts, Hannah. 2019a. "The dangers of securitizing health." December 4. Accessed May 1, 2020. https://www.e-ir.info/2019/12/04/the-dangers-of-securitizing-health/.

Roberts, Hannah. 2019b. "The dangers of securtitizing health." December 4. Accessed June 10, 2020. https://www.e-ir.info/2019/12/04/the-dangers-of-securitizing-health/.

Rodgers, G. 1989. "Precarious Work in Western Europe." In *Precarious Jobs in Labour Market Regulation: The Growth of Atypical Employment in Western Europe*, edited by G. Rodgers and J. Rodgers, Belgium: International Institute for Labour Studies, pp. 1–16.

SAARC TB & HIV/AIDS Center. 2017. "SAARC Regional Strategy on HIV/AIDS." Accessed 2020. http://www.saarctb.org/new/wp-content/uploads/2015/04/SAARC-Regional-Strategy-for-HIV-and-AIDS.pdf.

Sahni, Rohini, and V Kalyan Shankar. 2013. *Sex Work and its Linkages with Informal Labour Markets in India: Findings from the First Pan-India Survey of Female Sex Workers*. Working paper, Brighton: Institute of Development Studies.

Sangram/VAMP. 2011. "The VAMP/SANGRAM Sex Worker's Movement in India's Southwest." Accessed June 2, 2020. https://www.awid.org/sites/default/files/atoms/files/changing_their_world_2_-_vamp_-sex_workers_movement_in_indias_southwest.pdf.

Saunder, Penelope, Cristine Sardina, Katherine M. Koster, and Derek Demeri. 2015. "Silence is Still Death for Sex Workers: The National HIV/AIDS Strategy Implementation Plan." *Best Practices Policy*, December 2nd [Online]. www.bestpracticespolicy.org/2015/12/02/silence-is-still-death-for-sex-workers-the-nhas-implementation-plan/.

Schotten, Heike. 2005. "Men, Masculinity and Male Domination: Reframing Feminist Analyses of Sex Work." *Politics and Gender* 1 (2): 211–240.

Shani, Giorgio. 2020a. "Securitizing 'Bare Life'? Human Security and Coronavirus." April 3. Accessed April 6, 2020. https://www.e-ir.info/2020/04/03/securitizing-bare-life-human-security-and-coronavirus/.

Shani, Girogio. 2020b. "Securitizing 'Bare Life'? Human Security and Coronavirus." April 3. Accessed April 10, 2020. https://www.e-ir.info/2020/04/03/securitizing-bare-life-human-security-and-coronavirus/.

South Asian Association for Regional Cooperation (SAARC). 2002. "Convention on Preventing and Combating Trafficking in Women and Children for Prostitution."

UNAIDS. 2014. "Sex Workers." Accessed 2020. https://www.unaids.org/en/resources/documents/2014/Sexworkers.

UNAIDS. 2020. "Sex workers must not be Left Behind in the Response to COVID-19." Accessed July 2020. https://www.unaids.org/en/resources/presscentre/pressreleaseandstatementarchive/2020/april/20200408_sex-workers-covid-19.

United Nations Office on Drugs and Crime (UNODC). 2003. *United Nations Convention on Transnational Organized Crime and Protocols Thereto*. New York: United Nations.

Vogel, Lise. 1995. *Woman Questions: Essays for a Materialist Feminism*. New York: Routledge.

Vosko, Leah F. 1997. "Legitimizing the Triangular Employment Relationship: Emerging International Labour Standards from a Comparative Perspective." *Comparative Labour Law and Policy Journal* 19 (Fall): 43–77.

Weitzer, Ronald. 2000. *Sex For Sale: Prostitution, Pornography, and the Sex Industry*. New York: Routledge.

Yadav, Smita. 2018. *Precarious Labour and Informal Economy: Work, Anarchy, and Society in an Indian Village*. Palgrave Macmillan.

CHAPTER 8

Ready Made Garment (RMG) Factories During the Pandemic: Mapping the Effects in Bangladesh

Fahim S. Chowdhury, Afshana Choudhury, MD. Faizul Islam, and Sadril Shajahan

List of Abbreviations

BDT	Bangladesh Taka
BGMEA	Bangladesh Garment Manufacturers and Exporters Association
BKMEA	Bangladesh Knitwear Manufacturers and Exporters Association
BRPD	Banking Regulation and Policy Department
C&A	Clemens et August

F. S. Chowdhury (✉) · A. Choudhury · MD. F. Islam · S. Shajahan
Centre for Entrepreneurship Development (CED), Brac University, Dhaka, Bangladesh
e-mail: fahim.chowdhury@bracu.ac.bd

S. Hewamanne and S. Yadav (eds.), *The Political Economy of Post-COVID Life and Work in the Global South: Pandemic and Precarity*, International Political Economy Series,
https://doi.org/10.1007/978-3-030-93228-2_8

CED	Centre for Entrepreneurship Development
CPD	Centre for Policy Dialogue
DIFE	Department of Inspection for Factories and Establishments
EKN	Embassy of the Kingdom of the Netherlands
EPZ	Export Processing Zone
H&M	Hennes & Mauritz
ILO	International Labour Organization
LPP	Lubianiec, Piechocki and Partners
MFO	Microfinance Opportunities
MiB	Mapped in Bangladesh
MoLE	Ministry of Labour and Employment
NGO	Non-Government Organizations
NBR	National Board of Revenue
PPE	Personal Protective Equipment
PVH	Phillips Van Heusen
RMG	Ready Made Garments
SME	Small and Medium Enterprise
SANEM	South Asian Network on Economic Modeling
US	United States
VF	Vanity Fair

Introduction

The Covid-19 pandemic has not only emerged as a public health challenge worldwide but also has exacerbated the supply chain of the global apparel market. Bangladesh has been a major contributor to the global apparel market, and hence it was inevitable for the country to face a negative downturn as a result of Covid-19 Pandemic and the industry has been going through different phases since the finding of the first official case of Covid-19 patients in Bangladesh.

In an effort to explore all these phases including the operational status of the factories, the Mapped in Bangladesh (MiB) project of Centre for Entrepreneurship Development (CED) of Brac University has taken a phase-wise approach to initiate rapid surveys on export-oriented ready-made garment (RMG) factories of Bangladesh. MiB is a four-year-long project and is being funded by Laudes Foundation and the Embassy of the Kingdom of the Netherlands (EKN) with the strategic partnership of Bangladesh Garment Manufacturers and Exporters Association (BGMEA) and Bangladesh Knitwear Manufacturers and Exporters Association (BKMEA) and the Department of Inspection for Factories and Establishments (DIFE). MiB conducted the two phases of rapid surveys using its factory database generated through the countrywide factory census. Pursuing the objective of MiB to provide authentic factory information in a digital map (https://mappedinbangladesh.org) for enabling transparency in the RMG sector, it has also developed a Covid-19 RMG map (https://covid-19.mappedinbangladesh.org) where the data of these two rapid surveys were added to the factory profiles on the digital map.

The objective of the two rapid surveys was to explore the operational status of RMG factories during pandemic and digitally map the surveyed factories where the factory profiles have the collected information of rapid surveys in alignment with the previous information collected as part of original MiB project. As the two phases addressed two time periods of the RMG industry of Bangladesh during the pandemic, a pragmatic comparison between these two surveys can picture the recovering pattern of the industry from the crisis of Covid-19. From the perspective of the rigorousness of research, such comparison can also serve as a potential tool to propagate new research endeavours and additional study items that MiB can also leverage for the project itself and for the forthcoming rapid surveys.

Impact of Pandemic on the Garments Industry of Bangladesh

The first Covid-19 patient in Bangladesh was found on 8 March 2020[1] and the first death of Covid-19 infected patient was recorded on 18 March 2020.[2] Identification of infected patients and death as a result of the virus along with an increasing number of reported cases have led the Government of Bangladesh to the announcement of general holiday from

[1] "First Coronavirus Cases Detected in Bangladesh," The Business Standard, March 8, 2020, https://www.tbsnews.net/bangladesh/health/3-tested-positive-coronavirus-bangladesh-iedcr-53476.

[2] "Bangladesh Reports First Coronavirus Death," *United News of Bangladesh*, March 2018, 2020, https://unb.com.bd/category/Bangladesh/bangladesh-reports-first-coronavirus-death/47361.

26 March 2020[3] to keep the general public at home. Bangladesh Garment Manufacturers and Exporters Association (BGMEA) and Bangladesh Knitwear Manufacturers and Exporters Association (BKMEA) in a joint statement on 10 April 2020 announced that the RMG factories would remain closed until 25 April 2020.[4] The two apex trade bodies later decided to reopen the factories on 26 April 2020 to save the sector from the economic collapse.[5] Although the restrictive measures were officially in effect until 31 May 2020, apparel factories were allowed to start resuming their operations in phases and zones on a limited scale from 26 April 2020.[6]

Since then, Bangladesh apparel industry has gone through different incidents from March to June 2020 which were summarized from different media sources as follows for the sake of the literature to instigate the main emphasis of the data collection of rapid surveys.

Announcing and Receiving of Stimulus Package

On 25 March 2020, a financial stimulus package of BDT 50 billion was announced by the Honourable Prime Minister of Bangladesh—Sheikh Hasina—exclusively for the export-oriented industries to fight the impact of Covid-19.[7] The fund was formed to ensure that workers from the export-oriented sectors do not lose their jobs, and at the same time owners are at ease in paying three months of salaries to their workers

[3] "Lockdown Relaxed, Defeating Purpose of General Holiday," *Prothom Alo*, May 25, 2020, https://en.prothomalo.com/opinion/editorial/lockdown-relaxed-defeating-purpose-of-general-holiday.

[4] "RMG Factories to Remain Closed until April 25," *The Financial Express*, April 10, 2020, https://thefinancialexpress.com.bd/trade/rmg-factories-to-remain-closed-until-april-25-1586518829.

[5] Simon Glover, "Bangladesh to Reopen Garment Factories," *Ecotextile News*, April 16, 2020, https://www.ecotextile.com/2020041625965/materials-production-news/bangladesh-to-reopen-garment-factories.html.

[6] "Bangladesh Factories Begin to Reopen: Perspectives from a Factory," Better Work, Accessed August 12, 2020, https://betterwork.org/2020/04/28/through-the-eyes-of-a-factory-bangladesh-starts-to-reopen/.

[7] "Impact of Coronavirus: PM Announces Tk 5,000cr Stimulus Package for Export-oriented Industries," *The Daily Star*, March 25, 2020, https://www.thedailystar.net/coronavirus-deadly-new-threat/news/pm-announces-tk-5000cr-stimulus-package-export-oriented-industries-1885813.

from the loan they receive, which was set at just 2 percent service charge.[8] Bangladesh Bank issued a circular (BRPD Circular No. 07, dated 2 April 2020) where it was announced and stipulated that the package would act as an interest-free loan to the export-orientated employers for the sole objective of paying the wages and benefits of the workers for April, May and June 2020. According to the circular, the deadline for submitting loan applications to the respective banks was on 20 April 2020. Once the applications are received and accepted, the Bangladesh Bank would then approve and sanction the loans in three phases—that is disburse one-third of the total loan amount to the respective banks by the end of each month in question.[9] It was also decided that the eligibility criteria for receiving the fund would require the industries to export a minimum of 80 percent of their total production.[10] The central bank in the first phase released BDT 20 billion to the respective banks. During the same time, BGMEA certified about 1650 of their member factories to apply for the loan. The government later added BDT 30 billion more to another stimulus package of BDT 300 billion for industries and services sectors following requests from BGMEA and BKMEA.

The industries had to submit their loan applications to their respective banks by 2 May 2020 and the banks started to disburse the workers' wages from the government's stimulus package started from 3 May 2020.[11] The RMG factory owners got funds from the package to pay the workers for July 2020.[12]

[8] Abul Kashem & Jasim Uddin, "No Stimulus After Layoffs," *The Business Standard*, April 20, 2020, https://www.tbsnews.net/economy/industry/no-stimulus-after-layoffs-71794.

[9] Brac Institute of Governance and Development (BIGD), *Taka 5000 Crore Novel Corona Financial Stimulus Package for Export-Oriented Industries: RMG Trade Union Responses* (Dhaka: BIGD, June 18, 2020), https://bigd.bracu.ac.bd/wp-content/uploads/2020/06/Report_Trade-Union-Responses_Financial-Stimulus-Package.pdf.

[10] "RMG Workers Start Receiving Salaries from Stimulus Package," *The Financial Express*, May 8, 2020 https://thefinancialexpress.com.bd/trade/rmg-workers-start-receiving-salaries-from-stimulus-package-1588945130.

[11] AKM Zamir Uddin, "Garment Workers Salary Disbursement Stimulus Package Starts Today", *The Daily Star*, May 3, 2020, https://www.thedailystar.net/business/news/garment-workers-salary-disbursement-stimulus-package-starts-today-1898938.

[12] Abdur Rahim Harmachi, "Bangladesh Apparel Factory Owners Seek More Government Incentives to Pay Workers", *BD News,* August 27, 2020, https://bdnews24.com/business/2020/08/27/bangladesh-apparel-factory-owners-seek-more-government-incentives-to-pay-workers.

Additionally, the government of Bangladesh declared a BDT 20,000 crore package for Small and Medium Enterprises (SMEs), to primarily allow factories that do not directly export but supply their products to the export-oriented companies to avail the loan facility.[13]

Despite the government's support, an estimated 1090 industrial units, including more than 600 textile and RMG factories, according to industrial police and industry insiders failed to make payments to their workers before Eid.[14] A survey titled "Massive shift to Digital Wages Payments in Bangladesh's RMG Sector", conducted on 15 and 16 May 2020 by researchers working for the Dhaka-based South Asian Network on Economic Modeling (SANEM), and Microfinance Opportunities (MFO), a U.S.-based NGO[15] reported that 67 percent of workers in the RMG sector had reportedly been paid as of 16 May 2020. Quoting from a BGMEA personnel, Dhaka Tribune reported that 97.5 percent of factories paid salaries for April 2020 and 1449 factories paid a bonus, while as of 22 May 2020, 48 out of 1926 BGMEA member factories could not pay wages for April 2020 due to fund shortage.[16]

Different statistics have emerged from various sources regarding the number of factories that were actually able to pay their workers as well as pay bonus. Business Post[17] has compiled the numbers from the source of Industrial Police, and we have developed Table 8.1 based on their data:

In May 2020, several thousand workers of the ready-made garment factories in Dhaka city and other industrial zones across the country protested and staged demonstrations demanding full wages for the month

[13] Abul Kashem & Jasim Uddin, "No Stimulus After Layoffs", *The Business Standard*, April 20, 2020, https://www.tbsnews.net/economy/industry/no-stimulus-after-layoffs-71794.

[14] Monira Munni, "Workers of Nearly 1100 Industrial Units unlikely to Get Wages, Bonus", *The Financial Express*, May 18, 2020, https://thefinancialexpress.com.bd/national/workers-of-nearly-1100-industrial-units-unlikely-to-get-wages-bonus-158977484.

[15] "RMG Workforce Survey Reveals Seamless Shift to Digital Payments", *United News of Bangladesh*, May 22, 2020, https://unb.com.bd/category/Business/rmg-workforce-survey-reveals-seamless-shift-to-digital-payments/51980.

[16] Ibrahim Hossain Ovi, "48 RMG Ractories yet to Pay Salaries before Eid", *Dhaka Tribune*, May 23, 2020, https://www.dhakatribune.com/bangladesh/2020/05/23/48-rmg-factories-yet-to-pay-salaries-before-eid.

[17] Abdullah Kafi, "Frustration Grips RMG Workers as Factories Cut Jobs", *Business Post*, May 29, 2020 https://businesspostbd.com/post/1580#.XtEJNgsvlWV.twitter.

Table 8.1 Number of factories that paid salary and allowances, and Eid bonus (see Footnote 17)

Factory Membership	*Number of Factories*	*Factories paid April's Salary and Allowances*	*Factories Paid Eid Bonus*
BGMEA	1882	1721	1544
BKMEA	1101	1041	1016
BTMA	389	349	342
BEPZA	364	356	353
Non-member (factories that are not members of BGMEA, BKMEA, BTMA and BEPZA	3866	3089	(Data was not found)

Source The Business Post (see Footnote 17)

of April and arrears amid the risk of coronavirus infection.[18] As a result, a tripartite meeting was held between factory owners, government high-officials and trade union leaders with Home Minister, where it was decided that 50 percent of the workers' basic salary would be paid as Eid bonus before the festival and remaining 50 percent would be paid after the festival.[19]

However, stakeholders have remained sceptical regarding the eventual outcome of such packages. In an assessment report titled "Early Assessment of BDT 5000 Crore Incentive Package: Will the Target Groups Get the Benefits?", Centre for Policy Dialogue (CPD) made the observations that the government's stimulus package for export-oriented sectors

[18] "Unrest in RMG Sector Continues for Wages", *New Age*, May 13, 2020, https://www.newagebd.net/article/106309/unrest-in-rmg-sector-continues-for-wages.

[19] Refayet Ullah Mirdha, "Pay Half of Bonus Now, the Rest Later", *The Daily Star*, May 17, 2020, https://www.thedailystar.net/frontpage/news/pay-half-bonus-now-the-rest-later-1903318.

hardly benefitted the country's apparel workers, as there were irregularities in wage payment and retrenchment.[20] Their assessment[21] concluded the following:

- 63 percent of the respondent workers mentioned that they could not pay their house rents;
- 39 percent of the respondent workers mentioned they had unpaid utility bills;
- 36 percent of respondent workers mentioned they had unpaid school fees; and
- 85.5 percent of total interviewed workers reported that they received full payment for March 2020.

Only 14.8 percent of the respondents reported that they received full payment in April 2020, while about 27.3 percent received 50 percent or less of their gross wages.

On the other hand, many Trade Union leaders were not optimistic that the stimulus package would be adequate to cover the 4.1 million RMG workers' wages and benefits for three months. The minimum wage fixed by the government is BDT 8000, and multiplying this amount with the total number of workers of 4.1 million, the payable workers' wages for a month amounts to BDT 32.8 million, which for three months totals BDT 98.4 million. Thus, approximately 51 percent of the official target of three months wages is covered by the stimulus package.[22]

[20] "CPD: Govt's Stimulus Package Hardly Benefits RMG Workers", *RMG Bangladesh*, June 12, 2020, https://rmgbd.net/2020/06/cpd-govts-stimulus-package-hardly-benefits-rmg-workers/.

[21] "CPD: Govt's Stimulus Package Hardly Benefits RMG Workers", *Dhaka Tribune*, June 9, 2020, https://www.dhakatribune.com/business/economy/2020/06/09/cpd-govt-s-stimulus-package-hardly-benefits-rmg-workers.

[22] Brac Institute of Governance and Development (BIGD), *Taka 5000 Crore Novel Corona Financial Stimulus Package for Export-Oriented Industries: RMG Trade Union Responses* (Dhaka: BIGD, June 18, 2020), https://bigd.bracu.ac.bd/wp-content/uploads/2020/06/Report_Trade-Union-Responses_Financial-Stimulus-Package.pdf.

Closing and Reopening of Factories

As a preventive measure for reopening the factories, BGMEA published its own guidelines for opening the factories,[23] and the Ministry of Health and Family Welfare, Government of the People's Republic of Bangladesh provided hygiene and safety guidelines for garment factories.[24] Six teams were formed by BGMEA whose task was to ensure that the reopened factories followed physical distancing and other safety protocols. An important guideline by BGMEA was that factories that would reopen would do so with workers living nearby the factory; however, this rule was not maintained by several factory authorities where they allowed workers from other districts to come and join the factories.[25] The Covid-19 health guideline prepared by DIFE in association with International Labour Organization (ILO) state that workers with coronavirus symptoms be paid sick leave. The guideline also mentioned that paid sick leave, sickness benefits, and parental care leave should be adjusted and expanded by the employers and they should inform about such to all of their workers in line with the national standards.[26]

The two apex trade bodies—BGMEA and BKMEA reported that 419 ready-made garment factories did not reopen since 26 April after a month-long closure in addition to public holidays. Of these factories, 348 were BGMEA registered, while 71 were registered with BKMEA. As per BGMEA, out of the 348 factories, 268 factories were temporarily closed, while the remaining 80 factories were permanently closed.[27]

[23] *BGMEA Factory Opening Guideline*, Fair Wear, April 22, 2020, https://api.fairwear.org/wp-content/uploads/2020/05/BGMEA-Factory-opening-Guidelines.pdf.

[24] Ministry of Health and Family Welfare, *Directives of Maintaining Safety Measures and Hygiene in Industries* (Dhaka: Ministry of Health and Family Welfare, 2020), https://api.fairwear.org/wp-content/uploads/2020/05/Ministry-of-Health-and-Family-Welfare-Translated.pdf.

[25] "Most RMG Factories Fall Short of Reopening Criteria as Virus Lockdown Unwinds", *The Financial Express*, May 13, 2020, https://thefinancialexpress.com.bd/trade/most-rmg-factories-fall-short-of-reopening-criteria-as-virus-lockdown-unwinds-1589379753.

[26] "Covid-19 Guideline Suggests Workers with Symptoms Get Paid Sick Leave", *New Age*, June 10, 2020, https://www.newagebd.net/article/108096/covid-19-guideline-suggests-workers-with-symptoms-get-paid-sick-leave.

[27] "Many RMG Units Remain Shut for Lack of Work Orders", *The Financial Express*, May 21, 2020, https://thefinancialexpress.com.bd/economy/many-rmg-units-remain-shut-for-lack-of-work-orders-1590056382.

The Guardian on 11 May 2020 reported that the decision of reopening factories in April end was a result of pressure to revive the garment industry coupled with preventing orders from being diverted to Vietnam or Cambodian factories. This resulted in more than 1000 factories resuming their operations.[28] Even though factories were advised to restart their operations with 30 percent of their workforce and gradually increase the number of workers, country representative of Fair Wear reported that several factories reopened with 50 percent or more of its capacity. Additionally, they reported that a number of factories directly violated the Covid-19 health guidelines and engaged 70–90 percent of their workforce.[29]

Reopening of the factories and workers returning to their workplace was however not very smooth particularly since thousands of workers had to return from their villages despite lack of adequate public transport. Returning in crowded public transport and gathering at the industrial regions further risked the health conditions of the workers as well as the risk of spreading the virus (see Footnote 29). As the movement across the country was restricted, DIFE issued a special order for the workers where they would show their identity cards while entering Dhaka and would not be able to enter ferry terminals or any other entry points of Dhaka without their identity cards.[30] However, the government later decided to keep workers movement restricted to prevent possible transmission of the virus by not allowing them to leave their residential areas during Eid holidays.[31] At a meeting presided over by the State Minister of Ministry of Labour and Employment (MoLE) with the trade union leaders, ready-made garment owners and apparel workers, it was mutually decided that if any worker fails to join their factory as a result of the

[28] "Bangladesh Garment Factories Reopen despite Coronavirus Threat to Workers", *The Guardian*, May 11, 2020, https://www.theguardian.com/global-development/2020/may/11/bangladesh-garment-factories-reopen-despite-coronavirus-threat-to-workers.

[29] *Reopening Garment Factories in Bangladesh Despite of Covid-19 Threat*, Fair Wear, May 12, 2020, https://www.fairwear.org/covid-19-dossier/fair-wear-staff-share-covid-19-guidance/reopening-garment-factories-in-bangladesh-despite-covid-19-threat/.

[30] "Workers must Show ID Cards to Enter Dhaka", Dhaka Tribune, May 2, 2020, https://www.dhakatribune.com/bangladesh/2020/05/02/workers-must-show-id-cards-to-enter-dhaka.

[31] Ahammad Foyez, "RMG Workers not to be Allowed to Travel during Eid", New Age, May 9, 2020, https://www.newagebd.net/article/106014/rmg-workers-not-to-be-allowed-to-travel-during-eid.

countrywide shutdown, they will be paid 65 percent of their wage, instead of the earlier (April 2020) fixed 60 percent of their wage.[32] In addition to these, another praiseworthy step by the government was to identify Dhaka, Narayanganj and Gazipur as risky areas as they are densely populated, and form a committee and three sub-committees to oversee health care activities in these three areas.[33]

Order Cancellation and Reinstatement of Orders

Cancellation of orders by the global apparel buyers worldwide and disruption of apparel supply change at the global level has been in the limelight of discussion as countries across the world started to adopt lockdown measures in order to restrict and prevent the spread of coronavirus. Penn State Center for Global Workers' Rights administered an online survey on employers from Bangladesh during 21–25 March 2020. Research brief from the survey revealed that 58 percent of the surveyed factories had to shut down most or all of their operations as a result of order cancellations and lack of payment.[34]

While data from BGMEA reveals that at least 1931 brands including high street fashion brands, purse-friendly chain-stores and faceless buying houses, have either delayed, put on hold, or straight up cancelled their orders amounting to approximately $3.7 billion since the onset of Covid-19. Of these 1931 brands, about 470 were US-based, 280 were UK-based, 180 were Italy-based, 170 were Canada-based, 150 were Germany-based and 140 were France-based. Data from BGMEA also showed that there were at least 127 major brands who have cancelled contracts at various stages of production including rejecting to accept products that were lying at the port. Apart from these, there were brands

[32] Ibrahim Hossain Ovi, "Absentee Apparel Workers Salary Increased to 65%", Dhaka Tribune, May 4, 2020, https://www.dhakatribune.com/business/2020/05/04/apparel-workers-to-receive-65-wages-for-april.

[33] Ahammad Foyez, "RMG Workers not to be Allowed to Travel during Eid", *New Age*, May 9, 2020, https://www.newagebd.net/article/106014/rmg-workers-not-to-be-allowed-to-travel-during-eid.

[34] Mark Anner, "Abandoned? The Impact of Covid-19 on Workers and Businesses at the Bottom of Global Garment Supply Chains", Penn State Center for Global Workers' Rights, 2020, https://www.workersrights.org/wp-content/uploads/2020/03/Abandoned-Penn-State-WRC-Report-March-27–2020.pdf.

that demanded massive discounts for products already produced or deferring payments from six to twelve months (in the worst case—indefinite time). Primark, H&M, C&A, Marks & Spencer and Tesco—all renowned brands—were found to have postponed or cancelled the highest volume of orders. According to Worker Rights Consortium, an international labour rights monitoring body, among the top 50 brands that cancelled or postponed orders from Bangladesh, only 10 brands—particularly: H&M, Marks & Spencer, Tesco, Kiabi, VF, LPP, PVH, Inditex, Target and Ralph Lauren—have committed publicly to make payment in full for orders that were completed and/or in production. Vague promises to take back cancelled orders (without any specified time and payment details) were made by Bestseller, C&A, Primark and Walmart. However, Dr. Rubana Huq, President, BGMEA, on 20 May 2020 said that up to 58 percent of the initially cancelled orders were reinstated by these brands.[35]

New orders from international brands and retailers went down by 45 percent in June 2020 compared to same period in 2019 primarily because demand in the Western markets are yet to pick up as a result of the ongoing pandemic. On the bright side, of the $3.15 billion worth of cancelled orders, a portion have been reinstated after intense negotiation.[36]

Forbes, citing The Daily Star's new estimates, reported that the global brands and buyers owe an astonishing $5.1 billion (equivalent to 15 percent of the country's net export) to the factories in Bangladesh for completed and shipped orders.[37]

RMG Export

With most part of the world under lockdown, earnings from RMG exports dropped significantly. In April 2020, earnings from the RMG

[35] Sushmita S. Preetha & Zyma Islam, "Is Foul Play the New Normal", *The Daily Star*, June 26, 2020, https://www.thedailystar.net/business/news/you-suffer-we-survive-1920733.

[36] Refayet Ullah Mirdha, "Fresh Orders for Apparel Plunge 45pc", *The Daily Star*, June 10, 2020, https://www.thedailystar.net/business/news/fresh-orders-apparel-plunge-45pc-1911933.

[37] "Bangladeshi Garments Suppliers Held Hostage by International Clothing Brands, Retailers", *The Daily Star*, May 10, 2020, https://www.thedailystar.net/country/news/bangladeshi-garments-suppliers-held-hostage-international-clothing-brands-retailers-190 1218.

exports dropped to $360 million; however, apparel exports increased to $1.23 billion in May 2020 as economies started to reopen, to a further $2.25 billion in June 2020 and finally $3.24 billion in July 2020. The trend continued in August 2020, where during the first 22 days of the month, the apparel exporters were found to have sold apparel worth over $2.37 billion, which is nearly a 46 percent year-on-year growth.[38]

A year-on-year comparison of export data was made by BGMEA with provisional data compiled from the National Board of Revenue (NBR). RMG exports in March 2020 when the first coronavirus patient was detected was $1.97 billion which is a straight decline by 30.19 percent compared to same month of 2019 when the export was $2.82 billion. Data reveals that there was a 62.09 percent decline in the RMG exports during the 29 days of May this year compared to same time in 2019, specifically from $2.81 billion in May 2019 to $1.07 billion in May 2020. Furthermore, the country's export from RMG went down from $2.54 billion in April 2019 to $374.67 million in April 2020—it is an 85.25 percent year-on-year decline.[39]

BGMEA's President said that their member factories are operating at 55 percent of their capacity as a result of lower orders. BGMEA on the other hand estimated that the sector may lose as much as $5 billion in the 2019–2020 fiscal year due to the ongoing pandemic.[40] Fresh orders dropped from 454 in March–May 2019 to a mere 172 during the same period in 2020. BGMEA also reported that earnings from apparel export was $25.70 billion during July-May of the current fiscal, which is a 19 percent decline against $31.73 billion compared to same period in 2019.[41]

[38] Abdur Rahim Harmachi, "Bangladesh Apparel Factory Owners Seek More Government Incentives to Pay Workers", *BD News*, August 27, 2020, https://bdnews24.com/business/2020/08/27/bangladesh-apparel-factory-owners-seek-more-government-incentives-to-pay-workers.

[39] "Covid-19 Hammers RMG Exports for 3rd Month", *New Age*, May 31, 2020, https://www.newagebd.net/article/107345/covid-19-hammers-rmg-exports-for-3rd-month.

[40] Ibrahim Hossain Ovi, "BGMEA Chief: RMG in Crisis with Factories Running at 55% Capacity", *Dhaka Tribune*, June 4, 2020, https://www.dhakatribune.com/business/2020/06/04/rubana-factories-running-with-55-capacity-job-cut-soon.

[41] Ibrahim Hossain Ovi, "Apparel Exporters See 62% Drop in New Orders", *Dhaka Tribune*, June 15, 2020, https://www.dhakatribune.com/business/economy/2020/06/15/apparel-exporters-see-62-drop-in-new-orders.

Workers Losing Jobs

According to data from Industrial Police, some 19,409 ready-made garment and textile workers lost their jobs right after Eid-ul-Fitr. This was mainly attributed to the cost-cutting measures adopted by factory owners as a result of the pandemic. Labour leaders, however, argued that the figure would be much higher.[42] DIFE on the other hand provided a list of 24,860 workers who lost their jobs from 1 to 15 June 2020. DIFE also reported that 38 factories located in Dhaka terminated 13,750 workers, while 33 factories from Gazipur terminated 9839 workers, and 3 factories from Narayanganj terminated 560 workers.[43]

Methodology

Much has happened within the RMG sector of Bangladesh as a result of Covid-19 outbreak—the global pandemic. The reality is that it is not possible to cover all aspects and impacts of the pandemic on the RMG sector of Bangladesh through a single research. Mapped in Bangladesh (MiB) has put an effort to cover as much as possible within its scope. As the databases of export-oriented RMG factories developed as part of MiB census can leverage the rapid surveys, exploring the operational status of those factories during Covid-19 pandemic has been stressed for the rapid surveys, along with envisaging number of workers, the percentage of capacity at which the factories were operating and expectation of factories to resume their regular operation after May/June 2020. Additionally, the rapid surveys collected information on the production of masks and PPE considering the demand surge of these products due to Covid-19 pandemic. Such information coupled with information on factories arranging training or briefing about the pandemic, factories following Covid-19 safety guidelines and measures taken by factories to combat it have also been collected.

[42] "21,331 RMG Workers Lose Job after Eid", *New Age*, June 18, 2020, https://www.newagebd.net/article/108700/21331-rmg-workers-lose-job-after-eid.

[43] "Govt Urges Garment Owners to Stop Sacking", *The Financial Express*, June 23, 2020, https://today.thefinancialexpress.com.bd/first-page/govt-urges-garment-owners-to-stop-sacking-1592846930.

Methodology for both the Rapid Surveys: Phase 1[44] (Rapid Survey 1) and Phase 2[45] (Rapid Survey 2) was same:

- Using the list of factories from MiB dataset following the factory selection criteria[46] (i.e. Factory Definition) as per project's methodology;
- Utilizing the survey team who are already experienced in communicating with factories to collect data from factories over the phone;
- Assigning each team member with a list of factory names and contacts derived from the MiB database;
- Input the collected data through an electronic survey instrument using KoBoToolbox platform.

The only difference was that Phase 1 of the survey did not include factories from Chattogram, whereas, Phase 2 included Chattogram data.

Data Collection and Dissemination

The Rapid Survey: Phase 1 titled "*Operational Status of Export-oriented RMG Factories during Covid-19 Pandemic*" was conducted in May 2020, while Rapid Survey: Phase 2 titled "*Status of the Export-Oriented RMG Factories in Bangladesh during Covid-19 Pandemic*" was conducted in June 2020.

Data for the first phase of the survey was collected from 30 April to 7 May 2020, and data of the second phase was collected from 15 to 27 June 2020. The result of the first phase survey was shared in June 2020 while the report of the second phase survey was published in August 2020. While the first rapid survey has embraced a newspaper op-ed, the

[44] Centre for Entrepreneurship Development (CED), *Operational Status of Export-oriented RMG Factories during Covid-19 Pandemic* (Dhaka: Brac University, June 1, 2020), https://mappedinbangladesh.org/wp-content/uploads/2020/06/R-2_MiB-Research-Brief_Rapid-Survey.pdf.

[45] Centre for Entrepreneurship Development (CED), *Mapped in Bangladesh: Rapid Survey-Phase 2* (Dhaka: Brac University, July 2020), https://mappedinbangladesh.org/wp-content/uploads/2020/08/MiB_RAPID_SURVEY_PHASE-2.pdf.

[46] "Methodology of Mapped in Bangladesh", Mapped in Bangladesh, Accessed August 12, 2020, https://mappedinbangladesh.org/wp-content/uploads/2019/05/MiB-Methodology-.pdf.

second rapid survey has been received widespread media dissemination riding with the webinar based on its results. The webinar titled "State of the RMG Industry during the Pandemic: Is it on the Way to Recovery?" was organized on 20 July 2020 where three prominent international and national scholars of RMG sector of Bangladesh were present as discussants and they pointed out the policy relevance of MiB rapid surveys in terms of urgency for non-member factories to receive support from the government, importance of supply chain approach for addressing vulnerabilities of RMG workers and comparative aspects of two rapid surveys and further data points that could be included in the upcoming surveys.

Data Presentation and Discussion

The discussion on comparing two rapid surveys proceed as follows based on the major data points and findings of those two surveys.

Factory Distribution

Rapid Survey 1 was conducted on 2526 factories from Dhaka, Gazipur and Narayanganj, while Rapid Survey 2 was conducted on 3342 factories from Dhaka, Gazipur, Narayanganj and Chattogram from the MiB database. The sample distribution disaggregated by location and membership type, and type of factory is provided in Tables 8.2, 8.3.

Out of the 2526 factories contacted during Phase 1 of the Rapid Survey, 66.8 percent of the factories responded to the survey. The remaining 33.21 percent of the factories either did not respond to our calls or were unable to reach us. The response rate was higher during Phase 2 where 69.84 percent of the factories responded to the survey (Table 8.4).

Operational Status

Among those factories who responded to the surveys in Phase 1 and Phase 2, the incidence of factories being open was higher in Phase 2. In Phase 1, 64 percent of the factories that responded to the survey were found to be open, which was 79.3 percent in Phase 2. An unpaired t-test was also performed and we found the difference to be statistically significant at 5 percent level.

Table 8.2 Distribution of factories by location and membership type

		Dhaka	*Gazipur*	*Narayanganj*	*Chattogram*	*Total*
Only BGMEA	Rapid Survey 1	856	746	57	–	1659
	Rapid Survey 2	856	746	63	231	1896
Only BKMEA	Rapid Survey 1	109	111	256	–	476
	Rapid Survey 2	109	111	257	48	525
Both BGMEA and BKMEA	Rapid Survey 1	56	61	105	–	222
	Rapid Survey 2	56	61	106	22	245
Non-member	Rapid Survey 1	34	135	–	–	169
	Rapid Survey 2	150	135	187	204	676
Total	Rapid Survey 1	1055	1053	418	–	2526
	Rapid Survey 2	1171	1053	613	505	3342

Table 8.3 Distribution of factories by factory type

	Rapid Survey 1	*Rapid Survey 2*
Knit	1072	1384
Woven	870	995
Sweater	419	539
Non-RMG	8	69
Mixed	157	355
Total	2526	3342

Table 8.4 Factory response

	Rapid Survey 1		*Rapid Survey 2*	
	Freq	*Percent*	*Freq*	*Percent*
Responded to the survey	1687	66.8	2334	69.84
Did not respond/Could not communicate	839	33.21	1008	30.16
Total	2526	100	3342	100

About 28.6 percent of the factories were found to be temporarily closed in Phase 1 which dropped down to 12.3 percent in Phase 2 and this was found to be statistically significant at 5 percent. In Phase 1, 124 factories or 7.4 percent of the factories that responded to the survey said that they closed down permanently, which increased to 198 factories or 8.5 factories in Phase 2 (Table 8.5).

As we can see, 849 factories from both phases of the survey were found to be open. Among the open factories in Phase 1 of the survey, 17 reported that they closed down temporarily and 9 factories said that they permanently closed down during the second phase of the survey (Table 8.6).

Table 8.5 Operational status of the surveyed factories

Operational Status	*Rapid Survey 1*		*Rapid Survey 2*		*p-value (unpaired* t*-test)*
	Freq	*Percent*	*Freq*	*Percent*	
Open	1080	64.0	1850	79.3	0.000
Temporarily Closed	483	28.6	286	12.3	0.000
Permanently Closed	124	7.4	198	8.5	0.192
Total	1687	100	2334	100	

Table 8.6 Comparison of the operational status of the surveyed factories during the two survey phases

		Rapid Survey 2					
		Open	*Temporarily Closed*	*Permanently Closed*	*Did not respond*	*Could not communicate*	*Total*
Rapid Survey 1	Open	849	17	9	70	135	1080
	Temporarily Closed	226	113	45	21	78	483
	Permanently Closed	10	19	75	3	17	124
	Did not respond	68	7	1	40	30	146
	Could not communicate	216	45	35	31	366	693
	Total	1369	201	165	165	626	2526

We conducted a paired t-test on the factories which were reported to be open, temporarily closed and permanently closed in either of the two phases of the survey. With $n = 1363$, 64 percent of the factories were found to be open in Phase 1 which increased to 80 percent in Phase 2 and the difference was statistically significant at 5 percent level. About 28 percent of factories said that they were temporarily closed during Phase 1, which dropped significantly to 11 percent during Phase 2. Approximately 8 percent of the factories in Phase 1 and 9 percent in Phase 2 reported that they were permanently closed. One important finding from this table is that 226 factories those were temporarily closed during Rapid Survey 1, were open during Phase 2 of the survey (Table 8.7).

About 28 percent of BGMEA member factories reported that they were temporarily closed during Rapid Survey 1, which significantly dropped to 11 percent during the second phase of the survey. While 36 percent BKMEA member factories said that they were temporarily closed in Phase 1 of the survey, only 13 percent said the same during Rapid Survey 2, and the difference is statistically significant at 5 percent level. Among the factories who were members of both BGMEA and BKMEA, 16 percent in Phase 1 and only 6 percent in Phase 2 reported being temporarily closed and this decrease in the number of temporarily closed factories of this category was statistically significant at 5 percent (Table 8.8).

The difference between an average number of temporarily closed Non-member factories during Phase 1 of the Rapid Survey (35 percent) and 18 percent during the second phase was statistically significant at 5 percent level. This indicates that irrespective of membership, more factories were found to be temporarily closed down during Rapid Survey 1 which was conducted in May 2020, since this was during the early stage of the

Table 8.7 Paired t-test of operational status of the surveyed factories

Operational Status	*Observations*	*Rapid Survey 1*	*Rapid Survey 2*	*p-value (paired* t*-test)*
Open	1363	0.64	0.80	0.000
Temporarily Closed	1363	0.28	0.11	0.000
Permanently Closed	1363	0.08	0.09	0.006

Table 8.8 Comparison of temporarily closed factories in the two survey phases based on membership

Membership	*Rapid Survey 1*		*Rapid Survey 2*		*p-value*
	n	*Mean*	*n*	*Mean*	
Only BGMEA	1071	0.28	1316	0.11	0.000
Only BKMEA	343	0.36	395	0.13	0.000
Both BGMEA and BKMEA	165	0.16	170	0.06	0.004
Non-member	108	0.35	453	0.18	0.000
Total	1687	0.29	2334	0.12	

Table 8.9 Anticipation to continue operation after May 2020 and actual operational status in May 2020

Operational Status during Rapid Survey 2	*Anticipation to continue regular operation after May 2020*		
	Yes	*No*	*Do not know*
Open	362	53	433
Temporarily Closed	3	3	11
Permanently Closed	3	2	4

pandemic (March–May 2020) and therefore, the factories were not sure what was going on and what the situation would be in the future. Furthermore, this was the time when the factories, trade bodies and brands were in discussion regarding current, ongoing and future orders. Things began to settle down during May and June 2020, and therefore, we found a lower number of factories reporting to be temporarily closed down. This is also reflected in Table 8.6, where we see that 226 factories which reported to be temporarily closed during the Phase 1 survey were open during Phase 2.

From Table 8.9 we see that 433 factories who said that they did not know or were uncertain whether they would be able to continue their operation after May 2020 (this was asked during Rapid Survey 1), were found to be open during Rapid Survey 2 conducted in June 2020. Additionally, 53 factories that said that they will not be able to continue their regular operation after May 2020, were actually found to be open during Phase 2 of the survey conducted in June 2020. This indicates that the industry is gradually moving towards a stable situation where factories are opening up and are optimistic in terms of continuing their operations.

Employment and Capacity Utilization

We conducted both Unpaired and Paired t-test on the number of workers currently working at the factories. The results from both the unpaired and paired t-test shows that the difference between the average numbers of workers working at the factories during Rapid Survey 1 was significantly lower than Rapid Survey 2 (Tables 8.10, 8.11).

We re-ran the tests (unpaired and paired t-test) on the number of workers working by membership status of the factories. The difference in the average number of workers during the first and second phase of the survey was statistically significant in all cases. The average number of workers during Phase 1 was lower for all cases except one. Only in the case of unpaired t-test on the non-member factories do we see that the

Table 8.10 Paired and Unpaired t-test on the number of workers

	Unpaired t-*test*			*Paired* t-*test*		
	Observations	*Mean*	*p-value*	*Observations*	*Mean*	*p-value*
Rapid Survey 1	1026	663	0.003	816	668	0.000
Rapid Survey 2	1849	793		816	1061	

Table 8.11 Paired and Unpaired t-test on the number of workers by membership status

	Member			*Non-member*		
	Observations	*Mean*	*p-value*	*Observations*	*Mean*	*p-value*
Unpaired t-test						
Rapid Survey 1	970	686	0.000	56	258	0.024
Rapid Survey 2	1520	931		329	159	
Paired t-test						
Rapid Survey 1	783	685	0.000	33	268	0.015
Rapid Survey 2	783	1089		33	396	

average number of workers was higher during the first phase of the survey compared to the second phase of the survey.

Statistically, significant higher average number of workers during Rapid Survey 2 (compared to Rapid Survey 1) indicates that though the factories were operational during the first phase of the survey (in May 2020), they were deploying lower number of workers which might be due to orders being cancelled, held up or orders being negotiated. Another factor that could lead to lower the number of workers working could be health safety measures by the workers themselves and the factory itself—workers were not going to their workplaces to avoid getting infected by Covid-19, while factories allowed lower number of workers to lower the risk of spreading the virus in their factories. However, as time passed by, during June 2020 (when the second phase of the survey was conducted), things started to normalize with workers and factories taking preventive measures to combat being infected by the virus. Furthermore, with international as well as national pressure, many brands and customers have revised their initial decision about orders with the factories. With the revision of their decisions, the factories have gradually increased their production, which is reflected by the higher number of workers during the second phase of the survey (Table 8.12). This result is also reflected when we compare the average capacity utilization of the factories. Irrespective of a membership type and unpaired or paired t- test, we see that the capacity utilized by the factories were significantly lower during May 2020 compared to June 2020 (Table 8.13).

Capacity utilization of the factories during the two phases are presented in Table 8.14, and a comparison of capacity utilization among the factories is provided in Table 8.15. As we can see from Table 8.15, among those factories that were using 25–49 percent of their capacity during Rapid Survey 1, 26 factories increased their capacity to 25–49 percent and 120 factories increased their capacity to 50–74 percent during Rapid

Table 8.12 Paired and Unpaired *t*-test on capacity utilization

	Unpaired t-*test*			*Paired* t-*test*		
	Observations	*Mean*	*p-value*	*Observations*	*Mean*	*p-value*
Rapid Survey 1	1045	49.04	0.000	824	49.36	0.000
Rapid Survey 2	1850	68.64		824	72.27	

Table 8.13 Paired and Unpaired *t*-test on capacity utilization by membership status

	Member			*Non-member*		
	Observations	*Mean*	*p-value*	*Observations*	*Mean*	*p-value*
Unpaired t-test						
Rapid Survey 1	990	49.48	0.000	55	41.05	0.000
Rapid Survey 2	1521	70.55		329	59.83	
Paired t-test						
Rapid Survey 1	792	49.73	0.000	32	40.09	0.000
Rapid Survey 2	792	72.62		32	63.59	

Table 8.14 Average capacity utilization

Average Capacity	*Rapid Survey 1*		*Rapid Survey 2*	
	Freq	*Percent*	*Freq*	*Percent*
0–15 percent	59	5.65	29	1.57
16–24 percent	53	5.07	35	1.89
25–49 percent	389	37.22	213	11.51
50–74 percent	365	34.93	738	39.89
≥ 75 percent	179	17.13	835	45.14
Total	1045	100	1850	100

Table 8.15 Average capacity utilization by the factories during Rapid Survey 1 and Rapid Survey 2

Rapid Survey 1	*Rapid Survey 2*					
	0–15 percent	*16–24 percent*	*25–49 percent*	*50–74 percent*	*≥ 75 percent*	*Total*
0–15 percent	2	2	12	11	15	42
16–24 percent	–	–	6	18	17	41
25–49 percent	3	4	26	120	153	306
50–74 percent	–	3	19	111	162	295
≥ 75 percent	1	1	10	47	81	140
Total	6	10	73	307	428	824

Survey 2, and 153 factories were utilizing more than 75 percent of their capacity. Furthermore, among those factories that were using 50–74 percent of their capacity during the first phase of the survey, 162 factories were found to be utilizing above 74 percent of their capacity during the second phase of the survey (Table 8.15).

This increase in the number of current workers and capacity utilization in June 2020 compared to May 2020 suggests that things are gradually stabilizing and moving towards a positive situation.

Table 8.16 shows the comparison of the number of workers employed during Rapid Survey 1 and 2 with that of the respective baseline factory data. As we can see, the factories that responded to the first phase of the survey (1687 factories) employed a little over 1.5 million workers during the baseline, which dropped down to 1.2 million workers during Rapid Survey 1 from 1080 operational factories. About a little over 0.3 million workers (from 607 factories those were either temporarily or permanently closed) were not working during the survey period.

From the 2334 factories that responded in the second phase of the survey employed about 1.7 million workers during baseline. Of these factories, 1850 those reported to be operational during the survey period employed about 1.6 million workers, while 0.16 million workers from

Table 8.16 Comparison of workers employed during Rapid Survey 1 and Rapid Survey 2 with baseline employment

	Observations	*Total Number of Workers*
Total Number of workers in the factories from baseline data those responded to the Rapid Survey 1	1687	1,521,127
Total Number of workers in the factories that were Open during Rapid Survey 1	1080	1,206,052
Total Number of workers in the factories that were Closed (temporarily or permanently) during Rapid Survey 1	607	315,075
Total Number of workers in the factories from baseline data those responded to the Rapid Survey 2	2334	1,757,223
Total Number of workers in the factories that were Open during Rapid Survey 2	1850	1,594,173
Total Number of workers in the factories that were Closed (temporarily or permanently) during Rapid Survey 2	484	163,050

484 factories (those who reported temporarily or permanently closed) were not working at the time of the survey. Therefore, we note the incidence of unemployment during the first phase of the survey, which dropped down during the second phase of the survey. However, we do not know the exact status of these workers who were not working. In other words, we are not certain whether they have been laid off, terminated or on leave.

Diversity in Production

As a result of the pandemic, the RMG factories have started to diversify their production by including Personal Protective Equipment (PPE) and Face Masks in their production. Several factories were found to be producing a combination of PPE, Face Masks and their regular products. In Phase 1 of the Rapid Survey, 151 factories were found to be producing PPE and/or Face Masks along with their regular products. However, 143 factories were found to be producing PPE and/or Face Masks and/or regular products in the second phase of the survey. Interestingly, some factories were producing PPE and Face Masks on not-for profit basis.

Limitations

The following limitations can be envisaged regarding the data collection of the two rapid surveys:

1. Ensuring operational status along with data collection was not possible for those factories which could not be reached over phone.
2. It is expected that all the factories who responded to the phone call and participated in the survey would not be able to provide all data points with full accuracy while it is also not possible for the surveyors to confirm the full reliability of the data since the surveyors are not physically present while taking the interviews.
3. Name, address, membership, exporting status and other relevant information of the factories of Dhaka, Gazipur and Narayanganj clusters in MiB map, which were also surveyed in these rapid surveys, have been already verified and validated as per MiB data verification and validation protocol. But information of Chattogram factories surveyed was not verified and validated as per the mentioned MiB protocol as yet. Thus it cannot be said that after the

MiB data verification and validation process, how many Chattogram factories will be finalized to be uploaded on the map.

4. Factories of Export Processing Zone (EPZ) areas were not part of the survey as those factories are neither part of MiB map nor the MiB database although MiB is still approaching EPZ authorities to get access of their factories.
5. The total number of workers between "baseline" (which is referred to as "before pandemic") and "during pandemic" has been compared within two separate timelines of data collection. While the "baseline/ before pandemic" period refers to the data collection timeline of MiB Census which started from 2018, and the "during pandemic" period denotes the data collection timeline of the Rapid Survey Phase 1 and Phase 2. Therefore, as the "baseline" period is based on a broader timeline (from 2018 till February 2020), it cannot be said that the changes of workers' numbers are caused only by the pandemic; rather there could be other possibilities of influence from external factors active within such broader timeline.

Conclusion and Recommendation

The significance of these rapid surveys lies in unearthing the industry pattern through which export-oriented RMG factories in Bangladesh have geared up the required recovery during Covid-19 pandemic. Additionally, the evidence that these rapid surveys have drawn will remain evident as the factories were derived from Mapped in Bangladesh's digital map and the factory information of these rapid surveys are now being showcased in its Covid-19 RMG map. Using such evidence worthy feedback from the rapid survey data coupled with data from MiB database, stakeholders can play an active role in proposing short and long-term policies targeting the current Covid-19 crisis and forthcoming challenges of the garments industry in the post-pandemic global world of apparel sector. Such proposals can emphasize the relevance of these rapid surveys in terms of depicting region-wise RMG scenarios during pandemic period, identification of factories operating with different capacities, tracking the changes of total number of workers, RMG factories' involvement with the supply chain of Masks and PPE, and RMG factories' response to prevent Covid-19.

Our findings suggest that workers and capacity utilization during the early stage was low, which gradually started to pick up during the second phase of the survey. Factories' anticipation to operate in the following month of the surveys were also more positive in the second phase than the first phase. This can be attributed mainly due to the overall uncertainty and lack of knowledge and understanding on how to act and address the crisis moment. With increase in understanding of the situation and how to tackle the situation, factories started to open up and operate maintaining guidelines provided by the government and trade associations. We anticipate that the sector will return to its former position over the next couple of months.

However, a further in-depth research is required to explore order details of the factories, the terms of worker termination/ layoff and what they are doing now, whether operating cost of the factories have increased or not due to the pandemic, and whether there has been any change in the mode of shipment (air/ sea).

Annex 1: Questions Asked During the Surveys

Rapid Survey Phase 1 and 2

The following questions were asked in the both phases of the Rapid Surveys:

- Operational status of the factories
- Current products produced (PPE/ Masks/ Regular products)
- Production mode (with profit/ without profit) of Masks/ PPE
- Number of workers currently working
- The percentage of capacity at which the factories are currently operating
- Whether the factories are hopeful to resume their regular operation after May/ June 2020.

Phase 2 Additionally Covered the Following Issues

- Whether factories arranged training or briefing about Covid-19
- Whether the factories are following Covid-19 safety guideline (from Govt./ BGMEA/ BKMEA)?
- Measures taken by factories to combat Covid-19 in the factories

Bibliography

Anner, Mark. *Abandoned? The Impact of Covid-19 on Workers and Businesses at the Bottom of Global Garment Supply Chains*. Pennsylvania: Penn State Center for Global Workers' Rights, 2020. https://www.workersrights.org/wp-content/uploads/2020/03/Abandoned-Penn-State-WRC-Report-March-27-2020.pdf.

Brac Institute of Governance and Development (BIGD). *Taka 5000 Crore Novel Corona Financial Stimulus Package for Export-Oriented Industries: RMG Trade Union Responses*. Dhaka: BIGD, 2020. https://bigd.bracu.ac.bd/wp-content/uploads/2020/06/Report_Trade-Union-Responses_Financial-Stimulus-Package.pdf.

Centre for Entrepreneurship Development (CED). *Operational Status of Export-oriented RMG Factories during Covid-19 Pandemic*. Dhaka: CED, 2020. https://mappedinbangladesh.org/wp-content/uploads/2020/06/R-2_MiB-Research-Brief_Rapid-Survey.pdf.

Centre for Entrepreneurship Development (CED). *Mapped in Bangladesh: Rapid Survey Phase 2*. Dhaka: Brac University, 2020. https://mappedinbangladesh.org/wp-content/uploads/2020/08/MiB_RAPID_SURVEY_PHASE-2.pdf.

Ministry of Health and Family Welfare. *Directives of Maintaining Safety Measures and Hygiene in Industries* . Dhaka: Ministry of Health and Family Welfare, 2020. https://api.fairwear.org/wp-content/uploads/2020/05/Ministry-of-Health-and-Family-Welfare-Translated.pdf.

CHAPTER 9

Demoralizing Impacts of the COVID-19 on the Bangladesh Ready-Made Garment (RMG) Supply Chain

Shahidur Rahman

Abbreviations

BGMEA	Bangladesh Garment Manufacturers and Exporters Association
BGSS	Bangladesh Garment Shramik Sanghati
BIGD	BRAC Institute of Governance and Development
BKMEA	Bangladesh Knitwear Manufacturers and Exporters Association
BRAC	Building Resources Across Communities
CED	Centre for Entrepreneurship Development

S. Rahman (✉)
Department of Economics and Social Sciences, BRAC University,
Dhaka, Bangladesh
e-mail: shahidur@bracu.ac.bd

S. Hewamanne and S. Yadav (eds.), *The Political Economy of Post-COVID Life and Work in the Global South: Pandemic and Precarity*,
International Political Economy Series,
https://doi.org/10.1007/978-3-030-93228-2_9

COVID-19	Coronavirus Disease of 2019
CSR	Corporate Social Responsibility
DIFE	Department of Inspection for Factories and Establishments
EU	European Union
G2G	Government to Government
GDP	Gross Domestic Product
H&M	Hennes and Mauritz
IBC	International Building Code
ILO	International Labour Organisation
MNC	Multi-National Corporation
OSH	Occupational Safety and Health
PPE	Personal Protective Equipment
RMG	Ready-made garment
US	United States
USA	United States of America

Introduction

When Bangladesh became an independent nation in 1971, after nine months of war with Pakistan, the entire economy, particularly trade and industry, was in bad shape. The immediate concern was to restore the economy with a strong and restrictive policy. The new government implemented a socialist economy which had been promised during the independence struggle (Stepanek 1979). The nationalization of the economy ended in Bangladesh in the late 1970s and since then embraced trade liberalization and export-led growth strategy. The only success of this strategy is the significant development of the Ready-made garment (RMG) industry. By many measures, the Bangladesh RMG industry has performed very well over the last forty years. From a less than million dollar industry in the early 1980s, it has reached to a billion-dollar industry in 2000. In the next twenty years the export earning has increased to $30 billion. The industry now accounts for 11% of Bangladesh's GDP and its share of the country's exports rose from 4% in the 1980s to around 80% in the current decade (Kabeer et al. 2020).

Depending on the hard work of more than 4 million workers of whom 80% are women, Bangladesh is now the second-largest exporter of RMG, behind China. The socio-economic achievement in Bangladesh, however, also came with a steep price, one that resulted in the Rana Plaza collapse—the worst industrial tragedy of the world with more than 1100 worker deaths (Rahman and Rahman 2020).

It took some time for the Bangladesh garments industry to recover after the Rana Plaza tragedy, a wake-up call for the industry. Since then, more than a hundred programs have been introduced by the stakeholders. As a result of these initiatives, the moment we thought we had overcome the consequences of Rana Plaza and would achieve the $50 billion target of export earnings by 2021, our dream has been washed away by Covid-19, a pandemic that has shattered the Bangladesh RMG industry. Factories have reportedly opted to furlough and lay-off their workersworker, ultimately, threatened the livelihood of some four million garment workers, who are grappling with the repercussions of the virus outbreak. For the sake of survival, the whole world has been campaigning for social distancing and lockdown, which has triggered the shutdown of stores of retailers and buyers. Because of the cancellation of orders, the Bangladeshi garment exports have declined by 18.45%, the highest decrease in the history of Bangladesh's garment export sector (The Economist 2020).

Based on secondary sources such as local and international news as well as research reports of different research institutions, this chapter focuses on the impact of coronavirus on the Bangladesh garments industry. The objectives of this chapter are to understand the consequences of this pandemic on the Bangladeshi suppliers and workers. It will also shed light on the role of the buyers and the government of Bangladesh in mitigating the effects of the pandemic. It also focuses on the perspectives of local trade unions. The chapter concludes that the workers are the most vulnerable in the global supply chain and the buyers have failed to maintain Corporate Social Responsibility (CSR). It also explores the bleak future of the Bangladeshi RMG industry in the aftermath of the pandemic.

Evolution of the Bangladesh RMG and CSR

The first wave of the transition of the Bangladesh RMG was shaped by the global shift of production, which initiated the relocation of production from high-wage countries to low-wage countries (Rahman and Rahman 2020). From diverse backgrounds, the Bangladeshi garment entrepreneurs started to invest in this industry by taking advantage of cheap labour, and flourished with very limited labour surveillance (Rahman 2014). Attempts at intergovernmental regulation through the addition of a social clause including the core labour standards of the International Labour Organization (ILO) in the World Trade Organization (WTO) were not successful in the mid-1990s (Pahle 2010). Anti-sweatshop activists therefore turned their attention from governments to high-profile garment brands, who responded by developing Codes of Conduct and joining multi-stakeholder initiatives (Merk 2011). Such codes frequently included ILO core labour standards (though sometimes omitted freedom of association and right to collective bargaining) and were subject to regular auditing by the lead firm and/or a third party. This second wave of regulation through codes of conduct improved working conditions in the Bangladesh garment industry by removing child labour from the sector in the late 1990s, as well as forming a welfare committee in the EPZ (Rahman 2014). Yet evidence suggests that buyers' codes of conduct produced limited results in other areas such as health and safety, working time and wages (Locke 2013). In line with this, the implementation of prevailing social audit is bedevilled by low-quality inspections, poor value for money, unnecessary duplication of audits, inconsistent corrective action plans and audit fraud (Reinecke et al. 2019).

The above-mentioned flaws of both governance approaches—public (weak institutions) and private (buyers' code of conduct)—was starkly demonstrated by the Rana Plaza tragedy in Bangladesh, and this paved the way for the emergence of the third wave of regulation—a need multi-stakeholder governance approach known as Accord and the Alliance. Different scholars have focused on the governance logic of the Accord and

Alliance (Anner 2015), comparing the initiatives in terms of the politics of their emergence (Donaghey and Reinecke 2015, 2018), their achievements and weaknesses (Anner 2018; Scheper 2017), and their impact on the emerging power of domestic trade unions (Zajak 2017). Whereas some commentators argue that Accord is a 'game changer' (Ryan 2013), a 'new paradigm in the enforcement of labour and human rights', some criticize the Accord for not addressing social compliance (Smith 2014) and no firm obligation on buyers to support suppliers financially in factory remediation (Rahman and Rahman 2020). In spite of the criticism, the Accord and Alliance has been considered as a success story in CSR because the poor condition of fire, electrical and structural safety of the RMG factories of Bangladesh has improved immensely after the Rana Plaza tragedy in Bangladesh (Anner 2018). Such change is the outcome of the Accord and Alliance, which has pointed out the weaknesses of traditional CSR.

However, the glory of CSR through different mechanisms as mentioned above has entered into a new dark chapter in 2020. The slavery conditions of workers have unfolded again during the current coronavirus pandemic when workers have either been laid-off without pay, or forced to work in unsafe environments (Islam 2020). Over the past seven years, following the Rana Plaza tragedy, Western activists have manifested deep concern about workers' rights and safety, particularly, in the context of Bangladesh's RMG workers. The current pandemic brought forth contradictory responses, from the same group of Western retail and apparel brands. At the end of April 2020, orders for more than \$3.17 billion had been cancelled, reported by 1149 factories in Bangladesh. Anner's study (2020) shows that more than half of the suppliers have had the bulk of their in-process, or already completed, production cancelled. Cancellation of these current orders means a loss of resources with an imminent threat to the RMG backward linkage industries, as 72.1% of buyers refused to pay for the raw materials already purchased by the suppliers. While all the Western brands are recognized to advocate responsible sourcing, the livelihood of workers should be a fundamental priority, and there is no time like the present to exhibit their responsibilities towards them. The Covid-19 offers an opportunity to rethink of the CSR and the ways the business is going on.

Methodology

This study uses content analysis method to understand the impact of the COVID-19 on the Bangladesh RMG. On the basis of authenticity, popularity and scale of users I have selected 12 media outlets—7 international and 5 Bangladeshi. The Bangladeshi media outlets are The Daily Star, Dhaka Tribune, The Financial Express, The Business Standard. The international media outlets are The Economist, The New York Times, Forbes, The Guardian, NPR, Quartz, The New Daily. Another secondary source of data is the reports published by different research organizations. In this study, three reports from two leading organizations have been used and these are: Centre for Global Workers Right of Penn State University, Bangladesh Institute of Governance and Development (BIGD) and Centre for Entrepreneurship and Development (CED) of BRAC University. The timeframe of the news and reports is March–June 2020. More than one method is used to search news relevant to the research question of this study. I have searched the keywords in Google, the website of each newspaper is visited and other research organizations relevant to the area are explored in web. By following these search methods, I have collected 36 news from the media outlets and 3 reports based on primary data and used thematic analysis. Broadly the data has been analysed under six themes—origin of the crisis, buyers action, impact on the suppliers, vulnerability of workers, responses and lessons. The main limitation of the methodology is that it is entirely dependent on the secondary data since fieldwork has become very difficult during the lockdown situation after the pandemic and needs to maintain strictly preventive measures such as social distancing.

Origin of the Crisis

After the Rana Plaza tragedy retailers and apparel brands of the West began a major push to improve workers' rights through strict monitoring and collaborating with institutions and organizations committed to ensuring labour welfare and establishing safer workplaces. Subject to certain conditions and regulations, failure of compliance led to the termination of business contracts and in extreme cases complete shutdown of factories, thus, prompting local manufacturers to maintain safe working practices and uphold workers' rights. As a result, the Western brands were deemed to champion workers' rights, given their seeming interest on ethical sourcing. But this commitment has completely disappeared after the COVID-19. The virus-fueled global economic slump has not spared any major industry worldwide. According to the International Labour Organisation (ILO), 400 million people have lost their full-time jobs globally (The Economist 2020). The Covid-19 has effected a dire situation that has forced fashion retailers, brands and discount stores to shut. Large quantities of existing stock in the stores have been left unclaimed. The closed stores of EU countries and the USA—two prime destinations of the exports of Bangladesh RMG are a testament to the crisis within the apparel industry. To follow social distancing measures, shoppers have stayed home leaving a drastic plunge of demand for new clothes. As a result of the COVID-19, factory owners are facing financial ruin on one hand. On the other hand the livelihoods of more than 4 million garment workers are also at stake.

From an online survey of the Bangladesh suppliers in March 2020, Anner (2020) reveals the devastating impact of COVID-19 on the suppliers and the workers. According to the study, 45.8% of suppliers reported a cancellation of completed orders by their buyers, 72.1% of buyers refused to pay for raw materials, 91.3% of buyers refused to pay the production cost and as a result of cancellation of orders 58% of factories surveyed shutdown most or all of their operations. As per BGMEA data work orders dropped to 172 in March–May period which was 454 in the same period last year (Ovi 2020). The country's garments export declined by more than 62% in the first 29 days of May this year compared with that of corresponding period last year. The BGMEA data also shows the factories are now running at only 55% capacity due to lesser work orders (Ovi 2020). Rubana Huq, the president of the Bangladesh Garment Manufacturers and Exporters Association (BGMEA) said: "Our situation is apocalyptic. The cancellations and hold instructions coming in from Western fashion retailers are pushing us to the point of insolvency. Brands who were partners last month have all turned into strangers…For them (Western Retailers), it's a question of the survival of the businesses. For us, it's the survival of our 4.1 million workers" (Paton 2020).

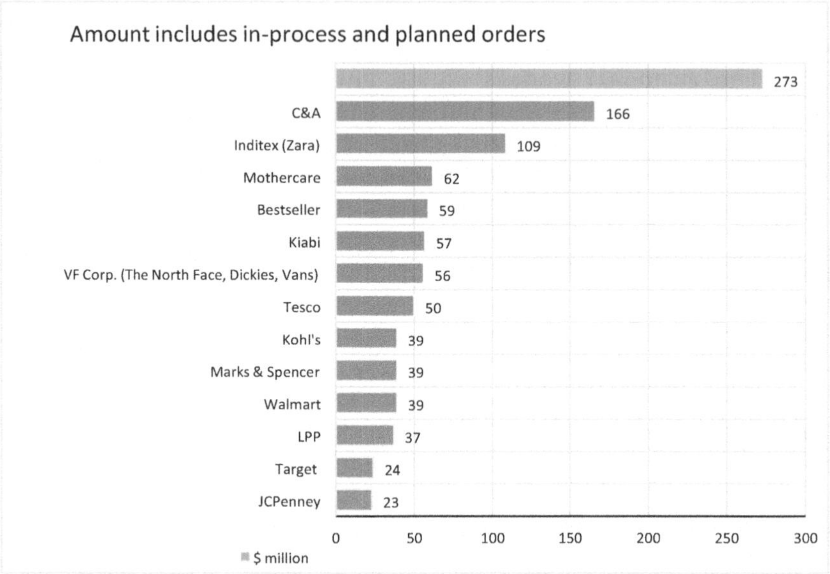

Estimated orders canceled or on hold at Bangladeshi garment factories (*Source* Bain 2020)

Dominating Role of Buyers

Fast fashion business model continues to squeeze suppliers by setting unrealistic targets. As a result, lead times have dropped by 8% and prices paid to suppliers have declined by 13% (Anner 2018). The COVID-19 pandemic has created another opportunity for the buyers to use their unequal power positions with suppliers to justify cancelling or postponing orders and refusing to pay for orders that suppliers have already produced. For a long time the buyers have taken advantage of cheap labour from Bangladesh and benefited from the lower bargaining power of the supplier. However, they have completely abandoned the workers of their supply chains in their hour of need (Saxena 2020). From both the CSR and business sustainability context the buyers should have accepted the goods which are currently in different stage of production at the factories. Additionally the brands should have paid the cost of manufacturing for the goods they have already ordered. Such action would have demonstrated a strong commitment to workers from the buyers. Instead they have decided to look after their own interests. For example, Paul Marchant, the chief executive of Primark stated "We recognize and are deeply saddened that this will clearly have an effect throughout our entire supply chain. This is unprecedented action for unprecedented and frankly unimaginable times. We have large quantities of existing stock in our stores, our depots and in transit, that is paid for and if we do not take this action now we will be taking delivery of stock that we simply cannot sell" (Paton 2020). Moreover, a H&M spokesperson is on record as saying, "We will stand by our commitments to our garment manufacturing suppliers by taking delivery of the already produced garments as well as goods in production. We will of course pay for these goods and we will do it under agreed payment terms. In addition, we will not negotiate prices on already placed orders. This is not only the case in Bangladesh, but for all production countries. We are at this instance intensively investigating how we can support countries, societies and individuals from a health and financial perspective. We hope to be able to communicate more around these initiatives within shortly" (Suhrawardi 2020).

Perception of buyers on the crisis

Buyers	*Order status*	*Comment from buyers*
C&A	Sent a letter to suppliers in March cancelling all orders through to June. Later backtracked, promising to pay for 93% of orders that are finished or in production and negotiate settlements for the remaining 7%. Has started to discuss new orders	Reaching out to our suppliers to identify ways to mitigate the devastating economic impact of this crisis on suppliers
Next	Cancelled some orders but will pay for orders that were due to leave supplier factories up to and including April 10. Selecting ranges and continues to order stock for later in the year	Product teams have cancelled stock that no longer need and identified stock that can carry over to future seasons. Made good progress and saved around 290 million pounds ($354 million) on stock purchases. Endeavoured to be fair to suppliers

(continued)

(continued)

Buyers	*Order status*	*Comment from buyers*
Walmart	Will pay for orders, with a few exceptions. Has placed new orders in South and Southeast Asia	Estimated that such exceptions will amount to less than 2% of estimated annual private brand apparel orders in Bangladesh
Gap	Reuters could not determine status of orders	Focused on reducing expenses while doing what is in the best interest of employees, customers and partners, as well as the long-term health of the company. Managing inventory, including identifying those products can sell in the short-term, those can store now to sell later, and those orders need to cancel
Bestseller	Committed to paying for orders already made and in production, but has negotiated changes in terms with suppliers. Says it is placing reduced volume of orders for Autumn	Any changes in terms and volumes have been agreed with all suppliers through these individual negotiations and all due invoices to suppliers have been paid enabling suppliers to cover their expense
H&M	Will pay for orders and is placing new ones, though the crisis is impacting plans	Highly value the relationship with suppliers and stand by commitments, being transparent and having responsible purchasing practices
Inditex	Will pay for orders, whether finished or in production	Ensure that all orders that are in production are completely paid according to the original payment schedule, making full payment even in the event that current circumstances mean that it's not yet possible for the products to be shipped

(continued)

(continued)

Buyers	*Order status*	*Comment from buyers*
Marks and Spencer	Paying for orders shipped before March 24, paying for all made garments for almost every order not shipped before March 24	Have paid for all shipped products and for the vast majority of orders will pre-pay for all garments and committed fabric—which is the most expensive cost for a supplier—and across all partners will aim to ensure that no fabric goes to waste and is used at a later date
Tesco	Committed to paying for orders, shipped or unshipped	Not changing payment terms or asking for discounts, and will use most of the fabric suppliers have already bought on future orders
Sainsbury	Has paid for everything manufactured for it	Have honoured every contract with clothing suppliers
ASOS	Delayed and canceled orders worth between 5 million pounds and 6 million pounds ($6 mln to $7.3 mln). Will pay for orders that were shipped by March 13. Negotiating settlements with suppliers individually	Reviewing stock intake, reducing reliance on categories that have been affected such as dresses and tailoring, and shifting into higher-demand product, like loungewear and activewear. As a result, have had to delay some orders and cancel others
Primark	Will pay for 370 million pounds in orders either finished or in production for handover by April 17. Primark did not say what percentage of its total commitments that represents	Committed to paying for some 370 million pounds ($450 mln) of additional orders for product over and above the 1.5 billion pounds of stock in stores, depots and in transit
Mango	Will pay for orders already shipped but delaying payment for those in production. Has made new orders from factories in China and Bangladesh	Have committed to pay for products already shipped and for those that are still in production have negotiated with the suppliers to extend the payment time by one month
Fast Retailin (Uniqlo)	Has committed to paying for orders and is placing new orders	Believe that brands have an important role to play in mitigating the humanitarian and economic threats posed by the Covid-19 pandemic

(continued)

(continued)

Buyers	*Order status*	*Comment from buyers*
New Look	Cancelled 20% of spring/summer orders from Bangladesh	Could not place new orders until further notice and would be temporarily postponing outstanding supplier payments until the situation improves
JC Penney	Delaying payment for orders	Extended payment terms to 60 days

Source Dhaka Tribune (May 19, 2020)

After a public outcry, some Western companies agreed to pay for orders that have already been shipped or are in production. Others asked for discounts or have delayed payment, leaving suppliers struggling to stay afloat. Asking for discounts and pushing back orders from the suppliers demonstrate the power of the buyers during this pandemic. Labeling the buyers' action as 'stunning hypocrisy', Boersma notes that the intention of the buyers seems to be to safeguard shareholder dividends at the expense of workers at the bottom of the supply chain (Black 2020). The buyers' legal obligations are complicated as well. To avoid liability, the buyers are using 'force majeure' clause that release them from their contractual duties in exceptional circumstances. Alan Behr, a partner at Phillips Nizer, a fashion law firm said, "If you have anything in there (force majeure clause) on disease, pandemics, quarantines, then you have a specific force majeure clause that will probably be effective for you in negotiations. If it simply says 'act of god,' which nearly all of them say, well you've got a basis for discussion there" (Bain 2020). The lawyer further added that if a supplier did try to sue for damages, they would first probably need to try to mitigate their losses which means, for example, if factory owners had purchased materials already, they would need to try to sell those materials to recoup whatever costs they could. However, the best solution for the buyers, as Behr argued, is not to go for legal action such as force majeure and for the suppliers not to sue the buyers but to sit together to reach an agreement beneficial for both parties because the pandemic will not remain forever and the buyers can't do business without suppliers (Bain 2020).

Struggling Suppliers

In order to complete those orders not yet cancelled, some owners kept factories open through lockdown without proper social distancing. Restrictions for factories were then relaxed in May despite the increasing number of coronavirus cases in Bangladesh. Understandably, many fear that more and more workers will get infected in the factories. The Covid-19 has pushed the suppliers' association BGMEA into a difficult position to decide whether or not to close the factories. On one hand, there has been pressure on the suppliers to keep the factories open for the sake of survival of the business. On the other hand, trade unions and activists from around the world are worried about the health and lives of the garment workers and demand shutting down of factories. Although the BGMEA initially has urged the owners to close their factories, it later allowed production for factories that have export orders and the ones that are manufacturing products to protect from coronavirus.

A study was conducted by the CED (2020) based on an online survey of 2334 factories in June reveals that the factories are reawakening from the disaster gradually. The key findings are: 79.26% factories were in operation, only 8.49% factories were permanently closed, 40.54% of the factories were found to be hopeful to resume their operation in full phase after June 2020, among the currently operational factories 27.08% of the factories were found to be currently utilizing more than 80% of their total capacity (CED 2020). The factories which are currently operational are using 92.1% of their workforce during the pandemic as compared to pre-pandemic period. 93% reported they were producing only their regular products while the remaining 7% of the factories produced a combination of masks, PPEs and regular products. However, 36 factories claimed that they were producing masks without any profit margin and 22 were producing PPE without any profit margin.

Factories that were members of any trade association had WPC, and had Safety Committee took higher number of measures in the factory to prevent Covid—19 than factories that were non-member, did not have WPC, and did not have Safety Committee (CED 2020).

A tale of a supplier, Mustafiz Uddin: Into a death trap

"I have been giving my life to save my factory from being perished last 4 months, and I have left no stone unturned in that effort. I was advised to explore the possibility of selling the cancelled / stocked items which were made for some of my buyers. I reached out to a few buyers and then discovered another harsh reality. I need to take no objection clearance from the buyer, who cancelled the goods unethically, to be able to sell it to another buyer, and I would get the permission if I can replace the buttons, rivets, zippers, etc. Honestly speaking, if I remove and replace those then the products will not be in a proper shape to sell to a consumer.

My question to this very civilized world, I won't either be paid for my goods, nor will the stocks be released by the buyers and paid for, nor will they allow me to sell those off to third parties without altering them to a non-sellable shape, where will we go? There is no law to protect me from unethical cancellations and non-payments, and there are laws to prevent me access alternate ways to live! How merciless! Is it the world where we talk so big and loud about responsibility, purchasing practices and sustainability!"

Source Cline (2020)

Even though demand for clothes has plummeted, many factory owners feel they cannot afford to remain closed because (a) some online retailers are still buying (b) demand may revive as lockdowns ease in parts of Europe and America and (c) demand for PPE. The exporters also raise a valid point that the competing countries such as Cambodia, China, Sri Lanka and Vietnam have already reopened. A leading Bangladeshi factory owner believed "If Bangladeshi suppliers remain on lockdown, he fears, customers may start to shop elsewhere" (The Economist 2020). There has been a change in the exporting product after the rise of this pandemic. The factory owners have received orders of making masks and hospital gowns for front line medical workers in the developed countries which offer some comfort for the Bangladeshi entrepreneurs.

Although the labour ministry and the DIFE have held several meetings with different stakeholders including the factory management, it has been difficult to avoid loss of income for workers. However, the pace of laying off has showed as a sign that large and medium factories are receiving orders from the buyers of Europe and the US. But the small factories are facing enormous difficulties as they do not have work orders and their financial strength is weaker than the large factories. The RMG industry has more than 30% shortage of work orders (Mirdha 2020a) and thus the factories are operating below full capacity.

Vulnerability of Workers

More than 80% of the workers of the industry are women who support their own families and send remittances to their parents as well. Their jobs are not protected due to the ineffective execution of labour laws, lack of union negotiations, capitalist mindset of the entrepreneurs and above all the absence of social safety net for the workers. For those workers, under these circumstances, loss of income is devastating because any pay cut can lead to deprivations and even starvation. Millions of garment factory workers in Bangladesh have been released from work in the wake of the coronavirus pandemic. According to the Department of Inspection for Factories and Establishment (DIFE), more than 25,000 workers have been fired till now (Mirdha 2020a, b). However, Amirul Haque Amin, the president of the National Garment Workers Federation has disagreed with this estimation arguing the actual number of lay-off workers is higher than the estimate of the DIFE. It has left them without income and basic resources to fight the pandemic. Some are returning to the villages and others are staying in their homes close to factories with the hope of resuming work. They have been left in a state of abject poverty.

Underlining the vulnerability of the workers, Nazma Akhtar argued "The cruel reality is that the sufferer is our worker. They are the most vulnerable. The manufactures will be losing profit, but it is the worker who will lose their food. We have to think about the people who made you [brands] profit for years. When they need you, you cannot leave them in a starving situation. All these years we worked to make your companies so much profit. We did that together. We should be in this together" (Suhrawardi 2020). Although the BGMEA directed all of its members not to ask their workers to return to Dhaka until a concrete decision was taken about reopening of factories, the workers were scared of losing their jobs. One of the factories sacked about 709 workers justifying the cancellation of orders from buyers (The Daily Star 2020). The same news report reveals the thoughts of a worker, who said: "We do not accept the decision. We want to get back our jobs. The prime minister said no worker will be sacked. We will have to starve." Garment workers across Bangladesh have protested outside factories over unpaid wages after the cancellation of orders and in some cases protests turned violent. The BGMEA has identified at least 46 factories which have not paid workers salaries for March 2020 (Mirdha 2020a, b). In some cases, the furloughed garment workers have been promised some compensation for the days of work they missed while their factories were shut. One of the furloughed workers shared the frustration in this way: "He (manager) told us we'll be paid 60% of our salaries for the days we missed. But he also said global orders have basically stopped, and he doesn't know how long he'll be able to keep paying us at all" (Frayer 2020). Strikes have happened in large non-union plants. The trade unions leaders have pointed out the usefulness of unions in managing workers' frustration and anger. In this context, the IBC Secretary General argued that if the owners allowed trade unions, the union leaders would be able to communicate with the workers on strike during this pandemic (Perera 2020).

Factory owners terminated workers under several sections of the labour law, such as sections 12, 16 and 20, showing that they have no available work orders, said Nazma Akhter, president of the Sommilito Garments Sramik Federation (The Business Standard, 2020). When factories are forced to close for a certain period in the event of a catastrophe, sections 12 and 16 of the Bangladesh Labour Act 2006 may become of relevance. According to Section 12 (subsection 8), if the period of stoppage of work due to any other cause out of control extends beyond three working days, the workers may be laid-off (Fair Wear 2020). These workers (laid-off) shall be paid compensation by the employer for all days during which he/she is so laid-off, except for such weekly holidays as may intervene as stated in section 16 of the Labor Act. In any case where, during a calendar year, a worker is to be laid-off after the first forty-five days, for any continuous period of fifteen days or more, the employer may, instead of laying-off such a worker, retrench him under section 20 (Fair Wear 2020).

After closing the factories for a while, the government later, in a directive, resumed operation of the export-oriented garment factories. This was a result of the pressure they received from the factory owners. The vulnerability of workers is expressed by a worker in this way: "When my line chief called and asked me to start working again, I asked him: 'Why are you doing this? Do you want to get us killed? He told me if we don't show the world the factory is ready and working, the orders will go to Vietnam, Cambodia or some other places and eventually we will all be kicked out of our jobs anyway" (The Guardian, May 11, 2020). The conditions for reopening factories were to maintain physical distance and protective measures to combat the pandemic. However, social distancing is near-impossible for Bangladesh, one of the world's most densely populated countries. The size of population of Bangladesh is 164 million who live in 57,000 square miles. A space roughly the size of North Carolina, but home to equivalent of half the population of the United States. The machine layouts in many plants have not been designed considering the COVID-19 and thus it is difficult to keep machines/workers distanced. Amid the community spread of the pandemic, the workers are concerned about the lack of safety measures at workplaces. In response, one of the BGMEA directors has noted that the larger business group has established a crisis management team with hotline phone numbers that would immediately respond to workers' calls (Perera, May 18, 2020).

According to a report of Bangladesh Garment Shramik Sanghati (BGSS), based on news reports published in 25 media outlets, the factories have resumed work without due preparations. The only new measure, after the pandemic, is hand-washing at the entrance of factories. However, no enforcement measures for physical distancing can be found. One worker said, "There was no change in the factory. I saw in the news that they promised protective gear like masks and social distancing, but our factory didn't give us anything. We paid for masks from our own pocket" (The Guardian, 2020). Taslima Akhter of BGSS demanded quick disclosure of information regarding infected and deceased workers and disinfection measures at factories (The Daily Star 2020). In a study by the BIGD (2020), the factory owners are held responsible by the trade unions for exposing the workers to health risks, transmitting the virus to the community, and effecting job insecurity. Instead of taking any responsibility for the distressed workers, factory owners and associations passed on all obligations to the government. The study further adds that in the face of the pandemic, the trade unions extended its cooperation by negotiating with the owners to reclaim the jobs of the workers, organizing awareness programmes about sanitary practices and supporting the DIFE to collect data on the number of closed factories, layoffs or retrenchments, amount of due wages, and the number of infections among the workers (BIGD 2020).

Response from the Government and Other Agencies

The government has announced a stimulus package of $590 million for the RMG industry in efforts to face the possible impact of the COVID-19 on the economy (Rahman 2020). According to the Bangladesh Bank (2020), this fund, as an interest-free loan, has been designed for the sole purpose of payment of wages and benefits to workers for up to three months. To access the stimulus package the RMG entrepreneurs must (i) export at least 80% of all manufactured products, (ii) show wages sheets confirming full wage-payment of workers for December 2019–February 2020; (iii) have established relationships with the banks for at least three months; (iv) ensure that all workers have MFS/bank accounts; and (v) authenticate the list of workers by submitting valid National ID cards or birth certificates. There is a service charge of 2% payable to the bank and the full repayment must be completed within two years with a grace period of six months. The unions raised questions about (a) the adequacy of the fund because the current size of government's fund is only about 51% of the amount needed to pay the minimum wage for three months and to cover at least 4000 factories (b) how much actually will be paid to each worker (c) the lack of a needs-based principle in implementing the package (BIGD 2020). No transparency of the disbursement of the stimulus package, inability of small factories to be eligible for this funding, lack of involvement of unions in the process and a database of workers to monitor and administer the status of payment are major problems.

The European Union (EU) has also proposed a €90-million grant for the Bangladeshi RMG workers who have either been laid-off or will permanently lose their jobs because of the Covid-19 pandemic (The Business Standard, June 2, 2020). This grant will be disbursed to one million workers and each worker will get cash support of Tk3000 for three months in the first phase—from June to August. The total size of the grant could be further increased to €500 million. However, the government has failed to develop a model for the wage disbursement and proposed to create a welfare fund with the grant instead of the wage disbursements (The Economist 2020). The workers have received a glimpse of hope after hearing of the EU's grant. One worker said, "when I learnt about the EU compensation for three months, it was my hope that it would help me till I find a new job. If it takes too long to disburse the fund, the ill fated workers will have to leave the city soon and will not be able to find another job" (The Economist 2020).

The key stakeholder of the industry, BGMEA has realized the importance of having an unemployment benefits scheme for the workers. Rubana Huq prescribed that with capacity reduction at 50% across the industry, the factories will need a revised business landscape for which a collective government to government (G2G) initiative is required (The Business Standard, June 2, 2020). Realizing the businesses in Germany receive adequate government support, the BGMEA has requested the German government to reassure buyers in Germany to take the apparel items already produced in Bangladesh. The BGMEA president predicted a situation to prompt social unrest if significant numbers of workers lose their jobs (Financial Express, March 26, 2020). Addressing the immediate needs of women garment workers in Bangladesh in the wake of the coronavirus outbreak, H&M is initiating a long-term project with a funding of $1.3 million (Ovi 2020). The BGMEA has issued guidelines to protect workers and urged the management to provide preventive measures such as wearing masks, washing hands and maintaining social distancing. Another measure of the organization is to reach out to hospitals to make sure that the infected garment workers get treatment. The ILO is working with the BGMEA and the BKMEA to launch a RMG 'Learning Hub' to address three areas: (1) raising COVID-19 prevention awareness among workers and factory management; (2) ensuring COVID-19 Occupational Safety and Health (OSH) preparedness guidelines are being followed and (3) continuing to promote strong social dialogue in the workplace (The Economist 2020).

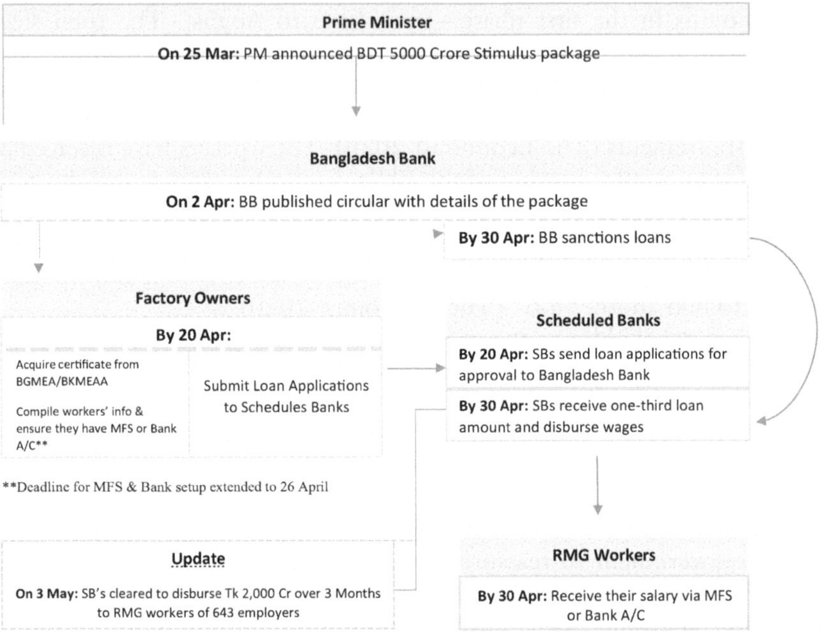

Flowchart for stimulus package (*Source* BIGD 2020)

The situation of public health in Bangladesh is far from ideal. For 164 million population, the country has about 2000 ventilators and around 1000 intensive-care beds (The Economist 2020). Although different stakeholders such as the government, EU, BGMEA, H&M have been offering different packages to fight back the pandemic, the magnitude of the sufferings is gigantic. Considering the limitations of the government some manufacturers like Chowdhury have taken matters into their own hands by paying workers' salary from their own packet. He asks, "For people at this level of society, it's impossible for them to have savings, and if you decide to lay them off, no one is going to hire them for the several months. So how are they going to survive?" (Suhrawardi 2020).

Lessons Learnt

A positive lesson to be taken from the Covid-19 as argued by Mostafiz Uddin is the need for greater collaboration among garment manufacturers globally (Uddin, June 15, 2020b). The solidarity of suppliers is required since all suppliers faced global and common problems. Criticizing the 'divide and rule' approach of the MNCs, Mostafiz Uddin (June 15, 2020a, b, c) has raised some questions for the global suppliers: "As garment manufacturers, can we not agree on some minimum acceptable standards that we all agree must be abided by from brands? Can we not - collectively - call on brands to avoid the questionable usage of the 'force majeure' legal remedy which is seeing brands walk away from contracts without any financial repercussions, while leaving the supplier financially liable? Can we not agree at a global level that the kind of behaviour we have seen from some brands - such as cancelling finished orders then ignoring all contact from beleaguered suppliers - will simply not be accepted?"

This is a difficult choice for the government—saving lives or the economy. Bangladesh is considered as a role model for other developing economies in achieving sustainable development. Bangladesh has the fastest-growing economy in the Asia-Pacific region and lately, it has been closing in on double-digit annual growth in its GDP. This achievement has been under threat due to the impact of the pandemic. In 2019, 20% of the people were living below the poverty line. Within a month after the pandemic, it has increased to 30% i.e.50 million people. The global strategy of lockdown, as argued by the policy-makers, seems to be ineffective in a country like Bangladesh where the informal sector contributes to more than 80% of the economy and the garment sector is the dominant export earning sector. Due to aggressive global competition, the industry that is already left with thin margins is now facing a complete breakdown. Consequently, million of workers and their families are facing financial ruin. It is imperative that Western brands and retailers uphold the values of worker welfare. All the Western brands are recognized now as advocating responsible sourcing. The livelihood security of the workers should be a fundamental priority within this advocacy but is the very thing that is lacking. There is no time like the present to champion brand responsibility towards workers, welfare and livelihood security.

References

Anner, M. "Labor Control Regimes and Worker Resistance in Global Supply Chains." Labor History, 56(3), 292–307. 2015.

Anner, M. "Binding Power: The Sourcing Squeeze, Workers' Rights, and Building Safety in Bangladesh since Rana Plaza." n.p.: Penn State University. CGWR Research Report. http://lser.la.psu.edu/gwr/documents/CGWR2017ResearchReportBindingPower.pdf (accessed 3 February, 2019), 2018.

Anner, M. "Abandoned? The Impact of Covid-19 on Workers and Businesses at the Bottom of Global Garment Supply Chains." n.p.: Research report, March 27, 2020. Centre for Global Workers.' Right, Penn State University. 2020.

Bain, M. "More Than a Million Garment Workers Are Out of Work Because of Coronavirus." Quartz, April 1, 2020. https://qz.com/1828541/covid-19-leads-to-one-million-garment-workers-unemployed.

BIGD. "Taka 5000 Crore Novel Corona Financial Stimulus Package for Export-Oriented Industries: RMG Trade Union Responses." Research Report Gender Series 6, Rapid Research Response to COVID-19, BRAC Institute of Governance and Development (BIGD), BRAC University. June 18, 2020.

Black, Z. "'Bullying' Clothing Companies Are Asking Struggling Suppliers for Discounts." The Daily Star. 2020. https://thenewdaily.com.au/finance/consum/kmart-mosaic-coroner/2020/05/13avirus.

CED. Rapid Survey: Phase 2 "Status of the Export-Oriented RMG Factories in Bangladesh During COVID-19 Pandemic." July 2020

Cline, E. "The Power of Pay Up." Ethical Fashion, Asia, July 14, 2020. https://atmos.earth/payup-bangladesh-factory-worker-social-campaign/.

Dhaka Tribune. "Covid-19: Fashion Brands Cut Orders from Bangladesh, Asian Garments." Dhaka Tribune, May 19, 2020. https://www.dhakatribune.com/world/2020/05/19/fashion-brands-cut-orders-from-bangladesh-asian-garments.

Donaghey, J. and J. Reinecke. "When Industrial Democracy Meets Corporate Social Responsibility—A Comparison of the Bangladesh Accord and Alliance as Responses to the Rana Plaza Disaster." British Journal of Industrial Relations, 56(1): 14–42. 2018.

Ellis-Petersen, H. and R. Ahmed. "Bangladesh Garment Factories Reopen Despite Coronavirus Threat to Workers." The Guardian. https://www.theguardian.com/global-development/2020/may/11/bangladesh-garment-factories-reopen-despite-coronavirus-threat-to-workers.

Fair Wear. "How Does Covid-19 Affect Women Garment Workers?" https://www.fairwear.org/covid-19-dossier/worker-engagement-and-monitoring/gender-analysis.

Fair Wear. "Covid-19 Impact and Responses: Bangladesh—Fair Wear." Fair Wear. https://www.fairwear.org/covid-19-impact-and-responses-bangladesh.

Frayer, L. "For Bangladesh's Struggling Garment Workers, Hunger Is a Bigger Worry Than Pandemic." NPR. 2020. https://www.npr.org/2020/06/05/869486297/for-bangladeshs-struggling-garment-workers-hunger-is-a-bigger-worry-than-pandemic.

Islam, M. "Coronavirus Measures Give Bangladeshi Workers for Global Clothing Chains a Stark choice: Disease or Starvation." The Conversation, June 30, 2020. https://theconversation.com/coronavirus-measures-give-bangladeshi-workers-for-global-clothing-chains-a-stark-choice-disease-or-starvation-138549.

Kabeer, N., M. Solaiman and L. Huq. "Paradigm Shift or Business as Usual?" Workers' Views on Multi-Stakeholder Initiatives in Bangladesh. n.p.: Development and Change. pp.1–39, 2020.

Locke, R M. "The Promise and Limits of Private Power: Promoting Labor Standards in a Global Economy." New York: Cambridge University Press. 2013.

Merk, J. "Production Beyond the Horizon of Consumption: Spatial Fixes and Anti-sweatshop Struggles in the Global Athletic Footwear Industry." Global Society, 25(1), 73–95. n.p., 2011.

Mirdha, R. "Orders Are Finally Trickling in, but Garment Factories Are Still Reaching Out for the Axe." The Daily Star, July 17, 2020a. https://www.thedailystar.net/business/news/orders-are-finally-trickling-garment-factories-are-still-reaching-out-the-axe-1930117.

Mirdha, R. U. "Failure to Pay Wages: BGMEA Asks Govt to Close 46 Factories." The Daily Star, May 19, 2020b.

Ovi, I. H. "Apparel Exporters See 62% Drop in New Orders." Dhaka Tribune, June 15, 2020. https://www.dhakatribune.com/business/economy/2020/06/15/apparel-exporters-see-62-drop-in-new-orders.

Pahle, S. "The Rise and Demise of the 'Social Clause' Proposal in the 1990s: Implications of a Discourse Theoretical Reading." Labor History, 51(3), 389–410. n.p., 2010.

Paton, E. "'Our Situation is Apocalyptic': Bangladesh Garment Workers Face Ruin." The New York Times, March 3, 2020. https://www.nytimes.com/2020/03/31/fashion/coronavirus-bangladesh.html.

Perera, W. "Growing Number of Bangladeshi Garment Workers Infected with COVID-19." https://www.wsws.org/en/articles/2020/05/19/bang-m18.html.

Rahman, Shahidur. "Broken Promises of Globalization: The Case of the Bangladesh Garment Industry." Lanham: Lexington Books. 2014.

Rahman, S. "What the Pandemic Means for RMG." Dhaka Tribune, May 5, 2020. https://www.dhakatribune.com/opinion/op-ed/2020/05/05/what-the-pandemic-means-for-rmg.

Rahman, S. and K. M. Rahman. "Multi-Actor Initiatives After Rana Plaza: Factory Mangers' Views." Development and Change, March 2020.

Reinecke, J. "After Rana Plaza: Building Coalitional Power for Labour Rights Between Unions and (Consumption-Based) Social Movement Organizations." n.p.: 22(5), 720–740. 2015.

Reinecke, J., J. Donaghey and L. Lauriano. "Business Models and Labor Standards: Making the Connection." London: Ethical Trading Initiative. 2019.

Ryan, T. "Experts: Bangladesh Accord Is a Game Changer Available." Solidarity Center. http://www.solidaritycenter.org/content.asp?contentid=1716 (Accessed January 7, 2016). n.p. 2013

Saxena, S. "Bangladesh's Garment Industry Unraveling." East Asia Forum. https://www.eastasiaforum.org/2020/04/24/persistent-danger-plagues-bangladeshs-garment-industry.

Scheper, C. "Labour Networks Under Supply Chain Capitalism: The Politics of the Bangladesh Accord." Development and Change, 48(5), 1069–1088. 2017.

Smith, J. "Rana Plaza and the Crack in Economic Theory." n.p.: The Third SPERI Annual Conference. The Global Contours of Growth & Development Beyond the Crisis. 2014.

Stepanek, J. F. "Bangladesh, Equitable Growth?" New York: Pergamon Press. 1979

Suhrawardi, R. "Collapse of Bangladesh's Garment Industry During Coronavirus Leaves Its Workers More Vulnerable Than Ever." Forbes, March 30, 2020. https://www.forbes.com/sites/rebeccasuhrawardi/2020/03/30/collapse-of-bangladeshs-garment-industry-leaves-its-workers-more-vulnerable-than-ever-during--coronavirus/#2afd9ccaf27e.

The Daily Star. "BGMEA Issues Reopen Timetable." April 26, 2020. https://www.thedailystar.net/frontpage/news/bgmea-issues-reopen-timetable-1896880.

The Economist. "Suffering from a Stitch—Bangladesh Cannot Afford to Close Its Garment factories." The Economist, April 30, 2020. Retrieved from https://www.economist.com/asia/2020/04/30/bangladesh-cannot-afford-to-close-its-garment-factories.

The Financial Express. "Virus Vexes Nearly $2.0b Apparel Export Orders." 2020. https://thefinancialexpress.com.bd/economy/bangladesh/virus-vexes-nearly-20b-apparel-export-orders-1585020318.

Uddin, J. "EU Plans to Pay 1m RMG Workers for 6 Months." The Business Standard, 2020a. https://tbsnews.net/economy/rmg/eu-plans-pay-1m-rmg-workers-6-months-87607.

Uddin, M. "Global Suppliers Are Stronger Working Together." The Daily Star, 2020b. https://www.thedailystar.net/opinion/rmg-notes/news/global-suppliers-are-stronger-working-together-1914321.
Uddin, M. "Garments Industry Needs Evolution, Not Revolution." The Daily Star, June 20, 2020c. https://www.thedailystar.net/opinion/rmg-notes/news/garments-industry-needs-evolution-not-revolution-1921957.
Uddin, M. "Time to Put Workers First." The Daily Star. https://www.thedailystar.net/opinion/rmg-notes/news/time-put-workers-first-1929269.
Zajak, S. "International Allies, Institutional Layering and Power in the Making of Labour in Bangladesh." Development and Change, 48(5), 1007–1030. 2017.

CHAPTER 10

Wither Labor and Human Rights? Precarious Work and Informal Economies in the Post-COVID-19 Global South

Sandya Hewamanne

Abbreviations

AFWA	Asia Floor Wage Alliance
BOI	Board of Investment
CSR	Corporate Social Responsibility
EPF	Employees Provident Fund
ETF	Employees Trust Fund
FTZ	Free Trade Zone
GCRF	Global Challenges Research Fund

S. Hewamanne (✉)
Department of Sociology, University of Essex, Essex, UK
e-mail: skhewa@essex.ac.uk

S. Hewamanne and S. Yadav (eds.), *The Political Economy of Post-COVID Life and Work in the Global South: Pandemic and Precarity*, International Political Economy Series,
https://doi.org/10.1007/978-3-030-93228-2_10

GSEU	General Services Employees Union
MSA	Modern Slavery Act
PHI	Public Health Inspectors

> Can we change the workshop's focus to talk about economic problems of factory workers resulting from the pandemic and lockdown? (Neetha—a NGO Staff member)

> No. We can't do that. Because the funding was to conduct a workshop on occupational health laws and practice. (Author)

> Oh! Okay. Then let's focus on occupational health stuff. But I am warning you, workers would want to talk about the difficulties created by factories shutting down. (Neetha)

This dialogue occurred between Neetha and me in May 2020, while we discussed a workshop scheduled for July 2020. The funding to organize the workshop (one of three) was provided in January 2020 and the grant was advertised before the world had any inclination of COVID-19. Thus, the funds were to be spent only on proposed activities with no flexibility. However, the pandemic caused the funding agency to be more flexible—allowing meetings to take place via zoom (as opposed to face-to-face) and some changes regarding budgeted expenses. Although not wholly satisfactory, I was happy to conduct zoom workshops as I felt occupational health concerns are paramount when a global pandemic is raging.

The workshops, however, saw impassioned factory workers take every opportunity to discuss how in the context of the pandemic and the lockdown their occupational health rights or human rights were going to be the least important concern for factory owners and global buyers. They talked over each other to relate how they were experiencing extreme depravations due to the rapidly unraveling global production networks. My attempts to revert the discussion back to health laws and human rights were continually thwarted. This was strikingly different from 2018 to 2019 when I conducted seven workshops that began by discussing occupational health and moved on to labor and human rights. Workers participated enthusiastically during those two years and some showed passionate interest in improving factory occupational health standards and educating others on laws and regulations. To this end, they formed working groups, which continue to function as of July 2021. However, the excitement on legal empowerment, monitoring, and negotiating rights has died down and the focus has changed to finding and maintaining factory jobs. This is a direct result of the global pandemic, the lockdown and the consequent breakdown in global production networks.

Informal economies and precarious work are highly vulnerable to external disruptions. Workers in global assembly line production, especially in the apparel sector, are more susceptible to external shocks. Below I explicate how the pandemic affected top of global networks and how factory workers at the bottom-most level experienced its cascading effects. In doing so, the chapter, highlights how the pandemic is reversing positive policy outcomes that resulted from decades of labor protests. It contends that the immediate post-pandemic future is bleak for labor and human rights struggles within the global production networks and argues for rethinking of informal economies beyond neoliberal development models.

Global Networks; Global Fallouts

Global production networks, or the cascading system of subcontracting, intensified when Western investors and multinational corporations took full advantage of the structural adjustment policies that the World Bank initiated for debt-ridden developing countries by establishing factories in tariff free export-oriented production zones. These corporations sought to minimize the production costs by utilizing the abundant low-cost labor available in the Global South. Countries such as Mexico, Vietnam, Thailand, Indonesia, Honduras, and China established demarcated zones for transnational manufacturing of garments electronics, toys, rubber products and medical equipment where people, mostly women, worked for very low salaries in harsh conditions.

The structure of global assembly lines remains gendered, with women doing assembly line work while men occupy managerial positions. Employing women for assembly line work is based on patriarchal stereotypes that suggest women are nimble-fingered, docile, and supplementary earners, whereas men are assumed to be family's main breadwinners. Reports of labor and human rights abuses within factories raised concerns among global consumers, with companies like Nike, Gap, and Apple being accused of subcontracting to factories in the Global South that operated under sweat-shop like conditions. Global consumer activism brought about some positive policy outcomes in the form of global auditing, corporate social responsibility policies, and the 2015 UK

Modern Slavery Act, which sought to eradicate forced labor within supply chains. Manufacturing jobs in these global assembly lines provide much-needed wages for unemployed youth, allowing subcontracting factories in the global south to thrive with varying levels of compliance to international labor codes and best practice models.

When COVID-19 struck, stores closed across North America and Europe. Western brands canceled orders already in production worth billions of dollars, leaving shipments of clothing with no takers. As global production chains unraveled, closed shops in Europe and North America translated into more and more closed factories in the Global South (Nilson and Terazono 2020). Hundreds of factories closed across Asia, including Vietnam, China, and Bangladesh. This has led to millions of garment workers in Asia, a vast majority of them women, been suspended or laid off depriving them of $6 billion in wages (Nilson 2020).

In the West, companies such as JC Penney and Neiman Marcus filed for bankruptcy protection. The chain reaction caused 20–30% of companies along the value chain—from brands to wholesalers and department stores—to close down, thereby affecting numerous job levels across the industry. Many factory owners in the Global South are finding it difficult to recover payments from major brands and retailers who refuse to pay or demand deep discounts for goods that were already in production or ready for shipment (Anner 2020). More significantly, not having a pipeline of new orders is leading to deep cuts within the labor force. Factories have overhead costs (i.e., rent and utilities), which makes it difficult to stay afloat without steady orders. As a result, factories are closing indefinitely, leading to massive loss of employment. For example, at least 110 garment factories closed between January–September in Cambodia alone, leaving over 55,000 workers unemployed (Clean Clothes Campaign 2020). By July 2021 Asian workers have lost 12bn in wages (Nilson 2021). Workers who migrated for work in global subcontracting factories were especially affected. Clean Clothes Campaign reported that in August 2021 around 2000 migrant workers from Myanmar are stranded in Laos without work or money for rent or food (2021b). Thus, the pandemic is endangering livelihoods associated with global production networks, which while rooted in exploitation provided rural women some expendable income and socially empowering opportunities.

Perhaps more alarmingly the reduced orders and subsequent cutting of jobs have created a context where there are a lot more workers waiting for jobs than available work, thus providing a more beneficial environment for the employers. In this climate of financial struggles, many governments of the Global South are turning a blind eye to factories violating rules and accepted best practices, such as cutting wages (sometimes up to half of what they were pre-pandemic) and canceling bonuses and incentives (Dabindu 2020; Hewamanne 2021a). Asia Floor Wage Alliance (AFWA), Asian labor led global social alliance across garment producing countries, following an in-depth six-country regional study surveying over 2000 mostly women workers in Bangladesh, Cambodia, India, Indonesia, Pakistan, and Sri Lanka, found massive wage theft in the global garment industry during the pandemic. Their global launch event (July 7 and 14) was unapologetically titled "Money Heist: Covid-19 Wage Theft in Global Garment Supply Chains." All country reports highlighted similar processes of wage reductions and slashing of benefits (AFWA 2021).

The intensified global movement against human trafficking saw the UK Government pass the Modern Slavery Act (MSA) in 2015. Article 54 of the MSA specifically requires British companies to eradicate forced labor within their global supply chains. Although a step in the right direction, it led to companies outsourcing compliance responsibilities to local factory managers, who in turn shifted responsibility on to workers' shoulders. The MSA thus inadvertently became another burden for workers and one that further controlled their activities (Hewamanne 2020a). The pandemic has seen even the changes that were instituted at the surface level to be reversed, given that workers now grab whatever assembly line job they can in order to survive (Hewamanne 2021a).

Decades of journalistic reporting, research, and highly publicized disasters in factories had led to a concentrated focus on Corporate Social Responsibility (CSR) policies within the global subcontracting realm. These policies have led to improvements in shop-floor organization and health and safety measures, such as improved ventilation, more bathroom and water breaks, medical center visits, time allocations for health education, etc. However, the improvements at times seem to be engineered to minimize buyer guilt than for workers' wellbeing (Ruwanpura 2011; Goger 2014). For instance, while workers who faint on the job are treated better now structural changes that would enable conditions where workers would not faint at work, such as reducing impossible targets and long work hours, have not been implemented. Furthermore, the scholarship on CSR (Cross 2011; Rajak 2011; Hewamanne 2017; Prentice and De Neve 2017) shows how some of these initiatives are limited to the shop floor and have no bearing on worker wellbeing outside the factories. This focus on the shop floor allowed companies to easily turn a blind eye to difficulties, which are connected to work yet experienced outside the factory premises, by their workers.

Notwithstanding the prohibition of unionizing within FTZ factories, workers throughout the Global South found creative ways to protest and agitate for their rights (Merk 2009, 2014; De Neve 2008; Ong 1991). These protests, while seemingly unsuccessful in the short run, brought about some important changes within global assembly lines over time. The local protests drew the attention of Western consumers whose activist work has driven the focus on CSR policies. However, the pandemic and subsequent unraveling of global production networks have stymied these efforts as workers find themselves in a position highly detrimental to labor rights bargaining.

Wage theft and modern slavery thrive within global assembly lines, while countries slowly move toward authoritarian politics under the pretext of pandemic-related difficulties (Lorch and Sombatpoonsiri 2020; Hewamanne 2021b; DeVotta 2021). Non-vaccinated workers toil within crowded factory conditions and get infected and quarantined at alarming rates in Sri Lanka and other subcontracting countries in the Global South. For example, in mid-August 2021 Bangladesh alone has two million global factory workers still waiting for vaccinations (Clean Clothes Campaign 2021b). The companies that profit from these workers' labor are offloading their setbacks to subcontracting companies, thereby exacerbating difficulties faced at the bottom most rungs of the global production networks—the assembly line workers. I discuss below how these pandemic-related setbacks are affecting labor and human rights education within global production networks in Sri Lanka.

Sri Lanka and Subcontracting

The first Sri Lankan Free Trade Zone (FTZ) was established in 1978 in Katunayake, a town about 35 km from Colombo and home to the island's premier international airport, after a newly elected government began pursuing structural adjustment programs. Unemployed rural women filled the newly created assembly line jobs, characterized by rigorous schedules, poor work conditions, and minimal wages. Since then, thirteen other zones of varied capacity have been established. Even though officially called export processing zones, the workers still call these demarcated areas "the zone" or "FTZs" and I thus will use the term FTZ throughout this chapter. Sri Lanka's FTZ factories demand maximum output for minimal wages in exploitative working conditions as is common in other transnational factories in the Global South. Similarly, they also practice a distinctively late-capitalist form of gendered working relations where men manage and supervise women. In 2020, over 40 years after the first FTZ was established, the basic worker salary is Rs. 14,000 (about US$ 80) per month. However, one could earn about Rs. 25,000 by working overtime. This chapter is based on research conducted among workers associated with the Katunayake and Biyagama FTZs.

About 45,000 rural women from economically and socially marginalized groups work as machine operators in the Katunayake FTZ's 92 factories but together with workers from subcontracting factories located around the zone the number rises to 275,000 (Praja 2020). Biyagama also has close to 30,000 workers within the zone while subcontracting outfits in the surrounding area employ a further 20,000 workers. Most women workers are unmarried, young, and well-educated, often with 10–12 years of schooling (Hewamanne 2020b).

There are few state or factory-run hostels for the women who migrate from rural areas. Thus, they rent hastily built, poorly ventilated rooms from area residents (Hewamanne 2012, 2016). Although working and living conditions are difficult, declining agricultural economies and dearth of other work opportunities in rural areas push women to migrate and work in factories within and just outside the FTZs. The experience of living with other young women in urban areas cause these workers to undergo social, cultural, emotional, and cognitive changes even as they acquire global knowledge flows. This socialization process in factories and boarding houses encourage them to dress, behave, think, and desire in new ways.

Despite strict rules of non-unionization within factories Sri Lankan workers have engaged in creative forms of protests. Most notably, in 2011 workers resorted to a forceful protest, which culminated in police brutality and the death of a worker, forcing the government to retract a pension bill that sought to curtail their ability to obtain their Employees Provident Fund (EPF) and Employees Trust Fund (ETF) savings early. Individual workers have also sought support from several NGOs in Katunayake and Biyagama FTZs to pursue legal action against factories breaching labor laws. Although the continuing prohibition of unionization is detrimental to labor rights, the workers and the NGOs continue to find creative ways to circumvent factory restrictions to organize collectively. These included using NGO conducted classes in English, dance, embroidery, and yoga as spaces for educating and organizing the workers, boarding house visits by NGO staff to distribute educational materials, and using internationally funded workshops to educate workers on their labor and human rights. Still the FTZs and General Services Employees Union (FTZGSEU) remains the only trade union open for FTZ workers.

Parallel to CSR initiatives gaining prominence, factories reduced their regular workforce and increased the number of daily-hired workers to complete specific tasks. By 2015, the hiring of casual workers on a daily basis had become quite common, with such individuals branded "manpower workers." Their daily hiring took place conspicuously at the entrance to the Katunayake FTZ where women gathered under a banyan tree and waited for contractors to sign them up. Several dynamics led to this increase of manpower workers. The "garments without guilt" initiative that sought to brand Sri Lankan apparel production ethical (Saxena 2014) mandates meeting certain standards for the regular workforce, leading factories to rely more on casual workers. Additionally, the demands of "just in time production" (Barrientos 2013) have put tremendous pressure on factories to hire workers daily to supplement their regular workforce at short notice.

Dabindu (2017) reports that factories now encourage casual labor to the extent of asking regular workers to quit and re-enter as daily-hired laborers. Such moves allow management to satisfy ethical codes without jeopardizing profit margins. As the workers choose when and how long to work, these workers are freer and enjoyed the time that they had to hang out with friends and visit family. But this freedom comes with a price—insecure work, hidden exploitation, and loss of benefits. Still many daily-hired workers preferred the freedom over being tied to assembly line work, day in and day out. This preference is created by the current global labor regimes characterized by target-oriented assembly line work that is extremely stressful, backbreaking and coercive. Ultimately, such exploitative labor regimes ensure the continuing success of "race to the bottom." with daily-hired workers jeopardizing the bargaining powers of the regular workforce. A ready pool of casual labor just outside the gates mitigated any threat of strikes that the regular workforce could have used as a bargaining tool.

Yet, NGOs continue to engage in labor rights educational activities by reaching out to manpower workers as well. In 2018, I received funding from the ESRC Impact Acceleration program to conduct workshops on occupational health policies for global factory workers. In 2019, I received two additional grants from the British Academy Global Challenges Research Fund (GCRF) to conduct further educational workshops on occupational health in particular, and labor and human rights in general. All workshops were to be conducted in partnership with two NGO's in the Katunayake area, Dabindu and SAFE. The additional grants were for workshops to be held in May–July 2020. As noted above the pre-pandemic and pandemic time workshops dynamics were acutely divergent.

Following a brief description of my participating, conducting, and sponsoring labor and human rights educational workshops, and how Sri Lanka's three COVID-19 waves affected global factory workers, I discuss the divergent workshop experiences during COVID-19 to demonstrate how the ground map for achieving labor and human rights within the global production networks has changed dramatically due to the pandemic.

Labor and Human Rights Education-Pre-Pandemic

The first NGO-sponsored educational workshop I attended was organized by Dabindu, one of the oldest activist organizations in the FTZ, and was held over three days in July 2000. This internationally funded workshop had discussion groups on topics as diverse as labor rights, reproductive rights, sexual health, globalization and personal accounting. Since then, I have participated in several one-day workshops held for global factory workers and collected information on others. It was clear that the number of educational workshops significantly increased during the past decade as CSR initiatives gained in importance. This was because holding workshops during shifts for selected workers, or weekend workshops in the factory premises, counted under factory CSR initiatives. Most educational workshops, however, took place outside factory premises and were organized by NGOs using their connections to large boarding houses.

I was invited to give lectures in several workshops when in Sri Lanka for fieldwork. These workshops generally followed the same program for different groups of factory workers and focused primarily on labor rights, i.e., how to obtain individual reparations through local labor tribunals for breaches of law. This stemmed from the precarity of global factory work and the resultant high turnover, which in turn necessitated new groups of workers being educated on their basic rights. Most presentations did not make a connection between labor and human rights.

Based on research conducted in three boarding houses, I presented a paper titled "Tamil Workers, Human Rights and 'Mundane' Politics in Post-War Sri Lanka," at the fifth Sri Lanka Roundtable hosted by the University of Edinburgh in 2016. It discussed how women workers have only a vague set of ideas about human rights and how the workers from the two main ethnic groups (Sinhala and Tamil) understood human rights in quite divergent ways with neither displaying an in-depth knowledge. While Sinhala workers showed more knowledge of labor laws, Tamil workers' knowledge of labor rights was relatively low. Furthermore, due to the civil war and post-war unemployment, the latter were especially grateful for their jobs irrespective of work conditions and showed a reluctance toward collective activism. They were, however, more interested in human rights and frequently utilized the words human rights even when confronted with everyday slights. Since the Tamil workers started arriving at FTZs only a few years after the civil war ended in 2009, the paper stressed the need to enhance meaningful labor and human rights education for both groups of workers together. Due to language differences the workshops for the Sinhala and Tamil-speaking workers are held separately leading to misunderstandings and mistrust.

Rajapaksha (2019) assesses the low awareness of labor ordinances among Sri Lanka's global factory workers and contends that workers' level of education made a difference in their awareness while their level of experience did not. She further shows that workers showed a greater awareness of the Factories Ordinance and showed the least awareness of the Maternity Benefits Ordinance. This is not surprising considering that FTZs are governed by an intricate and complex combination of national labor laws, BOI regulations, and voluntary initiatives such as buyer codes of conduct enforced through auditing, reporting, and inspections.

There are numerous writings on how NGO workshops empower women workers to stand up for their rights (Abraham 2017; Connell 2019). Dabindu, Kalape Api, SAFE, Women's Center, Solidarity Center, and several other NGOs received regular international funding for such workshops in pre-pandemic times. Their workshops reached fluctuating numbers of workers, usually from the same factories and same boarding houses where managers and boarding owners are supportive of such educational workshops. Thus at each FTZ, workers conversant with labor rights and human rights exist together with those who are unaware of their rights. The difference corresponds to their exposure to educational efforts.

The ESRC and GCRF funded workshops I conducted in 2018 and 2019 were organized in partnership with Dabindu and SAFE. The titular focus was on occupational health laws and practice. Both organizations recruited workers from boarding houses they interacted with on a regular basis. Thus the participants of the first two workshops in 2018 were already somewhat knowledgeable. Workshops included interactive sessions conducted by professional trainers and NGO officers, which broke down the research material I presented at the beginning into digestible parts. These sessions animated the workers and at the end of the three initial workshops four working groups were formed to carry out proposed actions. The fourth workshop in 2018 brought other major stakeholders—BOI officials, managers, and NGO staff—to the table to discuss worker proposals and improve occupational health. When the partners decided to make the final workshop exclusive to get the support of BOI officials and managers for the proposed action, working groups protested and demanded members be allowed to attend the third workshop and confront the BOI officials and managers.

In 2019, in an effort to reach different groups of workers, workshops were held for Biyagama FTZ workers and those in factories just outside the Katunayake FTZ. By then, the working groups formed in 2018 had created solid action plans and were pursuing negotiations with factories. Some of these members attended the 2019 workshops, which were more broadly on labor laws and human rights. More working groups were formed after the 2019 workshops, and inter FTZ communication channels were established to renegotiate the action plans in ways that are more inclusive. When I left Sri Lanka in August 2019, I felt I was on the brink of something very important resulting from these workshops. Thus I was overjoyed when I received funding to hold further workshops in mid-2020. Consequently, two workshops for workers and two for managers and BOI officials were planned between May and July 2020.

Pandemic Waves and Global Factory Workers

As of July 16, COVID-19 has killed 4,380,849, while 208,424,644 have contracted the virus worldwide. Sri Lanka reported its first COVID-19 case in late February 2020. The country went into full lockdown on March 19 and an island-wide curfew was imposed until 11th of May.

While lockdown and curfew prevented the virus from spreading, the abrupt declaration of curfew affected thousands of FTZ workers adversely. The factories shut down without paying workers for the month of March while the cancelation of public transport services made it difficult for many to return to their village homes. Workers who were stranded in boarding houses with little to no money lacked food and other necessities. Within two weeks measures were taken to send the workers home, although many, especially the casual workers, decided to stay in their boarding houses with the hope that the factories would open any day (Fazlulhaq 2020).

Workers soon found out that these immediate concerns were the least of their worries. Between March to May 30, 2020 Sri Lanka's apparel exports fell 50% compared to the same period in 2019. This was a loss of close to $680 million. By April, the apparel industry faced losses of over $1.5 billion and swiftly appealed to the government for support to re-open factories and pay salaries and rent (Financial Times 2020). In June 2020, Tuli Cooray, the Secretary-General of the Joint Apparel Association Forum (JAAF), claimed that no orders were forthcoming for the fall season (Jayasinghe 2020). By October, overall exports to the US alone fell by 22.15%, while exports to the European Union fell by 21.36% (De Silva 2020). This bleak outcome was the same in other countries that depended on global assembly line work for export income. The resulting factory closures saw millions of garment workers, a vast majority of them women, being suspended or laid off, depriving them of billions of dollars in wages (Nilson and Terazono 2020; AFWA 2021; Nilson 2020).

Recent bankruptcy filings by companies such as JC Penney, and Neiman Marcus set in motion a chain reaction along with value networks, including brands, wholesalers, department stores, and supplier facilities to close, resulting in numerous job losses. More significantly, the factories are anxious about not having a pipeline of new orders and the prospect of Western companies "near-shoring" production (Mandhana and Myo 2020).[1] All this is leading to massive loss of employment across the industry, especially in the Global South. The results were devastating for female workers of Sri Lanka, with 89% reporting temporarily being

[1] "Near Shoring" refers to production lines strategically moved to markets in Turkey, Eastern Europe, and North Africa to cater to the European market and Mexico to cater to the North American market.

retrenched with partial or no pay between March–May 2020. In addition, 65% reported higher debts, while 28% reported lower food intake by September 2020 (Southernvoice 2021).

By June 2020, a false sense of safety spread across Sri Lanka, and the FTZ factories and subcontracting outfits were allowed to resume work at 50% capacity subjected to strict rules of distancing and sanitization. Workers, especially the daily hired workers who remained in the area, jumped at the opportunity to work. NGOs and workers, however, reported that by August many factories have become lackadaisical about safety measures. This led to the second wave of the pandemic, centering at The Brandix, a large garment factory in Minuwangoda. The Brandix/Minuwangoda cluster grew to 10,000 cases within the next two months (Rathnayake and Lott-Lavigna 2020). In the Katunayaka and Minuwangoda FTZ areas four large factories had to be completely shut down due to infections, while several others reported large numbers of patients. Public Health Inspectors (PHI) with the help of the military hauled women workers suspected of associating with the infected to quarantine centers in faraway places without warning. Others who remained in boarding houses saw neighbors treat them with contempt and fear (Perera 2020). "These women are being treated like criminals and 'lepers'" lamented Chamila Thushari, an NGO leader (2020a).

As I write in mid-August 2021, Sri Lanka is experiencing a virulent wave of infections. This wave started in mid to late April following the Sinhalese and Tamil New Year celebrations and led to a four weeks country-wide lockdown in June. By 16 August the dreaded delta variant has arrived and the country's health services are overwhelmed with 358,608 confirmed cases and 6263 deaths. This wave exacerbated the already acute supply chain disruptions and made life worse for global factory workers. While many other groups of informal sector workers found the lockdown detrimental to their livelihoods, global factory workers who secured the few available jobs found that their work is essential but their lives expendable. In early June, the president asked local authorities to support the continuation of factory operations despite the high number of infections (Groundviews 2021). By the end of June 2021, 6000 workers in the Katunayale area alone had contracted COVID-19. Although strict health regulations are in place, there is no proper monitoring and workers reported varying levels of satisfaction with how factories adhered to guidelines. As NGOs in the area report, the workers suspected of symptoms are sent to their boarding houses where congested, shared conditions put many others from varied factories at risk (Collective 2021). The workers who are quarantined in boarding houses have trouble securing rations. Dabindu reported how the government agent distributed five bags of groceries to a group of 32 quarantined workers and when the workers protested the government agent asked them to share the groceries among them just the way they share 4 toilets among 32 workers (Personal communication-Dabindu 2021). On top of being treated with disdain, the third wave intensified the already rampant stigma of migrant workers as a group susceptible to contamination. Fears of contamination have always intersected with race and class (Preston and Firth 2020). The fears and anxieties of the pandemic in Sri Lanka seem to further ostracize already stigmatized and marginalized communities: poor Muslims in congested living circumstances in the first wave and the garment workers (predominantly poor women) in the second and third waves.

During all this, the lack of supply chain responsibility was clearly evident. Instead of monitoring how workers are treated during the pandemic, brands and retailers have turned a blind eye and focused squarely on protecting their profits (Clean Clothes Campaign 2021a; AFWA 2021). All this can be characterized as a case of necrocapitalism, which allows people to die in the name of making a profit (Groundviews 2021).

Wither Labor and Human Rights Within Global Production???

The pandemic is accelerating autocratization in Asia. Many leaders have used the pandemic as a pretext to increase their power. Writing about Southeast Asia, Lorch and Sombatpoonsiri (2020) identify five trends resulting from the pandemic. These include tougher government restrictions on civil society organizations, contentious civil society action, new mutual aid initiatives, organized relief efforts, and repurposed advocacy groups. These five trends, in different combinations, are apparent throughout South Asia, including Sri Lanka. Lockdowns are not conducive to the right to assemble and protest, and the region has seen how lockdowns are used to restrict movements and thwart collective action against the infringement of rights. In early July 2021, a wave of protests organized by the leftist party National Liberation Front (JVP) swept across Sri Lanka. The protests focused on many issues including the high price of fertilizer, paddy, and gas, low salaries of teachers, as well as a bill aimed at privatizing and militarizing higher education. The government responded by arresting the leaders of varied protests and then strictly applying the lockdown prohibition of inter-district travel and assembly to send protesters to quarantine facilities in faraway places. This included high-profile trade union leaders such as the leader of the National Teachers' Union (Progressive Women's Collective 2021; Wadabima.lk 2021). This development further discouraged FTZ workers who found themselves in even more vulnerable position as poor, migrant women (Hewamanne 2021b; Clean Clothes Campaign 2021a).

Lorch and Sombatpoonsiri (2020) stress the potential of the pandemic to increase social engagement in mutual aid and welfare provision. This could strengthen links between national and international civil society, as well as between formally organized civil society organizations and community-based groups. Youngs (2020) also notes that while initial responses to the virus galvanized big government and strongman politics, the crisis could sharpen and intensify organized civil society action. While the potential is clearly there, labor and human rights education in Sri Lanka are experiencing major setbacks that would have cascading effects over a long period of time. The titles of two Clean Clothes Campaign reports, "Un(der)paid in the Pandemic: An Estimate of What the Garment Industry Owes Its Workers" (2020) and "COVID-19 Pandemic: A Pretext to Roll back Sri Lankan Garment Workers' Rights" (2021) spell out the cause and effect of the current labor and human rights scenario respectively. From March to May alone global workers in Sri Lanka lost approximately 40% of their normal wages, equivalent to US $24 million. This loss mostly consisted of withheld bonuses and incentives. Moreover, 20% of the workers lost jobs (Clean Clothes Campaign 2020). In this climate of more and more people clamoring for the available factory work, owners find it easy to thwart hard-won labor rights. There are reports of workers being forced to do unpaid overtime, work on public religious holidays, and denied bonuses and incentives. For example, Hydramani (pvt) Limited in Katunayake reduced its 1400 strong workforce to 400 in February 2021 while being accused of non-payment of full wages, overtime or bonuses. Overtime payments and bonuses are some of the rights negotiated very early in the global assembly line production and workers have come to understand these as part of their salaries and benefits.

According to Clean Clothes Campaign (2021a), manufacturers have circumvented responsibilities under the guise of the pandemic by failing to pay full, regular wages equal to pre-pandemic levels and failing to pay workers their annual bonuses. While paying a bonus is not a legal requirement, many factories advertise twice-yearly bonuses when recruiting. As salaries are low, these bonuses are important for worker survival and well-being. NEXT Manufacturing Ltd., and Chiefway Katunayake have denied bonuses to workers while Sumithra Hasalaka Pvt. Ltd, Smart Shirts, and Hydramani are some large factories producing for H&M, LLBean, and Asda that have failed to pay the legally required minimum wage as well as bonuses (AFWA 2021). With higher levels of education, connections to left-leaning NGOs and two trade unions, and being exposed to educational workshops on rights, one would expect global factory workers to be up in arms against the non-payment of wages and bonuses. Unfortunately, the reality far differs from expectations.

Workers are desperate for available jobs as almost all subcontracting factories have cut their labor force, in many cases up to 50% or more. As a worker, who was previously very active in worker protests, said, "I have a small child, so my wife cannot work. I feel lucky my job was saved. Some of my friends are working in construction sites as they have lost garment work. I am not going to jeopardize my job by agitating for more rights. I feel horrible about this. But buying formula milk for my baby is more important to me at this moment." Wasana, a female worker who was in the forefront of the 2011 worker protests and was hospitalized due to police beatings, had lost her job in a garment factory. "I think my leading role in a two-hour strike at the factory in 2018 made the factory cut me off when they got the chance. We figured, by checking in with protestors of several factories, that how active we were in earlier worker agitations factored into how the factories decided to lay off workers. So I don't blame the workers who still have jobs for not fighting for regular wages and bonuses. I am right now looking for work even as a domestic servant to make ends meet. No one is hiring domestic servants due to the pandemic. So yes, these jobs are as precious as gold. I think it's natural the workers would try to be on good terms with managers to protect their jobs." Wasana later added, "Those days I really didn't understand why you were harping on about these jobs being short term. Now I know what it is to hold precarious jobs." She used the English words "precarious jobs," showing her familiarity with NGO staff vocabulary.

Clean Clothes Campaign (2021a, p. 3) notes "Unlawful retaliation against workers who have acted collectively to advocate for improved conditions' as one-way factory owners try to roll back worker rights during the pandemic." The union-busting and suppression of collective action have increased during this time (industryALL 2020). One of the few unionized factories, Esquel Group, had closed its factory citing that their major buyers PVH, Gap and Ralph Lauren have withdrawn orders. However, the activists believe that the factory is using the pandemic to get rid of the unionized workforce (Clean Clothes Campaign 2021a, p. 12). In this context, workers are reluctant to agitate for these obvious violations of their rights.

There were few instances of workers trying to organize collectively. In December 2020, the workers of Next Manufacturing Ltd held public protests demanding their December bonus that was promised pre-pandemic. In January 2021, workers joined the FTZGSE union amidst threats pressuring them to not do so. Although the number that joined was sufficient to form a recognized union, just over 50% did not join fearing this could jeopardize their jobs. Moreover, Next has not yet recognized the union, thus thwarting attempts at negotiation (Clean Clothes Campaign 2021a, p. 12).

More alarmingly, some workers expressed sympathy with factory owners by noting how in this climate workers should be grateful that the owners were keeping factories open. "There were many factories that shuttered when they found one or two infected people. But this factory regrouped within a week and tried its best to save everyone's jobs. Yes, they had to let go of many. And since orders are not plentiful, they are not hiring that many man-power workers. But they still cared enough to save our jobs. I am very grateful," Malithi said instinctively bringing her hands together in the traditional form of showing gratitude. A male worker who was very active pre-pandemic told me that this is a time to support the owners and managers to keep the factory going. "We should not strike for more wages and bonuses. That is like 'a bull goring you right after you fall from a tree.' We need to let the factories heal before we ask for more salaries. Yes, we are working for less than what we should be getting. But these are unprecedented times. There's a global pandemic going on. Nobody knows what the right thing is to do," Shehan further added. Piyumi, a female worker who was very close to unions and NGOs and was previously given to using leftist vocabulary in everyday conversations dismissively asked, "what (who is thinking of) rights at this moment?

Having work is a luxury." Obviously, the pandemic had presented an ideal situation for global buyers and local management to bring global assembly line workers to their knees.

What About Occupational Health?

Clean Clothes Campaign (2021a, p. 7) accuses factory owners of thwarting their responsibility toward worker health by failing to set up bipartite (employer and employee) health committees to deal with COVID-19 as mandated by the labor ministry task force. Only two factories have complied with this requirement as of February 2021. Unions opine that establishing such committees could have minimized the intensity of the second wave which broke out in global garment factories. The workers complained of no social distancing measures and substandard masks made of left-over fabric (p. 9). An NGO staff member who visited some factories said the distancing was just two to three feet at most and one factory had just one sanitization station for about 200 workers.

When the second and third waves saw factory worker infections soar, many owners disregarded the suffering of their work force. Most factories sent the infected workers and their immediate neighbors back to their congested boarding houses, thereby putting other workers at risk. The over-crowding of government quarantine facilities forced infected workers to share their dingy boarding rooms and toilets with healthy workers. When a boarding house did not have a Public Health Inspector's (PHI) notice denoting a quarantining space, those not infected had to report to work in order to prevent getting fired or having salaries cut. Few factories provided provisions for quarantined workers, while most forgot about the infected workers after they were sent back to boarding houses (Daily Mirror 2021). An open letter to factory owners and buyers signed by several Sri Lankan labor organizations (Collective 2021) demanded that the owners and buyers work to vaccinate all active workers immediately and support initiatives to reduce suffering when the workers contract the virus from congested factory environments. These included factory sponsored quarantine centers, full pay and provisions during illness and quarantine, and a Rs. 5000 a month in payment. The companies that had promoted their CSR initiatives and bragged about how they supported community water projects and beautified roundabouts are deafeningly silent at these demands. The buying companies in affluent countries maintained distance from inhuman conditions within factories even during pre-pandemic times. Now they seemed to have completely abandoned their claims of corporate social responsibility.

Occupational Health, Labor Rights, and Human Rights Education

Workers' apathy toward fighting for their labor rights extended to protesting against factories disregarding pandemic health regulations and thwarting responsibility after workers contract the virus. Workers I interviewed were more anxious, and angry about the latter. "I wake up a few minutes earlier now, so I can pray to Lord Buddha and all the gods properly before I leave for work. Before I take my first step on to the factory floor I say another prayer, 'From the blessings of all gods, don't make me get it today,'" Malithi said with a laugh that turned into a bitter frown.

Obviously, the workers are very concerned about having to go to work in crowded spaces and residing in even more congested boarding houses where they share rooms, toilets, and bathing wells. Factories that failed to form the mandated bipartite health committees to discuss COVID-19 related measures highlighted their disregard for assembly line workers and their health anxieties. I therefore assumed the workers would be more than willing to discuss workplace health measures and propose action with a view toward negotiating with their factories. With that understanding, when the British Academy and GCRF Essex University offered an opportunity to slightly modify the proposed workshop focus, I decided to keep the focus on occupational health, labor laws, and human rights intact.

As the quotes at the beginning of this chapter noted, the partner organizations wanted to change the focus of the workshop to discuss the dire situation with regard to workers. By then the focus has already been set and it was too late to tweak things. Besides, I did not think it was productive or appropriate to use these workshops as a venue to lament obvious bad conditions associated with the virus. As noted above, the workers tried their best to thwart my attempts to talk about legal rights to occupational health and get them to propose actions and brainstorm about new ways to negotiate with managers. They quite astutely pointed out to me that even in pre-pandemic times the managers disregarded occupational health laws and got away with it. As Sumudu said, "Our backs broke sitting at the same place, some workers lost eye-sight, some got asthma. Unions and NGOs shouted, and shouted for years. Did anything change? If someone complains of difficulties, they remove that position and later hire manpower workers to fill it. You think the factories will change now? The pandemic opened a new gold mine for them (*honda illamak paadune*)." During the same discussion thread, Sampath, a male worker, bemusedly and almost as if talking to himself said, "Factories got us by the neck." Later at another discussion thread an impassioned Sampath said, "The government and politicians have no compassion for us. They gave millions in support to the factory owners and told them to start production even if they paid only 50% of workers' salaries. After this, is there any use in agitating for occupational health? Only our families care if we live or die." Many agreed with him, some pointing out to the helplessness of the government at this time as well. At the end of this discussion thread workers seemed to question the neoliberal development model (not in the same vocabulary) and to long for earlier models of state-led slow development. "We all may have only little to eat; but we all will be somehow eating, at least a little," Dharshini said, summarizing their longing for equitable distribution.

Several workers across the three workshops noted that one reason they participated was that it paid Rs. 1500 to do so and provided data cards to get on zoom. This was in contrast to the previous two years when participants clamored to join later workshops without any payment and even volunteered to go without lunch. Working groups that formed in 2018 and 2019 still met via Whatsapp, but mostly talked about their everyday deprivations. Workers talked about how factories are being irresponsible and stealing their wages and bonuses but mostly as angry outbursts than a way to move forward toward collective action. In fact, in all three workshops there were heartfelt requests for me to get funding to provide bags full of groceries for worker boarding houses. These were highly uncomfortable moments for me, and I was questioning my own wisdom of going ahead with the workshops. As the funding was not deferrable, I am glad I took the opportunity to hold some workshops and attempt to further educate and galvanize three groups of workers into action. However, the experience disheartened me on the prospects of legal empowerment via rights education at this moment.

In addition to this personal experience, there were other noticeable differences in the rights education landscape. The NGOs that have been conducting periodic workshops with international funding had focused on distributing humanitarian aid. This included the distribution of grocery packages and monitoring of quarantining boarding houses. Even for these activities they needed international funding and several NGO staff members claimed they had run out of funds by December 2020 and no further funds were forthcoming (Personal communication-Women's Center 2020). In a situation where there is not enough funds to provide humanitarian aid, it is foolhardy to hope that donor agencies would be interested in sponsoring educational workshops. Even if they do and workers get legally empowered via these workshops, until the global supply and production networks stabilize such empowerment will not lead to collective action, as the employers are in a particularly beneficial position at the moment.

Conclusion

Precarious work is highly susceptible to external shocks. Successive governments in Sri Lanka and many other countries in the Global South relentlessly pursued neoliberal development models since 1977. To be fair, international financial institutions did not allow these governments other options as they forced draconian structural adjustment policies on debt-ridden countries in the Global South. Successive Sri Lankan governments as well as generations of rural people relied upon subcontracting for global production to provide jobs, and to take them at least a little out of poverty (Hewamanne 2018, 2019, 2020a, 2020b). Workers collectively organized at times to negotiate favorable conditions. Global consumer activism also helped procure some rights for the regular workforce in FTZs. Yet, the workers had a fair understanding that their jobs were precarious, and they needed to be prepared for a time when they would not be welcome as global factory workers. Lack of alternative livelihoods makes them accept such precarious conditions and motivates them to do their best to achieve social mobility within given conditions (Hewamanne 2019, 2020a).

The COVID-19 pandemic has sharpened their understanding about the precariousness of their livelihoods and gotten them talking about economic options beyond the neoliberal model. However, at present these discussions are more at the level of musings. With jobs dependent on global supply and value chains, the global pandemic is specifically detrimental to labor rights and human rights for global subcontracting workers. Although Lorch and Sombatpoonsiri (2020) and Youngs (2020) note that NGO advocacy and organic civil society action may lead to collective action, currently the scenarios are bleak for global factory workers. The funds for educational workshops are nonexistent, while even usually active workers are focused on safeguarding their jobs. As more and more new variants emerge and vaccination programs in the Global South lag way behind affluent countries, it is difficult to predict when Western economies will recover and global production networks stabilize so that Global South economies can also recover. Obviously, it is going to take years for these already poor economies to recover and people to achieve even a modicum of livelihood security via subcontracting. All this points toward the importance of imagining economic lives beyond the market-based neoliberal development models geared toward benefitting already affluent countries.

Bibliography

Abraham, M.R. Sri Lanka's Garment Workers Stand Up for Rights. 2017. https://medium.com/change-maker/sri-lankas-garment-workers-stand-up-for-rights-82e7a244639c.

Anner, Mark. Leveraging Desperation: Apparel Brands' Purchasing Practices During Covid-19. 2020. http://www.workersrights.org/wp-content/uploads/2020/10Leveraging_Desperation.pdf.

Asia Floor Wages (AFWA). Money Heist: Covid-19 Wage Theft in Global Garment Supply Chains. 2021. https://asia.floorwage.org/wp-content/uploads/2021/07/Money-Heist_Book_Finalcompressed.pdffbclid=IwAR2S6dESEv37HGydzd24ngjKa6cbWiamnU81If41oVIIr (Accessed July 7, 2021).

Barrientos, S. Labour Chains: Analysing the Role of Labour Contractors in Global Production Networks. *Journal of Development Studies* 49(8):1058–1071. 2013.

Clean Clothes Campaign. Un(der) Paid in the Pandemic: An Estimate of What the Garment Industry Owes Its Workers. 2020. https://cleanclothes.org/file-repository/underpaid-in-the-pandemic.pdf/view.

Clean Clothes Campaign. COVID-19 Pandemic: A Pretext to Roll Back Sri Lankan Garment Workers' Rights. 2021a. https://file:///C:/Users/Sandya/Downloads/Sri_Lanka_Brief_March_2021%20(4).pdf.

Clean Clothes Campaign. Live-Blog: How the Coronavirus Affects Garment Workers in Supply Chains. 2021b. https://cleanclothes.org/news/2021/live-blog-on-how-the-coronavirus-influences-workers-in-supply-chains (Accessed August 16, 2021).

Collective. 2021. https://globaldialogue.online/ally-en/2021/sri-lanka-key-demands-to-address-the-covid-19-crisis-in-the-free-trade-zones-an-open-letter-to-the-gosl-factory-owners-buyers/.

Connell, Tula. Sri Lanka's Garment Workers Stand Up for Rights. 2019. https://www.solidaritycenter.org/sri-lanka-garment-workers-stand-up-for-rights/.

Cross, Jamie. Detachment as a Corporate Ethic: Materializing CSR in the Diamond Supply Chain. *Focaal: Journal of Global and Historical Anthropology* 60:34–46. 2011.

Dabindu Collective. *Living for the Day: Contract Workers in Sri Lanka's Free Trade Zones*. Nugegoda: NEO Graphics, 2017.

Dabindu Collective. NEXT Strike. 2020. https://www.facebook.com/chamila.thushari.18/videos/387335592729044 (Accessed December 22, 2020).

De Neve, Geert. Global Garment Chains, Local Labour Activism: New Challenges to Trade Union and NGO Activism in the Tiruppur Garment Cluster, South India, in G. De Neve, L. Peter, J. Pratt, and D.C. Wood (eds), *Hidden Hands in the Market: Ethnographies of Fair Trade, Ethical Consumption, and Corporate Social Responsibility* (*Research in Economic Anthropology, Vol. 28*), pp. 213–240, 2008. https://doi.org/10.1016/S0190-1281(08)28010-8.

De Neve, Geert and Rebecca Prentice (eds). *Unmaking the Global Sweatshop: Health and Safety of the World's Garment Workers*. Philadelphia: University of Pennsylvania Press, 2017.

De Silva, C. Apparel Exports Drop by 22% to 3.1 b in 9 Months. *Financial Times* (Lanka). 2020. ft.lk/front-page/Apparel-exports-drop-by-22-to-3-1-b-in-9-months/44-707531 (Accessed October 15, 2020).

DeVotta, Neil. Ethnoreligious Nationalism and Autocratization in Sri Lanka, in Sten Widmalm (ed), *Routledgehandbook of Autocratization in South Asia*. London: Routledge, 2021.

Fazlulhaq, N. Chaos as Thousands Crowd Transport Home for Free Trade Zone Workers. *The Sunday Times*. 2020 (Accessed March 29, 2020).

Financial Times (Lanka edition). Apparel Appeals to Government for Swift Support. 2020. ft.lk/front-page/Apparel-appeals-to-Govt-for-swift-support/44-698740 (Accessed April 10, 2020).

Groundviews. Avoiding Necrocapitalism in Sri Lanka's Free Trade Zones. 2021. https://groundviews.org/2021/06/13/avoiding-necrocapitalism-in-sri-lankas-free-trade-zones/.

Goger, A. Ethical Branding in Sri Lanka: A Case Study of Garments Without Guilt, in J. Bair, M. Dickson and D. Miller (eds), *Workers' Rights and Labor Compliance in Global Supply Chains: Is a Social Label the Answer?* London: Routledge, 2014.

Hewamanne, Sandya. *Stitching Identities in a Free Trade Zone: Gender and Politics in Sri Lanka*. Philadelphia: University of Pennsylvania Press, 2008.

Hewamanne, Sandya. Negotiating Sexual Meanings: Global Discourses, Local Practices and Free Trade Zone workers on City Streets. *Ethnography* 13(3): 352–374. 2012.

Hewamanne, Sandya. *Sri Lanka's Global Factory Workers: (Un)Disciplined Desires and Sexual Struggles in a Post-Colonial Society*. London: Routledge, 2016.
Hewamanne, Sandya. Health and Safety for Ten Hours Plus: Why CSR Policies Are Not Successful as Envisioned, in Geert De Neve and Rebecca Prentice (eds), *Unmaking the Global Sweatshop: Health and Safety of the World's Garment Workers*. Philadelphia: University of Pennsylvania Press, 2017.
Hewamanne, Sandya. Sewing Their Way Up the Social Ladder? Paths to Social Mobility and Empowerment Among Sri Lanka's Global Factory Workers. *Third World Quarterly* 39(11):2173–2187. 2018.
Hewamanne, Sandya. From Global Workers to Local Entrepreneurs: Former Global Factory Workers in Rural Sri Lanka. *Third World Quarterly* 41(3). 2019.
Hewamanne, Sandya. Surveillance by Another Name: The Modern Slavery Act, Global Factory Workers, and Part-Time Sex Work in Sri Lanka. *Signs*: *Journal of Women in Culture and Society* 45(3). 2020a.
Hewamanne, Sandya. *Re-Stitching Identities in Rural Sri Lanka: Neoliberalism, Gender and Politics of Contentment*. Philadelphia: University of Pennsylvania Press, 2020b.
Hewamanne, Sandya. Pandemic, Lockdown and Modern Slavery Among Sri Lanka's Global Assembly Line Workers. *Journal of International Women's Studies* 22(1):54–69. 2021a.
Hewamanne, Sandya. Global Worker Protests, and Tools of Autocratization in Sri Lanka: Rendering them Silent, in Sten Widmalm (ed), *Routledge Handbook of Autocratization in South Asia*. Routledge, 2021b.
IndustryALL. IndustryALL Global Union Calls on Isabella Private Limited Sri Lanka to Reinstate Dismissed Workers Immediately and Respect Their Right to Organize. 2020. https://industryall-union.org/sites/deafault/files/uploads/documents/2020/Sri_Lanka/industryall-global-union-letter-to-isabella-private-limited-sri-lanka-28-08-2020.pdf.
Jayasinghe, U. (2020). Apparel Stretched by Lack of Fall Season Orders. *Financial Times* (Lanka). https://Ft.lk/topstory/Apparel-stretched-by-lack-of-fall-season-orders/26-701412 (Accessed June 10, 2020).
Lorch, J. and J. Sombatpoonsiri. *Southeast Asia Between Autocratization and Democratic Resurgence*. 2020. https://carnegieeurope.eu/2020/12/07/southeast-asia-between-autocratization-and-democratic-resurgence-pub-83139 (Accessed December 22, 2020).
Mandhana, N. and M. Myo. Pandemic Crushes Garment Industry: The Developing World's Path out of Poverty. *The Wall street Journal*. 2020 (Accessed July 11, 2020).
Merk, Jeroen. Jumping Scale and Bridging Space in the Era of Corporate Social Responsibility: Cross-Border Labour Struggles in the Global Garment

Industry. *Third World Quarterly* 30(3):599–615. 2009. https://doi.org/10.1080/01436590902742354.

Merk, Jeroen. The Rise of Tier 1 Firms in the Global Garment Industry: Challenges for Labour Rights Advocates. *Oxford Development Studies* 42(2):259–277. 2014. https://doi.org/10.1080/13600818.2014.908177.

Nilson, P. Garment Workers in Asia Lose $6bn Wages. *Financial Times* (US edition, p. 10). 2020 (Accessed August 10, 2020).

Nilson, P. Asia Garment Workers Lose 12bn Wages and Jobs, Says Labour Group. *Financial Times* (US edition, p. 4). July 19, 2021.

Nilsson, P. and E. Terazono. Can Fast Fashion's $2.5tn Supply Chain Be Stitched Back Together? *Financial Times*. 2020. https://www.ft.com/content/62dc687e-d15f-46e7-96df-ed7d00f8ca55 (Accessed May 17, 2020).

Ong, A. The Gender and Labor Politics of Postmodernity. *Annual Review of Anthropology* 20:279–309. 1991.

Perera, A. Government's Extreme Measures to Contain the Garment Factory Outbreak Put Workers at a Great Disadvantage. 2020. https://adnasia.org/2020/11/09/in-tatters-sri-lankas-excessive-pandemicresponse/?fbclid=IwAR1L5VRWA62WDVZe9rvIjI5312yp4lihybIas-bwKbebM0TdEHuk-82KEjk (Accessed November 11, 2020).

Praja. Sri Lankan Garment Workers Face Difficulties During and After COVID-19 Curfew. 2020. http://praja.lk/sri-lankan-garment-workers-face-difficulties-during-and-after-covide-19-curfew (Accessed June 3, 2020).

Preston, J. and R. Firth. *Coronavirus, Class and Mutual Aid in the United Kingdom*. London: Palgrave, 2020.

Progressive Women's Collective. "Media Release." Progressive Women's Collective | Facebook. July 10, 2021.

Rajak, Dinah. *In Good Company: An Anatomy of Corporate Social Responsibility*. Stanford, CA: Stanford University Press, 2011.

Rajapaksha, Wasantha. Awareness Level of Workers to Labour Laws in Sri Lanka. *South Asian Journal of Social Studies and Economics*. 2019. https://doi.org/10.9734/sajsse/2019/v3i130094.

Rathnayake, Zinara and Ruby Lott-Lavigna. COVID Is Exposing How the Global Fashion Industry Value Workers. *VICE*. November 19, 2020. https://www.vice.com/en/article/z3vnpa/sri-lanka-covid-brandix-coronavirus-outbreak.

Ruwanpura, Kanchana. *Ethical Codes: Reality and Rhetoric: A Study of Sri Lanka's Apparel Sector*. (Report) Economic and Social Research Council: University of Southampton, 2011.

Saxena, S. *Made in Bangladesh, Cambodia, and Sri Lanka: The Labor Behind the Global Garments and Textiles Industries*. New York: Cambria Press, 2014.

Southernvoice.org. Stitching Solutions: Protecting Sri Lanka's Apparel Workers During COVID-19. March 22, 2021. http://southernvoice.org/post_covid/stitching-solutions-protecting-sri-lankas-apparel-workers-during-covid-19/.

Thushari, Chamila. Condemn the Uncivilized Media. Youtube clip. 2020a. https://www.youtube.com/watch?v=Tb7d4fDAC6E&fbclid=IwAR2pltIabAdHuF_uPtj2aNWUKM_MYJtdnCPKUfGyk3L-o8F02CyDWt8URPE (Accessed December 15, 2020).

Thushari, Chamila. 2020b. Workers Are Treated Like Criminals and Lepers. Youtube clip. 2020b. https://www.facebook.com/progressivewomensc/videos/2745646225692122 (Accessed December 15, 2020).

Youngs, R. How the Corona Virus Tests European Democracy. 2020. https://carnegieeurope.eu/2020/06/23/how-coronavirus-tests-european-democracy-pub-82109 (Accessed December 15, 2020).

Wadabima.lk. Free the Trade Union Leaders. 2021. https://www.facebook.com/photo?fbid=278260367424838&set=a.109724774278399 (Accessed July 10, 2021).

Wickramasinghe, K. Exploitation in Garment Factories: Rights Groups Demand Urgent Health Care for Workers. *Daily Mirror*. March 25, 2021. dailymirror.lk/news-features/Exploitation-in-garment-factories-rights-groups-demand-urgent-health-care-for-workers/131-212683.

CHAPTER 11

Supermarket Workers: Discovered and Uncovered During Covid-19 Pandemic

Patrícia Rocha Lemos

Abbreviation List

ICT:	Information and Communication Technology
IPE:	Individual Protection Equipment
GDP:	Gross Domestic Product
RSI:	Repetitive Strain Injury
WRMD:	Work-Related Musculoskeletal Disorder

Introduction

This article explores working conditions of supermarket employees in Brazil during the pandemic crisis. It examines the ways in which poor working conditions from before this crisis are being revealed for the public

P. R. Lemos (✉)
Centro de Estudos Sindicais e de Economia do Trabalho (CESIT), University of Campinas, Campinas, Brazil

S. Hewamanne and S. Yadav (eds.), *The Political Economy of Post-COVID Life and Work in the Global South: Pandemic and Precarity*, International Political Economy Series,
https://doi.org/10.1007/978-3-030-93228-2_11

at this moment. However, the need for these activities in times of self-isolation has not been enough for improving their living and working conditions. This paper aims to demonstrate in which ways the pandemic context highlights the already unsettled working conditions and deepens the situation of vulnerability and insecurity experienced by these workers.[1]

Studies on retail, especially on the characteristics of work in this sector, are very limited and arouse little interest, as already recognized by authors such as Grugulis and Bozkurt (2011) and Wrigley and Lowe (1996). Although it remains understudied, as Grugulis and Bozkurt (2011, 4–10) explain, the retail work is significant, diverse and problematic. Therefore, its study contributes to the understanding of the dynamics of labour relations in the current context of employment expansion in the service sector, both in the face of the internationalization and globalization of retail (Wrigley et al. 2005; Dawson 2007) and of the broader process of precariousness of work on a global scale.

The health crisis that hit the world and arrived in Brazil in early 2020, ended up aggravating the social, economic and political crisis in which the country was already immersed. The arrival and spread of the COVID-19 has highlighted two major problems that most severely affect precarious workers. The first concerns the difficulties in practising social distancing and home isolation both due to the need for income and structural problems that prevent them from having access to basic conditions such as housing and basic sanitation. The second aspect is the precarious working conditions of those who work in the retail trade and which is aggravated in the pandemic due to the lack of minimum hygiene conditions, access to IPE (Individual Protection Equipment) and social protection to those who need to be absent from work.

The precariousness of this type of work is not a novelty in Brazil, but results from a historically unorganized labour market in the country that has been aggravated in recent decades by the economic crisis and the flexibilization of labour legislation. This paper supports the argument that the process of degradation of the living and working conditions of

[1] As working conditions I am considering: (a) the salary and other types of remuneration (as profit-sharing, bonus etc.); (b) working hours; (c) ways of hiring; (d) occupational injuries or illnesses; (e) labour outsourcing; (f) benefits and incentive programs offered by the company; (g) complaints of harassment; (h) turnover and mobility; (i) work organization and managerial practices (related to the hierarchy, duties, levels of autonomy, skill requirements, training, engagement with the corporate ideology etc.).

the supermarket workers are being intensified during the pandemic. The paper is organized as follows. First, an overview of working conditions in supermarkets and how precariousness is part of the retail restructuring dynamics and the historical and structural precariousness of work in Brazil will be presented. Second, how the crisis of Covid-19 pandemic has impacted the working condition and life of these workers.

The presented arguments have been derived from a field of research carried out across three different supermarket stores, one in the Northeast and two in the Southeast of Brazil. From 2015 to 2019, I have conducted observation and I have interviewed 22 employees (19 women and 13 men occupied in different activities: salesperson, cashiers, low managers, butchers, etc.), 10 Union Leaders (four of them were also supermarket workers) and a Labour Judge. These and other additional materials are the ground of our analyses of working conditions and are more deeply developed in Lemos (2019). In addition, we interviewed in July 2020 three union leaders from different organizations to extend the informations about the pandemic period. The research is also based on: (i) a national administrative database that provides information on all formal (or legal) employees in the country; (ii) some institutional and media reports and (iii) documents from unions and labour organizations.

Precarious Work in Brazilian Supermarkets

Economically, the commerce sector is significant in Brazil, since it represents about 13% of the country's GDP (Gross Domestic Product), of which 40% corresponds to retail. The retail work in 2018 concentrated more than 16% of formal employment contracts in Brazil. Among these jobs, the supermarket and hypermarket segment is the largest, with more than one million employees. Although establishments with up to 04 employees (32%) predominate in the country,the greatest growth has been observed in businesses with more than 20 employees (Data from RAIS, presented in Lemos 2019).

During the 1990s the process of economic restructuring in Brazil has impacted labour in different ways. The process of economic opening stimulated the entry of Foreign Direct Investment and, with this, there was the consolidation of large retail chains in the country. The concentration and centralization of retail capital in large multinational networks has intensified until the mid-2000s (Dalla Costa 2005). Even today, the three largest retail chains are Carrefour and GPA (Grupo Pão de Açúcar)/

Cassino (French) and Walmart (American). Together they represent around 40% of the income in the segment.

The internationalization and the globalization process in retail have been articulated with the development of ICT (Information and Communication Technology) and have become a key component of businesses' retail strategies with implications on labour all over the world (Bonacich and Wilson 2008). Chris Tilly points out three main trends. First, the "supermarketization" process, that "brings larger enterprises and the replacement of self-and family employment with more standard capitalist employment relations". Second, globalization, represented by the "consolidation and saturation of domestic retail markets in richer countries", that lead to the concentration of retail industry in many countries and stimulate the centralization of management and control at the top of the company. Finally, the modern discounting that has made low wages a key part of business strategy in retail (Tilly 2007, 1).

The process of "supermarketization", with the expansion of self-service, the introduction of new technologies and the growth of big retail companies changed the labour process and pressed forward a new dynamic of labour relations (Lichtenstein 2009). With regard to employment relations, low-wage jobs, low skills requirements and low status are what predominate in the retail sector (Grugulis and Bozkurt 2011). Besides these characteristics of retail work in most countries, also stands out in the Brazilian case the large contingent of informality, with a significant number of small family businesses. In addition, high turnover rates and long working hours are much higher than in other industries.

With the expansion and consolidation of large transnational retail chains, another aspect that spreads with the internationalization and the increasing control of the companies' headquarters are the emerging labour management practices. As discussed by Ferner (1997) and Meardi et al. (2009) some issues are more likely to be transferred from the country-of-origin to the country host than others (Ferner 1997, 22). In the same direction, researchers indicate that the transfer of employment practices influences some dimensions, especially concerning corporate culture, functional flexibility and working time flexibility (Meardi et al. 2009, 497).

From the research conducted in Walmart stores in Brazil (Lemos 2019) it is possible to identify that the transformations in the work process in supermarkets had a strong impact on the precariousness of working conditions. Nevertheless, compared to the opportunities available in the national labour market, employment in supermarkets is not the worst. In other words, we can say that supermarkets are a "good job, but a bad work". To understand this difference, it is necessary to consider the labour policy of large retailers and their power to shape working conditions from various management mechanisms supported by innovative technologies. In addition, changes in the labour process in supermarkets are also related to market institutions and national regulation (Carré and Tilly 2017).

Regarding the power of companies to determine working conditions, Walmart's experience in Brazil highlights the dissemination of management practices focused on various coercive mechanisms. The pressure for achieving the goals is highlighted without being given the necessary conditions to accomplish them. So-called "motivational" practices and performance evaluation policies that represented harassment practices were also found, which were even condemned by the labour justice. In face of the lack or fragility of punitive measures, Walmart was able to circumvent labour laws in different ways and diffuse jobs with long working hours, excessive workloads, as well as mentioned policies for the intensification of work that have caused illness in several employees. The workers testify feeling diminished in different ways and in their point of view the company treats them only as a number or a machine.

> Lá a gente via coisa que tava errada, mas quem sou eu pra falar alguma coisa, né. Eu sou um número pra empresa. [...] É complicado isso, porque você trabalha numa empresa...A gente geralmente quando trabalha pensa: - 'Essa empresa vai crescer, que nem eles falaram, a gente cresce junto', mas não é nada disso. Você continua lá e quando você ainda fica com problema que nem eu fiquei você é posta de lado (Rute).[2]

> A gente sabe que é [uma empresa] americana. É uma empresa que visa muito mão de obra, muito trabalho. E assim, tem suas vantagens, mas tem algumas desvantagens, porque *ela visava o funcionário não como pessoa, mas sim como uma máquina*, entendeu (Rosana).[3]

[2] There, I saw some wrong things, but who am I to say something? I am a number for the company. [...] This is complicated because you work in a company, so you usually think:—'This company will grow, as they say, we will grow together', but it is not like this. You are still there and when you have a problem, as what happened to me, you are put aside (Rute, cashier and salesperson).

[3] We know that it is an American company, it is a company that aims mainly labour, a lot of work. So, it has its advantages, but it has some disadvantages because the company

Some workers even compare the situation with the smaller retail chains that were bought by these big companies. According to some workers, previous employment in national or family chains contained small benefits and "delights" in addition to a more direct, personal and sometimes more humanized relationship:

> Quando era uma rede [de supermercados] familiar, o dono, ele vinha pra dentro da empresa, vinha conhecer os funcionários, chamava a gente pelo nome. Tratava cada um com certo grau de respeito né, com um respeito por ser um cidadão, com um respeito por ser um trabalhador. Quando essa empresa chegou ao ponto de ser vendida pra uma empresa estrangeira, começaram a sucatear as lojas, começaram a diminuir os quadros, começaram a ter outra visão: a visão só de lucro, lucro, lucros... É o capitalismo selvagem. [...]O discurso é muito lindo... mas [a empresa] tem uma definição do que é a pessoa. A pessoa é um papel. [...] A pessoa é a visão somente de quê? Um cifrão, é dinheiro, é lucro. [...] Então... aos poucos foi mudando, mudando, mudando... e hoje nós somos isso: nós somos apenas aquilo que a empresa precisa. E o que é que a empresa precisa? A empresa precisa de uma pessoa que dê lucro (Lucas).[4]

However, if in these aspects of work and management organization companies have vast freedom to establish the conditions that suit them, in other aspects they face some limits established by national regulation. An example of this is that supermarket employees in big retail chains receive at least the minimum wage and generally more than small shops employees do.

The main explanation for the low but above minimum wage in Brazil is related to national regulations (Krein 2013). It is necessary to consider

sees the employee not as a person, but as a machine. Do you know what I mean? (Rosana, cashier).

[4] When it was a family business, the owner, he came into the company, came to meet the employees, called us by name. He treated everyone with a certain degree of respect, you know, with respect for being a citizen, with a respect for being a worker. When this company got to the point of being sold to a foreign company, they started to scrap the stores, they started to reduce the number of employees, they had another vision: the vision of profit, profit, profits ... It is wild capitalism. [...] The speech is very beautiful ... but [the company] has a definition of what a person should be. The person is a role. [...] The person is the vision of what? It's money, it's profit. [...] So ... little by little it was changing, changing, changing ... and today we are that: we are just what the company needs. And what does the company need? The company needs a person who makes a profit (Lucas).

that the legal union representing a segment settles a collective agreement every year. Because of that, wages are usually a little higher than the national minimum wage and are the same for all firms competing locally in a particular industry. Nevertheless, compared to other formalized jobs, data from the Labour Office show that in 2016, the entry-level salary at the retail sector was the second lower compared with other industries (R$ 1219.07), just slightly higher than agriculture (R$ 1122.77) (DIEESE 2017).

Another aspect that differs from many other countries is that in Brazil, full-time jobs are almost the totality of employment in the retail sector. Brazilian part-time regulations were created in 1998 but this variety of contract is not much worthwhile due to labour laws that prevent part-time jobs as a way of cutting working costs by compelling the employer to pay proportionate benefits for part-time employees.

These could lead us to the misplaced idea of a strong regulated and protected labour market. On the contrary, these factors are related to the argument developed by Krein and Castro (2015), who indicates that the regular full-time employment (the indefinite contract regulated by the "Consolidação das leis do Trabalho") in Brazil is already flexible enough and operates to reinforce an already high turnover rate. A prime example of this is the period of experience included on the indefinite employment contracts of full-time workers that determines the employer can dismiss the employee without costs in the first three months of "experience" (at least until the late labour reform) (Krein and Castro 2015).

Besides that, companies can largely benefit themselves from outsourcing as a much more efficient way of cutting costs. In most companies in the retail sector, outsourcing has spread through the rise of people employed as "sales promoters" who are hired by the supply company or by employment temporary agencies. Usually these workers do the tasks made in the past by direct supermarket employees, which is the case for shelves replacement.[5]

As mentioned earlier, the management power of companies and the national regulation is not enough to understand the dynamics of the precarization process in the retail sector in Brazil. It is also crucial to analyse these issues in the light of a broader historical process. It is known

[5] One of the most significant changes allowed by the Brazilian labour reform of 2017 was to generalize legal permission to outsource in all kinds of occupations that was restricted to non-essential activities.

that working conditions are historically precarious in Brazil. As a colonized country with a history of slavery, Brazil is still shaped by remaining features from its export-oriented and dependent capitalist development. Characterized by a large inequality gap and poor living conditions, as argued by Ruy Braga, it is necessary to note that the "precariat", understood as the most exploited and dominated fractions of the working class, has been the rule in the Brazilian history (Braga 2012, 2016).[6]

Considering the prevalence of low wages, high informality and high turnover, it is possible to argue that most workers in Brazil has been situated between the threat of social exclusion and the increase of economic exploitation (Braga 2012, 16). This constitutes a key issue to understand workers' point of view about their own employment situation. Having a job in a big retail company can be a good option in terms of owning labour rights and a legal job. For many people, this job seems to be the best they can get against the large informality and the structural unemployment.

Additionally, the process of working conditions "precarization" has been reinforced by neoliberal policies deployments. During the 1990s, labour market flexibility in the service sector in Brazil increased. Legislation reforms from this period gave greater freedom to companies in determining the conditions of use, hiring and remuneration of labour. This allowed companies to adjust the volume and price of the workforce to the production demands in order to reduce its costs (Krein 2007). Two pieces of evidence of these adjustments in the 1990s that stand out in the retail sector are the extension of opening hours on weekdays and the clearance for working on Sundays.

Recently, the labour reform approved in 2017, deepened this flexibilization process by creating a variety of new types of hiring as the intermittent employment contract. Furthermore, a set of mechanisms were legalized to allow a greater adjustment of work to the employer's demand and the prevalence of agreements over labour legislation. Thus, in addition to weakening social protection, this reform legalized and

[6] In this sense, Braga goes along with (Standing 2011, 2014) in the purpose of analyze the "precariat" as "a group of people who are deprived of any work-related guarantees, subjected to uncertain income, and without a collective identity that is rooted in a labour world". Despite that, Braga follows a Marxist agenda and conceive this group as an expression of the metamorphosis of working class. His argument is also focused on the Global South and particularly in Brazil (Braga 2016).

generalized the total availability of workers with an impact both on the extension of the workday and on the intensification of work (Krein et al. 2019; Krein 2018).

Impacts of the Pandemic Crisis on Work in Supermarkets

The explosion of the Covid-19 emergency in Brazil hit the country at a time of severe economic crisis, with unemployment of around 13 million people and increased social inequality and poverty. In addition, the crisis spread under an extreme-right government, closely aligned with Trump's policy having a denialist discourse with criminal and genocidal practices. The absence of an effective and coordinated national policy to fight the virus made the isolation measures and the guarantee of minimum conditions for the population performing activities considered essential difficult.

The very definition of what are considered essential activities was the object of dispute, which has been one of the multiple obstacles to face the crisis. On one hand, it is evident that these are essential activities for the reproduction of people's life. On the other hand, the definition of essential activities has been an object of dispute, which obstructs immediate measures to deal with the crisis.

The government decree of March 2020 defines public services and essential activities in the country as "those indispensable to meet the unavoidable needs of the community".[7] The generality of this conception allowed the legislation to include call centre services but did not initially consider labour inspection activities or research and scientific activities related to the pandemic. Shortly thereafter, contrary to what it would be recommended, religious activities of any nature were also added to the regulation as essential activities. Finally, in another attempt to undermine governors and other institutional powers, on May 11th, President Bolsonaro included in the decree as essentials the beauty salons, barbershops and gyms.[8]

[7] Decree 10.282 of March 20, 2020. Available in: http://www.planalto.gov.br/ccivil_03/_ato2019-2022/2020/decreto/D10282.htm.

[8] "Coronavírus: Bolsonaro inclui salão, barbearia e academia como 'atividades essenciais'" (Bolsonaro includes hair salons, barber shops and gyms as 'essential activities'),

This pressure to expand essential activities comes on one hand, from business sectors that sustain a false dichotomy between health and economy. They argue that measures of distancing and social isolation would bring more harm than benefits to the extent that the shutdown of economic activities would generate an income decline and unemployment. In this sense, they exempt themselves from calling on the State to build a political agenda that can guarantee the preservation of life in relation to both health and income security.

The pressure to "get back to work" is thus proposed as a strategy to avoid the implementation of the basic income policy, contrary to what has been done in other countries. This argument forces a polarization and is based on a discourse that places unemployment as an evil greater than the virus. In the omission of the State's public responsibility to ensure the right to live, for the majority of the population who depends on the public health service and does not have financial reserves to support itself during the crisis, the real "choice" to be made is between dying from the virus or starving to death.[9]

Moreover, the pressure of the Federal Government empowers the business discourse when the President shares the speech that opposes health and economy, in order to open trade and resume economic activities. One of the objectives of this resumption of commerce and service activities is to reduce the number of people who can access the Emergency Income Assistance Program during the pandemic. An example of this was the release of activities related to personal care and beauty services by the President since most professionals in the sector are self-employed and meet the requirements of this benefit.[10]

May 11, 2020. Available in: https://g1.globo.com/politica/noticia/2020/05/11/coronavirus-bolsonaro-inclui-salao-barbearia-e-academia-como-atividades-essenciais.ghtml.

[9] This debate was presented and deepened in the report "Emprego, trabalho e renda para garantir o direito à vida" (Employment, work and income in order to guarantee the right to life) prepared together with other members of the Working Group "Mundos do trabalho", CESIT.

[10] The Emergency Income Assistance Program was established by law 13.982 of April 2nd, 2020. The program is oriented to informal workers, individual microentrepreneurs (MEI), self-employed and unemployed. It lasts 3 months, with a monthly benefit of R$600.00, which does not reach 58% of the minimum wage. In addition to a late and insufficient measure, so far around 39 million people have claimed the benefit and had their claim denied. At the beginning of May, 6 million people were still awaiting analysis and 12.4 million would need to reapply. By that time 50.52 million people had received

Among the essential activities are supermarket workers who, as around the world, are on the front line now. Regarding these workers, two phenomena that develop in this context of the pandemic and social isolation stand out: their "discovery" and the deepening of their social "unprotection" and insecurity.

First, it is noted that these workers, previously invisible to the eyes not only of consumers, but also of many labour scholars, come to have their social importance to some extent recognized. The recognition of the need for these activities to be performed at this time has generated manifestations such as applause and various forms of symbolic gratitude. However, this greater visibility has not been translated into a vision that breaks social stigma or the low prestige of this work, distinctive features of many service jobs.

This devaluation is evident in two aspects. The first is by the permanence of a certain neglect of consumers with the health preservation of these workers. A report carried out in a supermarket chain in Rio de Janeiro showed that a significant part of people does not follow the recommendations of distancing and the necessary care to avoid contact and contamination, mainly of cashiers.[11] Unfortunately, the absence of a coordinated national policy to combat the virus ends up legitimizing, by Bolsonaro's stance, the attitude of part of the population who supports this denialist view of the lethality of the virus and the effectiveness of social distancing measures. With this, these workers are more exposed not only during their shift in the supermarket, but also in the use of public transport and other services.

Another aspect to be highlighted, even more serious, concerns the irresponsibility of employers who not only refuse to ensure minimum working conditions but also use this moment of exception to deepen the exploitation of this work through flexibility measures, excessive working hours and increased pressure at work.

the first part of the aid. It is estimated that about 97 million people fit the program's requirements. An additional serious problem is that a significant portion of the payment is being made at the state bank's agencies in person. Hence, thousands of people have been crowded at the bank doors for hours, in huge queues, exposed to the risk of virus contamination.

[11] Gonçalves, Juliana. Coronavírus: 'tem gente que tosse em cima da gente', conta caixa do supermercado carioca Mundial. (Coronavirus: 'There are people who cough over us' said a cashier from the Mundial supermarket chain in Rio de Janeiro), April 14, 2020.

In relation to working conditions, on April 20th, a letter was published by the Undersecretary of Labour Inspection of the Ministry of Economy with "General Guidelines for Employers and Workers in the Supermarket Sector due to the Covid-19 Pandemic". It is a very general set of recommendations. The guarantee of masks to workers, the screen protection for cashiers, the distance in the queues is only suggested. Similarly, it is also recommended to dismiss workers who are part of the risk group, but it considers the possibility of them being essential and relocated in activities of less contact with the public. Hence, not only it does not establish a limit and control of the number of people in the establishment, nor does it create any type of obligation that can be subject to supervision and punishment. Some cities and states will establish slightly stricter rules, but at the national level, the neglect and paralysis prevail. This reality also results from the instability of the Federal Government, which has already changed the Health Minister three times during the pandemic staying, most of the time, in the explicit control of military service members with no experience in health issues whatsoever.

The irresponsible and criminal stance of some enterprises is evident at this time when, unlike most commercial establishments, supermarkets have expanded their sales and their revenues. One evidence of this is the decrease in the number of dismissals pointed out by union leaders. However, maintaining the profitability of these businesses has not been a concern in preserving their workforce. At least two chains were reported in different states, where a high number of employees were contaminated without urgent measures being taken for isolation and testing. In different cases, it came to the point that the supermarket had to be closed by the Health Surveillance Agency.[12]

In light of the looseness of the guidelines and the irresponsibility of many companies, workers remain at the mercy of employers. The lack of

[12] The media has publicized cases as in Florianópolis and Vila Velha cities where the sanitary surveillance department order the closure of supermarket stores after a significant number of employees have been contaminated by Covid-19 virus. Read more in: "Supermercado em Florianópolis é fechado para desinfecção após funcionários contraírem Covid-19", April 8, 2020. Available in: https://g1.globo.com/sc/santa-catarina/noticia/2020/04/08/supermercado-em-florianopolis-e-fechado-para-desinfeccao-apos-funcionarios-contrairem-covid-19.ghtml; "Com funcionários com Covid-19, supermercado é interditado em Vila Velha", Abril 28, 2020. Available in: https://www.agazeta.com.br/es/economia/com-funcionarios-com-coronavirus-supermercado-e-interditado-em-vila-velha-0420.

individual protective equipment was already a recurring problem even in large supermarket chains before the pandemic. Complaints were common, for example, the lack of suitable gloves for the handling of food and the cutting of meats, as well as jackets for circulation in cold chambers. This problem, therefore, only worsens at a time when there is a need for more rigorous and frequent cleaning procedures and use of other protective equipment to avoid contamination by the virus. In many cases, the employees themselves provide alcohol and masks for their own use.

Reports from unionists also call attention to the expansion of the work hours as one of the main problems that has worsened during the crisis. This was already an old demand of employers and had already been occurring gradually with the changes in the legislation already mentioned: reduction of break schedule, work on Sundays, etc. Many labour lawsuits were filed against large chains, such as Walmart recording 12, 14 hours of continuous work without respecting time off before the pandemic crisis. This extra time not only exceeded the overtime legally permitted, but also was not recorded or paid as additional working time. Hence, the practice of "time stealing", as Basso (2014) pointed out, was already a common practice in the sector. The crisis only intensified the problem with a high record of reports of overwork and suspension of the days off to which these workers were entitled to. These practices hurt at least two important measures that were guaranteed to these workers in collective negotiation. The first is the right to a fixed day off on the week. That is, after working six days, the day off on the seventh day always takes place on the same day of the week. The second concerns the right of a day off on Sundays, usually once every three weeks of work at least.

Overtime work, apart from increasing the risk of accidents and exposure of workers, intensifies very serious problems that were already recurrent before the pandemic, such as the development of diseases like RSI (Repetitive Strain Injury) and WRMD (Work-Related Musculoskeletal Disorder), as a result of repetitive effort mainly by cashiers. Another problem is the recurrence of urinary infections in this activity, since the checkout cannot be closed without authorization, so operators need authorization from the superior and must wait for replacement so that they can be absent to use the toilets. Because of the low number of workers on staff, situations, where cashiers must wait for hours or until the end of their shift to go to the bathroom, are very common. There are many disputes in the labour justice against companies in which cashiers had urinated at the checkout and stay there until the end of their shift.

In one of these cases, the woman was pregnant.[13] A union leader also mentioned one case in which the worker felt so humiliated that she gave up on opening a public dispute in the labour justice.

Another very serious aspect that takes on greater proportions with the pandemic is the development or worsening of psychic illnesses such as depression and panic attack. The mechanisms of strong pressure at work by management goals and practices already made these problems the most recurrent reasons for health leave in the sector. The emergence of the health crisis resulting from Covid-19 emerges as another strong component of suffering. The statements point to anxiety and fear because they are exposed to the risk of contamination, the weight of the obligation to be attentive and vigilant to all acts and movement to avoid contagion. Due to the fact that these workers cannot self-isolate as they are not able to work from home, they fear exposing their children and family members to the virus.

In this sense, is important to notice that supermarket workers and their families are very vulnerable because, on one hand, they are more exposed to the virus contamination than the population that can practice self-isolation. On the other hand, the fact that they have a low income means that they are constantly exposed to more precarious and vulnerable living conditions as poor access to supply of water and basic sanitation facilities. Another aspect is that these families usually rely on the public health system, which has been overwhelmed all over the country, specially during the pandemic crisis. Data has shown that the virus has been more lethal for the population under these poor conditions.[14]

In this scenario, a union leader from São Paulo built in his testimony an image that seems to express not only the current situation, but the perspectives of future problems that originated in this crisis:

> O que pode trazer de sequela e está trazendo é realmente a questão psicológica. Porque as reclamações vem muito nesse sentido: "estamos aqui expostos". Então, na minha visão, realmente é a pressão psicológica. Hoje,

[13] "Caixa de supermercado que estava grávida e urinou na roupa por estar impedida de ir ao banheiro deve ser indenizada" (Supermarket cashier who was pregnant and urinated on clothes for being prevented from going to the bathroom should becompensated), 10 April, 2019. https://www.trt4.jus.br/portais/trt4/modulos/noticias/226188.

[14] Read the report on: https://www.cidadessustentaveis.org.br/noticia/detalhe/mapa-da-desigualdade-renda-e-mortalidade-por-covid-19-nas-capitais-brasileiras.

se a gente for pegar as estatísticas sobre o afastamento de trabalhadores por doença ocupacional, o comércio é um dos setores que tem mais afastamento. Por que? Porque por depressão? Pela pressão que as empresas fazem, principalmente para bater meta. Então na minha visão, as sequelas e as consequências durante o período dessa pandemia está sendo a questão dos supermercados e a pressão dos trabalhadores sobre eles mesmos. Ao sair de casa e pensar: "olha, eu estou indo realmente trabalhar no supermercado, como operadora, e eu posso, a qualquer momento, ser um positivo pro covid. Então, trata-se da autocobrança psíquica da pessoa. A pessoa já fica realmente com os nervos à flor da pele. Segundo ponto, isso não vai parar nesse momento. Após passarmos desse problema, acredito que o problema vai aparecer com muito mais volume. Por que? Porque as coisas vão estar mais relaxadas, o convívio social vai voltar (...) Eu não sou psicólogi, mas acho que vai ser mais ou menos como a perda de um ente querido, que fica um trauma e que depois é que vai cair a ficha. Então eu acho que após a crise vai ter muito mais afastamento, principalmente no setor dos supermercados, por conta de doenças que vão encontrar o organismo dessas pessoas debilitado e vai atacar. Eu acredito que vai aparecer muito esse quadro (Union Lider from São Paulo).[15]

This situation is aggravated by the need for this job, often the only source of income for the family. This leads many workers to agree to work even without the necessary protection, even when they belong to the risk group. This reality brings up two problems already mentioned earlier.

[15] What can, and is causing, consequences is really the psychological issue. Because the complaints are very similar. "We are exposed here!" So, in my view, it is the psychological pressure. Today, if we go to get the statistics on the work leave due to occupational illness, commerce is one of the sectors that have the highest numbers. Why? Why depression? Because of the pressure that companies put on workers, mainly to reach goals. So in my view, the consequences during the period of this pandemic and after that are the pressure of workers on themselves. When they leave their houses and think: "Look, I'm really going to work in the supermarket, as a cashier, and I can, at any time, be positive for covid-19". So, it's about the person's psychic self-charge. The person is already really nervous. The second point, this is not going to stop right now. After we get past this problem, I believe that the difficulty will appear with much higher volume. Why? Because things will be more relaxed, social life will come back (...) I am not a psychologist, but I think it will be more or less like the loss of a loved one, when people become traumatized and then sink in. So, I think that after the crisis there will be much more sick leave caused by mental health problems, especially in the supermarket sector, due to diseases that will find these people's bodies weakened and will attack. I believe that this picture will appear a lot (Union Lider from São Paulo).

Firstly, the structural precariousness and unstructured character of the labour market specific to peripheral capitalism. In light of the strong social inequality, informal work relationships and different activities that configure survival strategies predominate in the country. This reality creates a situation of strong coercion in the labour market, that is, in the face of the threat of unemployment, poverty and hunger, workers end up under pressure to accept jobs under the most degrading working conditions. In this sense, apart from State control, Brazilian society has been profoundly ruled by despotic market labour control (Anner 2015).

The second issue that makes this moment more difficult is the current process of dismantling social protection and the already fragile guarantee of more basic social rights. Although after the end of the military dictatorship in Brazil some rights were guaranteed by the Federal Constitution approved in 1988, this legislation has undergone a series of deconstructions through reformulations in labour laws and in the social security system since then. In this process, the mercantilization of these rights already of fragile and limited access and supervision was expanded (Andrietta and Lemos 2017; Andrietta et al. 2020).

In continuity with the process of dismantling the rights guaranteed to formal workers in Brazil, this moment of exception ends up becoming, for entrepreneurs, an opportunity to impose certain more degrading working conditions and to pressure the State to implement an agenda that deepens the flexibility and precariousness already promoted in previous labour and pension system reforms.

Final Considerations

This article draws attention to how retail transformation processes have impacted working conditions in recent decades in the sense of a greater precariousness in a sector in which work characteristics have always been problematic. Although we are considering the formal and protected jobs portion in retail, it is clear that the intensification of working hours and a set of management mechanisms has generated a process of degradation of working conditions.

First of all, in Brazil the existence of a labour legislation that guarantees some rights to these employees stands out. This makes retail jobs in supermarket chains a less unstable form of employment. However, the process of transforming the legislation in order to dehydrate it from within has increasingly brought the conditions of formal employment contracts closer to the unprotected situations of informal workers. Moreover, the structural precariousness of the work typical of the periphery of capitalism is also a fundamental pressure for workers to accept or have less power to challenge the downgrade of working conditions. Market coercion remains an efficient mechanism for overexploitation of labour and worsens in times of crisis.

In this scenario, the current health crisis has not represented a movement against these processes already underway. Supermarket workers were seen for their fundamental importance at that time, but this did not translate into the greater appreciation of their activities or to a guarantee of better working conditions. On the contrary, it is observed that the strategy of profitability of capitalist businesses does not have moral and humanitarian barriers. Not only do the problems of unprotection and overtime work worsen, but the sources of suffering and illness at work are expanded, given the high risk of contamination.

At this moment, however, what is observed is a deepening of social inequalities and the worsening of the already precarious situation of life and work of these workers. As Butler (2020) said, new ways of strengthening and reproducing inequalities, nationalism and capitalist exploitation are quickly witnessed. Additionally, we are testifying not only the omission of the State in the guarantee of social rights and the continuity of neoliberal policies. In this sense, a process of dismantling public services that have already been insufficient in countries such as Brazil has been under way.

After one year in this pandemic crisis, almost every day goes public in Brazil more evidence that the Federal government has been acting constantly to favour the dissemination of the virus as part of an "immunization by contamination" strategy.[16] At the moment of the final review of this text, in June 2021, Brazil has reached the tragic mark of 500.000 deaths from Covid- 19, in official numbers.[17] Based on the data from formal workers that have died during the pandemic, studies have shown that the occupations with highest increase of deaths are domestic workers, truck and bus drivers and salespeople (Freitas 2021; Gravas 2021). More research needs to be done but this desperate situation, unfortunately,

[16] Important part of these evidences are gathered in the report published by CEPEDISA and CONECTAS (2021).

[17] Real numbers are probably higher given evidence of underreporting in the lack of systematic testing and of a national source of reliable data.

points to a deepening process of vulnerability for the most invisible and precarious though essential workers.

The preservation of life, therefore, needs to be imposed as a fundamental social principle. It is not only a defence of the right to health, but the guarantee of health and life as a social obligation. As Butler (2020) inquires, "why are we as a people still opposed to treating all lives as if they were of equal value?" In the same direction, why are inequalities between workers also perpetuated, which place some as more worthy of rights than others? These are the questions that people around the world are still asking not only at the academy but also in public spaces and social demonstrations. As the manifest of the international movement "democratizing work" points out, one of the core lessons of the current crisis is that "working humans are so much more than 'resources.'" In this perspective, as an imperative of life it is urgent to "democratize firms, decommodify work, and remediate the environment".[18]

Dedication The book is dedicated to the world's low-income workers and informal labourers who are coping with the pandemic and lockdowns while enduring challenging working conditions exacerbated by COVID-19.

References

Andrietta, Lucas Salvador, and Patrícia Rocha Lemos. 2017. "O Sindicalismo Da CUT e a Mercantilização Do Sistema Previdenciário Brasileiro (2003–2014)." *SER Social* 18 (39): 501–19. https://doi.org/10.26512/ser_social.v18i39.14635.

Andrietta, Lucas Salvador, Patrícia Rocha Lemos, and Eduardo Fagnani. 2020. "Pensions and Commodification under the PT Governments (2003–2015)." *Latin American Perspectives* 47 (2): 117–30. https://doi.org/10.1177/0094582X19880907.

Anner, Mark. 2015. "Labor Control Regimes and Worker Resistance in Global Supply Chains." *Labor History* 56 (3): 292–307. https://doi.org/10.1080/0023656X.2015.1042771.

Basso, Pietro. 2014. "A Jornada de Trabalho No Início Do Século." In *Riqueza e Miséria Do Trabalho No Brasil III*, 73–83. São Paulo: Boitempo.

[18] To access the international manifest in different languages: https://democratizingwork.org/.

Bonacich, Edna, and Jake B. Wilson. 2008. *Getting the Goods: Ports, Labour and the Logistics Revolution*. New York: Cornell University Press.

Braga, Ruy Gomes. 2012. *A Política Do Precariado: Do Populismo à Hegemonia Lulista*. São Paulo: Editora Boitempo.

Braga, Ruy Gomes. 2016. "On Standing's A Precariat Charter: Confronting the Precaritisation of Labour in Brazil and Portugal." *Global Labour Journal* 7 (2): 148–59.

Butler, Judith. 2020. "Capitalism Has Its Limits." *Verso*, March 30, 2020. https://www.versobooks.com/blogs/4603-capitalism-has-its-limits.

Carré, From Françoise, and Chris Tilly. 2017. "The Surprisingly Changeable Wal-Mart around the World." In *Where Bad Jobs Are Better: Retail Jobs across Countries and Companies*, 172–93. New York: Russel Sage.

CEPEDISA, and CONECTAS. 2021. "DIREITOS NA PANDEMIA: Mapeamento e Análise Das Normas Jurídicas de Resposta à COVID-19 No Brasil." São Paulo.

Dalla Costa, Armando João. 2005. "A Internacionalização Do Varejo a Partir Dos Casos Wal- Mart e Carrefour." *Análise Econômica* 44 (23): 189–215.

Dawson, John A. 2007. "Scoping and Conceptualising Retailer Internationalisation." *Journal of Economic Geography* 7 (4): 373–97. https://doi.org/10.1093/jeg/lbm009.

DIEESE. 2017. "Comércio Em 2016: Um Balanço Dos Principais Indicadores." São Paulo.

Ferner, Anthony. 1997. "Country of Origin Effects and HRM in Multinational Companies." *Human Resource Management Journal* 7 (1): 19–37. https://doi.org/10.1111/j.1748-8583.1997.tb00271.x.

Freitas, Clayton. 2021. "Motoristas, Domésticas e Pedreiros Estão Entre Os Que Mais Morrem de Covid-19 Em SP." *Jornal Folha de São Paulo*, June 1, 2021. https://agora.folha.uol.com.br/sao-paulo/2021/06/motoristas-domesticas-e-pedreiros-estao-entre-os-que-mais-morrem-de-covid-19-em-sp.shtml.

Gravas, Douglas. 2021. "Trabalhador Essencial e 'Invisível' é Maior Vítima Da Pandemia No Brasil." *Jornal Folha de São Paulo*, June 19, 2021. https://www1.folha.uol.com.br/mercado/2021/06/trabalhador-essencial-e-invisivel-e-maior-vitima-da-pandemia-no-brasil.shtml?origin=folha.

Grugulis, Irena, and Ödül Bozkurt. 2011. *Retail Work*. Edited by Irena Grugulis and Ödül Bozkurt. London: Palgrave Macmillan.

Krein, Jose Dari. 2007. "Tendencias Recentes Nas Relações de Emprego No Brasil: 1990–2005." Universidade Estadual de Campinas. http://www.bibliotecadigital.unicamp.br/document/?code=vtls000430974&fd=y.

Krein, José Dari. 2013. *As Relações de Trabalho Na Era Do Neoliberalismo No Brasil*. São Paulo: LTr.

Krein, José Dari. 2018. "O Desmonte Dos Direitos, as Novas Configurações Do Trabalho e o Esvaziamento Da Ação Coletiva: Consequências Da Reforma Trabalhista." *Tempo Social*. https://doi.org/10.11606/0103-2070.ts.2018.138082.

Krein, José Dari, and Barbara Castro. 2015. "As Formas Flexíveis de Contratação e a Divisão Sexual Do Trabalho." *Friedrich Ebert Stiftung Brasil Análise* 06: 26. http://www.cesit.net.br/wp-content/uploads/2016/06/TD_FES_Dari.pdf.

Krein, José Dari, Roberto Véras de Oliveira, and Vitor Araújo Filgueiras. 2019. *Reforma Trabalhista No Brasil: Promessas e Realidade*. Campinas: Curt Nimuendaju.

Lemos, Patrícia Rocha. 2019. "'Custo Baixo Todo Dia': Redes Globais de Produção e Regime de Trabalho No Walmart Brasil." Universidade Estadual de Campinas.

Lichtenstein, Nelson. 2009. *The Retail Revolution: How Wal-Mart Created a Brave New World of Business*. New York: Metropolitan Books.

Meardi, Guglielmo, Paul Marginson, Michael Fichter, Marcin Frybes, Miroslav Stanojević, and András Tóth. 2009. "Varieties of Multinationals: Adapting Employment Practices in Central Eastern Europe." *Industrial Relations* 48 (3): 489–511. https://doi.org/10.1111/j.1468-232X.2009.00570.x.

Standing, Guy. 2011. *The Precariat: The New Dangerous Class*. London: Bloomsbury.

Standing, Guy. 2014. *A Precariar Charter: From Denizens to Citizens*. London: Bloomsbury.

Tilly, Chris. 2007. "Global Restructuring in Retail: What Impact on Labor?" *For Submission to International Labor Brief, Korea Labor Institute*.

Wrigley, Neil, and Michelle Lowe. 1996. *Retailing, Consumption and Capital: Towards the New Retail Geography*. Edited by Neil Wrigley and Michelle Lowe. Essex: Lognman.

Wrigley, Neil, Neil M. Coe, and Andrew Currah. 2005. "Globalizing Retail: Conceptualizing the Distribution-Based Transnational Corporation (TNC)." *Progress in Human Geography* 29 (4): 437–57. http://journals.sagepub.com/doi/pdf/10.1191/0309132505ph559oa.

Index

S. Hewamanne and S. Yadav (eds.), *The Political Economy of Post-COVID Life and Work in the Global South: Pandemic and Precarity*, International Political Economy Series,
https://doi.org/10.1007/978-3-030-93228-2

The manufacturer's authorised representative in the EU is Springer Nature Customer Service Centre GmbH, Europaplatz 3, 69115 Heidelberg, Germany. If you have any concerns regarding our products, please contact ProductSafety@springernature.com

Printed and bound by CPI Group (UK) Ltd, Croydon, CR0 4YY
30/09/2026
02225661-0008